W9-DEO-022

Psychological Consultation in Educational Settings

Casebook for Working with Administrators, Teachers, Students, and Community

Judith L. Alpert
and Associates

Psychological Consultation in Educational Settings

JASON ARONSON INC.
Northvale, New Jersey
London

THE MASTER WORK SERIES

First softcover edition 1995

Library of Congress Cataloging-in-Publication Data

Alpert, Judith L.
Psychological consultation in educational settings : casebook for working with administrators, teachers, students, and community / by Judith L. Alpert and associates.
p. cm.
Includes bibliographical references and index.
ISBN 1-56821-485-5 (pbk. : alk. paper)
1. Educational consultants. 2. Counseling in education.
I. Title.
LB2799.A46 1995
371.2'07 – dc20 94-45754

Manufactured in the United States of America. Jason Aronson Inc. offers books and cassettes. For information and catalog write to Jason Aronson Inc., 230 Livingston Street, Northvale, New Jersey 07647.

Contents

Foreword

Two complaints are ubiquitous among those in the educational and clinical professions (in psychology, at least). First, it is hard to read journal articles and feel secure that you understand precisely what the authors did and why; furthermore, you rarely feel that you understand what made it possible to conduct the study—how the authors managed to be "allowed" to do what they did as well as what they were unable to do. Second, journal policy does not allow authors to go into meaningful detail about the intervention they are attempting to describe. The writer, therefore, knows that the reader will possess not all of the truth but just the "facts" constituting very partial truths. If replication remains a massive methodological obstacle in these fields, it is in part because of the way we are required to write for our professional journals. I am not suggesting that the journal format is inappropriate for all problems but rather that for some important issues, such as consultation and other forms of intervention, that format tends to defeat rather than contribute to illumination. Nor am I suggesting that because an intervention or the process of a consultation has been described in detail it is automatically a contribution to knowledge. Format influences the scope and depth of substance, but it in no way ensures quality. Too frequently, the terms *clinical* and *case study* are excuses for sloppy thinking and reporting.

My enthusiasm for this book needs to be seen in light of the preceding comments. What we have here are detailed reports in which the consultant-writer is not an impersonal reporter but shares center stage with a complex, tradition-bound setting buffeted internally and externally by diverse, frequently conflicting forces. What we get are the intricate relationships between who the consultant is and how he or she thinks, plans, and acts, on the one hand, and the hierarchically organized actors who comprise the school setting on the other. There is a degree of candor and courage in these reports that is exemplary, regardless of whether the consultant has goofed or succeeded. What comes through is a sensitivity to the culture of schools that, in my experience, is rare. To the would-be consultant, this book will be invaluable. It may also be intimidating, because the neophyte will be aware that consulting in schools is demanding in three respects: the knowledge of the setting that is required, the interpersonal-conceptual skills that can only be acquired over time, and the obstacle course that one must expect to experience and that sets limits on what one hopes to accomplish. There is a fourth demanding factor, and I can only put it in this way: the obligation to reflect and to avoid the worst features of the prepotent tendency to project blame outward as if one is locked primarily in an interpersonal battle. What is so impressive about these reports is the clarity with which the consultant-writers came to understand that people are in roles that inevitably, almost regardless of personality, color their view of the consultant and his or her role.

This book will stand up over time, not only because it demonstrates that we have learned something important about consultants and schools but also because it describes that learning in a way that those who are entering the field will find instructive and inspiring. On my more despairing days, I find myself concluding that the many efforts to improve our schools over the past three decades have pitifully little to show. When I feel that way again I will remember this book, which demonstrates to me that some people learn and accomplish a lot. Educational psychology has a surfeit of studies and facts that get disseminated rather widely; it is short on wisdom. This book contains a kind of wisdom that educational psychology has lacked.

Seymour B. Sarason
Professor of Psychology
Yale University

Preface to the 1995 Edition

Consultation has had a short history and a long prehistory. We could say that the history of consultation began in the 1960s, with the consultative activities and writings of Gerald Caplan, Seymour Sarason, and Ruth Newman.

The prehistory of consultation is fascinating and begins with Lightner Witmer's Clinic. It had a community orientation, a concern with prevention, and an interest in the educational process. The workers in this clinic were involved in entering the schools, setting up programs for public school teachers, and helping to establish special classes in public schools. The visiting teacher service is also part of the prehistory of consultation. It developed out of the settlement house movement and provided a link between the school and the community. Visiting teachers were involved in developing programs in order to deal with the general problems of the school and the community. Essentially they adopted a situational approach in which the teachers were involved in visiting the homes of problem children, interpreting the child's behavior to school staff, and working to modify the way the school staff responded to the child. The community child guidance clinic is also part of the prehistory. Rather than providing treatment, the function of the clinic was to enable a variety of social, child welfare, and educational organizations to handle problems of children. The community child guidance clinic was involved in identifying gaps in service and working with the community toward correcting those gaps. The goal was to alter the environment and to make it better for the child. Witmer's Clinic, the visiting teachers, and the child guidance clinic sounded contemporary. Yet they existed from seventy to one hundred years ago.

The present book was written when consultation was about fifteen years old. Today, consultation is thirty years old, and is an adult by developmental standards. I recently re-read the book. It still seems current. My hunch is that if we were to have read this book in Lightner Witmer Clinic days (1896), it would have been contemporary. My second hunch is that if we were to read this book in 2096, it would still seem modern. While the examples could be altered to delineate up-to-date problems, the intervention techniques and the conceptualization of consultation experiences still have bearing. It is not that consultation is stagnant. Rather, the consultative framework continues to have relevance as it did back in 1896, when Witmer founded his clinic.

I guess my mother was right. She was talking about furniture, but it applies to consultation as well. The good stuff lasts.

New York, New York Judith L. Alpert
November 1994

Preface

The purpose of this book is to promote understanding of what experienced consultants do, how they do it, and how they make sense of it. Composed of case studies about successful consultations, it is intended for professionals and students alike —for university trainers, field trainers, and practitioners, as well as for students in mental health and allied fields who train consultants, continue to learn about consulting, or are beginning to consult. Although the material focuses on consultation in educational settings, the lessons from the cases are applicable to other settings as well.

The book is organized on the basis of level of school in which consultation occurred. The introduction, in highlighting the main thrust of each chapter, points out similarities and differences among various consultations. Then, ten case studies deal with consultation at progressive school levels (elementary school, middle school, high school, college, and entire school system, with one case involving consultation outside a school system). The concluding chapter identifies some common themes and discusses issues that are as yet unresolved in consultation practice.

Since consultants engage in many different consultative

activities, use a diversity of intervention techniques, and conceptualize their consultation experiences in a variety of ways, the cases were solicited with this diversity in mind. The cases differ with respect to *type* of consultation—for example, mental health, organization development, behavioral, and advocacy. They focus on the several consultative *stages* (entry, diagnosis, intervention, and evaluation). And they consider the *person(s)* consulted with, such as students, school staff members, and parents.

To help readers grasp what consultation consists of—what it actually *means*—when carried out by professionals, I encouraged the authors to write frank and detailed narrative accounts. I asked them to relate the puzzles, problems, and ethical issues they faced and to spell out the assumptions they made and the conflicts those assumptions produced. Although the contributors are distinguished in the areas of consultation to schools and although their cases represent good consultation practice, within most successes there are some errors. Thus, I also asked the authors to reflect on the errors. And, wanting the cases to have a storytelling quality, I requested "first-person" accounts and a minimum of references. Finally, to encourage similarity of coverage in all chapters, I asked authors to consider such issues as the school and community culture, entry, diagnosis, intervention, and evaluation. The contributors responded to my initial requests in ways I assume they respond to consultation contracts offered them by school systems. They questioned, asked for clarification, and suggested alternatives. And, together, we worked to make the standards for their contributions clearer and better.

What I hoped for, and what actually materialized, were detailed, informative accounts—the kind that would enable both professionals and soon-to-be professionals to learn more about the practice and theory of consultation than they could from most other written material. There are few published case studies of psychological consultation in schools; the chapters in this book help make up for that lack.

For the contributors' active stance and for the delight and excitement I experienced in working with them, I am thankful. I am also indebted to three other groups of people. First, to my students, who had a great deal to do with the writing of this book; through their desire for case materials written by "seasoned" consultants, through their expressed wish for exposure to experiences beyond what my courses could offer, and through their wanting to know more about a variety of large and small consultation activities, they stimulated me to conceive of and pursue this project to completion. Second, I am grateful to my mentors—particularly Seymour Sarason, who had nothing to do directly with the editing of any part of this book but who is responsible for the volume's existence. He did more than teach me how to be a consultant; he taught me to think in a consultative framework, and for this I owe him a great deal. Finally, I am thankful to and for my husband Gordon and my daughter "Ivanya the Great"—just because.

New York, New York
July 1982

Judith L. Alpert

The Authors

Judith L. Alpert is Professor in the Doctoral Programs in School Psychology and Child/School Psychology at New York University and is on the faculty in New York University's Postdoctoral Program in Psychotherapy and Psychoanalysis. A past president of the Division of School Psychology of the American Psychological Association, she is a recipient of numerous awards including that division's Distinguished Service Award. Dr. Alpert is the editor of three books, over 25 chapters, and 75 articles. In addition to her focus on consultation, she does research and writing in the areas of child sexual abuse and gender studies. She is presently editing a book on delayed memories for childhood abuse.

Dr. Alpert began her activity in consultation in 1969, when she interned at the Yale University Psycho-Educational Clinic under the direction of Seymour Sarason. Subsequently she consulted in parochial schools in New York City. In 1973 she developed a two-semester practicum course in school consultation, which she continues to teach. She is presently involved in supervising the work of school consultants and school consultants-in-training. Also, she is involved in consultation projects around the disclosure and prevention of child sexual abuse and the evaluation of child sexual abuse programs.

Jack I. Bardon is Excellence Fund Professor of Education at the University of North Carolina, Greensboro.

Claire Bloomberg is a mental health consultant at the Child Centre, Rockville, Maryland.

Lauren Ann Carner is adjunct assistant professor of psychology at Pace University and a practicing school psychologist.

Cary Cherniss is a research psychologist at the Illinois Institute for Developmental Disabilities.

Michael D'Antonio is coordinator of the Pennsylvania Sudden Infant Death Syndrome (SIDS) Center, Children's Hospital of Philadelphia.

Ellis L. Gesten is associate professor of psychology at the University of South Florida.

P. Ross Loomes is a psychologist at Saskatchewan Penitentiary, Prince Albert, Saskatchewan.

Frederic J. Medway is associate professor of psychology at the University of South Carolina, Columbia.

Richard J. Nagle is associate professor of psychology at the University of South Carolina, Columbia.

Ruth G. Newman is associate professor of psychiatry at the University of Maryland and member of the executive committee of the Washington School of Psychiatry.

Patrick O'Neill is associate professor and chairperson, Department of Psychology, at Acadia University, Wolfville, Nova Scotia.

Richard A. Schmuck is professor of educational psychology at the University of Oregon.

Katy Tracy is a graduate student in the Clinical/Community Psychology Program at the University of Maryland.

Edison J. Trickett is professor of psychology and director of the Clinical/Community Psychology Program at the University of Maryland.

Rhona S. Weinstein is associate professor of psychology at the University of California, Berkeley.

Roger P. Weissberg is a research associate and assistant professor of psychology, Center for Community Study, at the University of Rochester.

Psychological Consultation in Educational Settings

Casebook for Working with Administrators, Teachers, Students, and Community

Introduction: Psychological Consultation in Educational Settings

Judith L. Alpert

Sometimes I feel that I approach a school with a bag of garden tools, only to find that the school has plumbing problems. I do, however, have a way of *thinking* about a problem and what might be done. Together the school staff and I try to find a plumber or else learn plumbing skills ourselves. Then I leave the school with my way of thinking about school problems and my well-developed gardening skills and my new plumbing skills, and head off to another school. The garden grows well in the next school, the sinks drain with ease, but there is an electrical problem in the kitchen. I have a way of thinking about things, I remind myself, as I try not to panic. Perhaps we'll find a dishwasher expert to help out the school. Or perhaps I'll learn how to fix dishwashers myself. In any event I do know that the most important tool of my trade is the consultative way of thinking about issues—a perspective exemplified in the chapters that follow.

This is a book of case studies dealing with successful consultation in educational settings. The contributors are professors, former professors, trainers of consultants, and psychological consultants to schools. Each author is a distinguished consultant, and most have written extensively on the subject. Each case exemplifies good practice and brings out the puzzles and problems inherent in this field. Even though the contributors are distinguished and the cases exemplify good practice, the reader is encouraged to approach the cases critically. Yes, this is a book of successes, but even successes can be improved. I hope readers will reflect on what they would have done differently—and why—and weigh the ethical issues the cases present.

This book discusses consultation on all levels: elementary school, middle school, high school, college, the entire school system. One case involves consultation outside a school system. Since more consultation is directed to elementary schools than to any other level, our emphasis lies there.

Chapter One, by Lauren Ann Carner, may be particularly helpful to school-based consultants who would like to assume more of a consultative role. Carner, a full-time school psychologist, describes how she restructured the position of school psychologist from one with a psychometric focus to one with a consultative focus. She indicates that the effort to structure the role in two elementary schools began early, involved many meetings with many people, and necessitated "persistent work with much backtracking and repetition." It is clear from this chapter that a psychologist working in schools can, at least in some settings, develop a consultative role.

In Chapter Two, I concentrate on the diagnostic phase of the consultation process. There I conceptualize the role of school staff and consultant in the diagnostic process, explain how to use school faculty meetings as a diagnostic tool, and urge the labeling of schools as a means of understanding them and their needs. In describing my work and the work of my students in a Catholic elementary school over a three-year period, I focus on how I learned about the school's needs and the implications of this learning for intervention. As the neighborhood of the school changed from residential to industrial, the needs of the school changed also. It no longer needed help in developing; rather, it needed help in accepting its end. There were decisions to be made about the emptying building and the relocating of students and staff. I discuss my role in helping the school to accept its end and consider the implications of the support given to the dying school. The chapter raises certain important issues. What is organizational health? How do you decide whether you can consult in a school? Who should diagnose? Who should determine interventions?

A group headed by Fritz Redl and Ruth Newman and assisted by Claire Bloomberg and Howard Kitchener was invited into a school to provide weekly consultation where it was needed. In Chapter Three, Newman and Bloomberg describe this work—which involved developing relationships with school staff, working with teachers to help specific children, providing demonstrations, assisting teachers with parent conferences, and helping the principal deal with problems. While Chapters One and Two focus on a specific aspect of consultation, structuring a role and diagnosis respectively, this chapter exemplifies a larger part of the consultation process. Newman and Bloomberg were not called in to develop a specific program or work on a concrete project; rather, they made themselves available where they were needed. This case should be particularly helpful to those working in an elementary school since it illustrates the range of activities and approaches used by mental health consultants at that level.

In Chapter Four, Rhona S. Weinstein describes her work as an external consultant, which extended over a period of two years and involved the creation of a collaborative mental health team in a middle school. The team's objective was to explore innovative ways of helping problem children within the school setting while relying on the school's own resources, both real and potential. She traces the team's history, specific problems the group dealt with, and the reactions of the superintendent and principal to the group's nontraditional means of handling mental health problems in schools. In considering the institutional constraints to the team's work, the author illuminates the factors that might support or hinder the development of new organizational structures. This case should be of particular interest to those involved with group consultation as well as those who wish to develop new structures within a school.

In Chapter Five, Cary Cherniss, Edison J. Trickett, Michael D'Antonio, and Katy Tracy discuss the school effectiveness committee—a student group they created to involve high school students in governing the school. They describe the town and school, the consultant relationship, how they discovered the need for such a group, and how they formed the committee. Further, they explain the various phases of the group's work and their interaction with the group and also the social structure. The authors focus on both the content and the process of their intervention effort and draw implications about the role of the consultant and the problems of change. Chapters Four and Five both involve the creation of a group with a specific objective. Moreover, there are parallels in the phases of group development and in the institutional constraints to their work. Together the two chapters throw light on the relationship between organizational factors and institutional change.

In Chapter Six, Frederic J. Medway and Richard J. Nagle review literature concerning variables affecting high school consultation. Specifically they consider the physical environment of the high school and the relationship of the high school to the community. They then present a case illustrating high school consultation. The authors describe how they introduced themselves to school staff and students, how they learned about the problems facing students and faculty, and how they used a formal needs assessment. From this survey a decision was made to work on discipline. Thus Medway and Nagle worked with problem adolescents, a discipline policy committee, and a study skills program. They conclude by indicating the lessons they learned and the principles they believe are basic to high school consultation. They find that high schools are fertile ground for mental health consultation.

Chapter Seven concerns a new setting for consultation: the college or university. Jack I. Bardon describes his involvement in faculty development at a college and his use of consultation at that level. Specifically he describes entry into the system and details the intervention, which involved a faculty study group. After outlining what the group did to further faculty development, he explains why he recommended that the study group be discontinued after two years. Throughout the chapter, Bardon indicates mini-lessons he learned as he consulted. His chapter, moreover, raises an interesting question: Is every faculty member with consultative skills a consultant within the setting, or is the faculty member only a consultant when labeled as such by the institution?

In Chapter Eight, Ellis L. Gesten and Roger P. Weissberg describe a training program for social problem-solving skills designed to teach children a cognitive-behavioral approach to the resolution of daily interpersonal conflicts. The program involved 100 second, third, and fourth-grade teachers, and school staff were trained to operate it. The focus of the chapter is on the problems and processes associated with entry, program development, expansion, and dissemination. This discussion should be particularly helpful to those interested in setting up large-scale programs.

Chapter Nine, by Richard A. Schmuck, also exemplifies large-scale intervention. He describes the activities of a formal group in a school district that carried out organization-development consultation. The cadre of consultants was composed of teachers, counselors, principals, and central office personnel; the intervention involved peer consultation on organizational issues. Thus it is the school members themselves—with the aid of the voluntary, collegial, part-time consultants—who examine school problems and take part in the statement of goals, the development of skills, the redesign of structures and procedures, and the evaluation of results. Schmuck contends that the concept of "peer-colleagues as consultants" offers a healthy alternative to the traditional professional-client helping relationship in schools.

Chapter Ten, by Patrick O'Neill and P. Ross Loomes, discusses consultation outside the school system. The authors were involved in drawing teachers out of the schools to join parents in a collaborative enterprise to press an economically poor and conservative school system to introduce services for learning-disabled children. This case history documents the rationale behind their strategy, the tactics involved in enlisting parents, and the difficulties they encountered.

Some common themes emerge from a reading of these ten cases, even though there are some obvious differences in consultation practice in various settings. For example, in order to point out differences in consultation at elementary and high school levels, Chapters Six and Three could be contrasted. The reader should keep in mind that the two groups of consultants differ and neither school in which they consulted can be seen as representative of the school level. Nevertheless, the reader might consider whether Medway and Nagle could have worked in the high school as Newman and Bloomberg worked in the elementary school—or alternatively, whether it makes more sense to focus on projects at the high school level. Chapter Six could also be compared with Chapter Two, as both focus on the diagnostic phase of the consultation process. Whereas in Chapter Two I label and utilize faculty meetings, in Chapter Six Medway and Nagle administer a needs assessment survey. The reader might consider how intervention may have differed if I had used the survey or if Medway and Nagle had utilized faculty meetings or labeling for diagnostic purposes.

An interesting, and as yet unresolved, issue is apparent when one considers the various studies. In contrast to the rest of the book, Chapters One and Five describe cases in which the authors were internal consultants. By reading the two chapters consecutively, the reader is able to consider the advantages and disadvantages of serving as internal consultant. Clearly, in both settings the authors' position enabled them to know their system better. Could Bardon have accomplished his goal more readily had he been a consultant outside the system? This case could also be contrasted with Medway and Nagle's (Chapter Six) and with Newman and Bloomberg's (Chapter Three), in order to throw light on the different consultative problems one meets in the college, high school, and elementary school.

Schmuck (Chapter Nine) and O'Neill and Loomes (Chapter Ten) also consider the value of internal versus external consultants. Schmuck holds that the organization-development cadres combine the virtues of both internal and external consultants. They are internal consultants in that they work for the same school board and superintendent and are on the same pay schedule and receive similar benefits; they are external consultants since they never consult within their own departments, teams, committees, or schools. O'Neill and Loomes functioned as community organizers and worked outside the system to create change within the system; their case exemplifies advocacy consultation. Chapters Nine and Ten can be compared to gain an understanding of the differences in values, goals, strategies, and problems implied by working for change from within or without.

In the conclusion to the book, I will deal further with both the common themes and the unresolved issues in consultation practice.

Developing a Consultative Contract

1

Lauren Ann Carner

For every graduate student in school psychology, no doubt there exist unsettling fantasies of the first working days in the chosen profession. While seminars, practica, and internships give ample opportunities to discuss issues and develop skills, the nature of such preservice activities usually precludes any restructuring of the role itself. Work done at the preservice level must serve the demands of the school and the university. The intern or practicum student may concentrate on certain activities, but generally he or she steps into a preexisting role. Once employment in a school system has been gained, the former student may see this position as fixed and inflexible. The rigidity with which such role definitions are held depends on many institutional features—such as the state of the economy and its effect on the school budget, the size and complexity of the school system, and the history of psychological services in the district. However, these systems variables interact with individual variables—such as the new psychologist's training, orientation, and willingness to work at changing the established order. For those trained in consultation theory and practice, the traditional job description of school psychologist may seem limiting. Of course, training programs have for some time been emphasizing the "renaissance" school psychologist, but an approach that would enable one to move from psychometrician and counselor to a broader role remains elusive. Perhaps by keeping in mind certain basic principles offered by consultation theory such an approach can be articulated.

The following case study is a description of efforts to restructure a position as a school psychologist so that consultation would not be a peripheral service but rather a foundation. These efforts began as early as the first interview for the position and were most deliberately applied during the first weeks of the school year. Thereafter, a continuing pattern of assessment, adjustment, maintenance, and further evaluation was established. This pattern has changed little after nearly two years, although new and unanticipated difficulties continue to emerge. Despite the number of additional duties that have been imposed, the passage of time has confirmed to me that there can be a great deal of latitude in creating a consultative role in school psychology—and, moreover, that it is up to the psychologist to demonstrate what is possible. While some of these efforts took place in a secondary school, this account focuses on work done in two small elementary schools. Names and certain characteristics have been changed to protect the privacy of those mentioned.

The Setting

Westvale, an affluent community of about twelve thousand people, is situated near a large metropolitan area. Once a bastion of white, upper-middle-class values, it has clung with remarkable tenacity to its own deeply felt sense of history and purpose. The local weekly carries regular features on what was "news" ten, twenty, and fifty years before. Bronze tablets adorn schoolhouse walls with the names of both honor students and those who died in the last several wars. The town is politically conservative with a citizenry active in both country club life and school affairs. Like similar communities nationwide, however, Westvale has been forced to contend with changes not entirely to its liking. These have been experienced less as a tidal wave, perhaps, than as a persistent, ominous lapping against the bulwarks. The comfortable distance Westvale would prefer to keep between itself and the grim realities of the urban world has been eroding steadily in the last several years. Drug and alcohol abuse, vandalism, declining motivation and achievement of children, lack of respect for authority figures and their traditional values—such problems have caused considerable concern and much anxious discussion among parents and school personnel. As in many systems that perceive threats to their stability, the response in Westvale has often been to turn to traditional solutions that are believed to have worked in the past. Traditional teaching methods with an emphasis on basics are overwhelmingly preferred, and very high achievement is expected. With the average reading score two years above grade level, a demanding academic program is the norm. Children who are "merely" average, who may have less support at home, who may be less interested in academic pursuits, as well as those with specific learning problems, sometimes find it difficult to function well in such a rarefied atmosphere.

Inflation has exacted a toll on Westvale as well as the more publicized urban school districts. With the fastest-growing item in the school budget listed as heating and maintenance costs, and with an aging population less able to contribute to tax revenues, some teaching positions have been eliminated and every expenditure is carefully scrutinized by a vigilant school board.

The school system is small. Led by a superintendent and assistant superintendent, there are three elementary schools and a junior and a senior high school. Since the late 1950s, the district has been served by two psychologists—one responsible for the two smaller elementary schools and the junior high, the other responsible for the larger elementary school and the senior high. Other districtwide duties, such as Committee on the Handicapped, kindergarten screening, and in-service training programs, were divided between them.

When one of the positions became available, I immediately submitted an application. Because I had completed a part-time internship in the district some years before, an interview was granted as a courtesy. Although I had state certification in school psychology and a variety of relevant experience, it seemed an obvious disadvantage to have neither a doctoral degree nor the several years' experience the screening committee was looking for. In thinking about the impending interview, two related needs became evident. First, I would have to compensate for my lack of credentials by demonstrating an ability to handle some of the real-life difficulties faced by school psychologists; second, I would have to establish a contract to do consultation were I to be chosen for the position. Unlike consultants who are called in to help with a specific problem, school psychologists may not be perceived by administrators as having a negotiable role. Particularly since the enactment of Public Law 94-142 and related state regulations for the identification and education of handicapped pupils, psychologists may have lost some of their freedom to determine their own role and function. As Alpert and Trachtman (1980) point out, however, such legislative "restrictions" can actually serve as a springboard to consultative activity. They argue that if school psychologists wish to modify administrators' notions of what constitutes appropriate and useful activity, they must know *how* they want to function and be ready to seize opportunities that would allow them to function in that way. Accordingly, if I wished to develop a different approach to school psychology in Westvale, it would have to be understood and sanctioned by the administrators most affected by it: the principals.

The internship that I served, before going on for additional graduate training, gave me some familiarity with the system and taught me how the departing psychologist had functioned. This psychologist was personable, knowledgeable, and hardworking. Although she had allotted certain days to specific schools, she was almost never there for an entire day and would travel to the schools when requested to work with a child or meet with a teacher or parent. She maintained an extremely hectic pace, dashing from meeting to meeting and from school to school when summoned by a principal. This working style made an orderly follow-through and evaluation of efforts difficult to attain. It also tended to discourage referrals, since many teachers assumed she was too busy to help them. A more consultative approach would encourage teachers to come to the psychologist with a wide array of questions about student learning and behavior. Only through such contacts, and a relationship of trust and respect, would teachers be able to sharpen their ability to detect subtle signs of trouble and recognize behavior capable of being handled by the teacher.

My impression of this psychologist was that she was rather more successful with the principals than with teachers. Certainly she tended to share the administration's point of view. While the importance of the principal in implementing change is crucial, Caplan (1970) warns that the consultant's success depends also on negotiating sanction through all levels of the hierarchy—in this case, including teachers. To the extent that this did not take place, some referrals were not made, recommendations not always implemented, and effective evaluation of efforts did not always take place. This did not necessarily mean that she was a traditional school psychologist armed only with testing kit and counseling skills. Indeed the many meetings she attended suggested that group consultation was an important focus. But a critical element of planned change is that it must be orderly and systematic and take into account all the elements that will affect the outcome of an intervention. What I most wanted to convey in the interview was that I understood these elements and could act on that knowledge—a very important skill in the school psychologist's repertoire.

The Interview

The interviewing committee consisted of the two elementary principals with whom the prospective psychologist would be working, the assistant superintendent, and the remaining school psychologist. They were to select their three leading candidates, and the superintendent would base his decision on their recommendations and on his own interviews with the finalists.

The interview began with questions familiar to anyone who has ever sought a position in school psychology. Dr. Telford, the psychologist, asked about previous experience, my orientation toward special education and children with learning disabilities, and, finally, what I could bring to the position. I began to explain that the year-long laboratory course in consultation had been a particularly useful part of my training. When invited to elaborate, I said that, prior to taking the course, many situations had arisen in schools that appeared hopelessly beyond the expertise of even a skilled psychologist. Although a psychologist might understand a child's difficulties and have good suggestions to make, these recommendations would have to be acted upon by parents and teachers. Too often written recommendations appeared on a test report only as empty testimony to a psychologist's ingenuity, while the conditions responsible for the child's difficulties remained unchanged. It was the difficult terrain between understanding a problem and effectively helping others to make changes that had troubled me most as a beginning school psychologist. I went on to explain how consultation theory examines the basic dilemma of how to effect change. Situations that may have appeared hopeless and incomprehensible in the past could now be understood and dealt with by the consultant. Such situations could no longer be attributed to the child's unchangeable psychopathology; rather, they should be regarded as a combination of system variables and individual variables capable of assessment and treatment. Resistance, for example, usually seen in a school setting as hostility or stubbornness, could alternatively be understood as providing a useful defensive function against hasty or unwarranted change (Klein, 1976). Once seen in that light, a more appropriate strategy could then be devised to deal with it—a strategy sensitive to the individual's need to control the rate or scope of change.

The interviewing committee appeared to be interested, so I went on. A basic premise of consultation is that it must be a collaborative relation. Insisting on coequal status with teachers reduces the unrealistic pressure on the psychologist for magical solutions and encourages teachers to take responsibility for positive change in the classroom. After this last assertion, Mrs.

Hodges, the principal of Oak Street School, broke in with a somewhat dismayed tone of voice: "Isn't the psychologist supposed to be the expert?" Ms. Ferguson, the other principal, with less dismay in her voice than incredulity, added: "Shouldn't we be able to rely on the authority of the psychologist to induce teachers to change?" I thought a moment and replied that certainly there were areas of expertise that belong to psychologists and need to be shared in schools. Knowledge about child development, how children learn, environmental factors that promote cognitive and affective growth—all forms part of the "knowledge base" of psychologists working in schools. Nevertheless, the teacher is still the expert in the classroom and any strategies for change must take into account the teacher's range of skills, understanding of the problem, and teaching style. While the principal, as the executive in the school, does have the power to decree change, the psychologist has no such authority—nor would that approach make best use of the psychologist's skills. Rather than assume a role of authoritarian expert, I preferred to function as a team member, working in a collaborative manner, making use of the knowledge specific to psychology, but aiming always to facilitate the effective use of skills, talent, and energy in a school.

This statement appeared to mark a turning point in the interview. The committee members abandoned their prepared questions and began to ask how such an approach might work in certain situations they had faced. I tried to explain how the cases they mentioned might be handled in a consultative way, what outcomes might be expected, and why. I was careful not to portray consultation as a cure-all for every problem in the school, and, as Caplan (1970) recommends for consultation with teachers, I reflected on the enormously complex problems faced by school personnel today. This discussion not only provided an opportunity to give specific illustrations of how consultation works but also revealed the kinds of problems that particularly troubled these principals. In fact, the interview itself could be considered a preliminary assessment: a rich source of information in which the problems posed by the principal reflected her conception of what a school psychologist should be.

From this initial assessment, a few observations could be made. First, their examples did not concern situations that would call for testing or counseling but, rather, typified their own difficulties. There appeared to be tacit agreement among them that since the psychologist's knowledge was not accessible to them, questions about diagnostics or methodology did not arise. In looking for other measures to gauge the candidate's worth, the main criterion appeared to be the psychologist's ability to help the principal meet her own objectives. Judging from their previous remarks about "relying on the psychologist's authority," it appeared that they expected such help to be delivered in a direct, authoritarian way—that is, with the psychologist functioning as the principal's agent. Their evident interest in my remarks about consultation, however, suggested that they were open to a renegotiation of that role.

One main theme emerged: the issue of control. The principal appeared to be most concerned by what she saw as intrusion in school affairs by articulate, intelligent, sometimes aggressive parents who were not always in agreement with the aims and efforts of school personnel. It was not unusual for parents to take even minor complaints to the superintendent or members of the school board, and the principal would then be asked to account for her actions in the situation. Understandably, then, a psychologist's ability to defuse a tense encounter with an angry parent would be seen by the principal as an important skill indeed.

Another major concern was the "difficult teacher"—one who is unresponsive or hostile to the principal's suggestions for improvement. With pressures emanating from the superintendent and school board, the principals would not infrequently be frustrated by their failure to establish complete control over those in their purview.

Sarason (1971, p. 126) analyzes the difficult relations between principal and teacher as deriving from the "context of power and evaluation" in which they occur. He goes on to say that the potential for conflict between the principal and psychologist resides in the principal's dilemma of being dependent on the expertise of someone who is not administratively accountable to him. It is possible, however, that the unsteady alignment of expertise versus power may provide creative possibilities rather than conflict. The principal may be willing to relax control over the psychologist if the latter truly helps to implement the school's educational goals. Certainly the psychologist needs sufficient autonomy to refuse to perform actions antithetical to professional standards. What these principals seemed to be saying was that they would welcome assistance with many of the larger issues confronting them. I tried to make it clear that I too wanted to work with them and that, however our methods might differ, we would be working in a complementary way toward the same educational goals. Evidently my approach struck a responsive chord. A week later I was offered the position.

Preparation

In the absence of a written job description, I regarded my appointment as something of a mandate to work in the consultative way I had described in the interview. I had already stressed my desire to build collaborative helping relationships with teachers, and I had acknowledged the importance of working within the framework of the principal's objectives. The extent to which I could become involved in a broader role, one that would include program planning and implementation, was yet unclear. In terms of what I hoped to accomplish in the next year, I could identify three broad goals: first, to establish good working relationships with staff members; second, to enhance smooth teamwork within each school; third, to strengthen the schools' responsiveness to children in need—in terms of effective identification of such children and flexible individualized arrangements for them. In addition to knowing what I wanted to accomplish, I was quite clear about how I wanted to do it. I wanted to work toward prevention, at least part of the time. That is, some proportion of my efforts should be directed toward building a foundation that would reduce problems in the future as opposed to ameliorating a specific problem in the present. Moreover, it was my intention to emphasize indirect service as much as possible. This would mean working with staff members on the problem rather than working directly with the problem.

Meetings with the superintendent and with Dr. Telford led to an agreeable distribution of quasi-administrative, district-wide responsibilities traditionally shared by the two psychologists. Apart from that, no specific tasks were assigned. Since the departing psychologist had prepared summaries of cases she had worked on in the past year, in the weeks before school opened I spent hours going through the files of children who had been referred for psychological services. From this information it was possible to list the children who might need some follow-up action in September. This list would serve as a useful departure point in the initial meetings with principal and teachers. Since I wished to become part of the fabric of each school I worked in, I made a point of arranging to spend the entire designated day at the school rather than dropping in and out. Despite some disadvantages of this arrangement, the regular presence of the psychologist in the school has proved to be an important prerequisite for structuring a consultative role.

The first week of school after summer vacation is an exciting time. Teachers return to work tanned and refreshed, the frustrations and failures of the previous year soothed by the healing rituals of summer. Classrooms are newly decorated and thoughtfully organized, and there is a tangible atmosphere of hope and renewal. Since learning and behavior problems rarely emerge during this honeymoon period, it is a good time for a psychologist to get to know teachers and pupils in a calm atmosphere. I made appointments with Mrs. Hodges and Ms. Ferguson, the two principals, for the first week of school.

Beginning Work with the Principal

If the interview for the position was the first stage in structuring a consultative role, the initial meetings with the principals inaugurated the second. Armed with the list of children who might require follow-up, I visited Mrs. Hodges of Oak Street School first. She was a pleasant woman, in late middle age, who would be retiring the following year. She offered coffee and we began talking about the specifics of my work in the school. When I mentioned my wish to become part of the school by being available to teachers on a consistent, scheduled basis, Mrs. Hodges seemed pleased. There was no indication that she would be threatened by my attempts to develop relationships with teachers. I then expressed my hope that we could meet regularly every week and coordinate my activities with her objectives.

After these preliminary matters were settled, I asked Mrs. Hodges which of her yearly objectives I could help to implement. Without hesitating, she talked at length about the fourth-grade class, which had a reputation for unruliness and conflict despite good academic ability. She reflected on the history of this group and the factors that had contributed to its dynamics. She expressed interest in working with me to develop an affective program for this group of children. We discussed the possibility of starting an affective program in the kindergarten and first grade as well. As a beginning step, I offered to bring information describing different approaches so that she could decide on a suitable one for Oak Street School. I also offered to give a mini-workshop for the teachers on the rationale behind affective programs and their various characteristics, including programs developed by teachers. This was the beginning of a long-term multifaceted intervention in the school. It covered several grade levels, led to joint efforts by parents and teachers, and appears to have become a well-integrated part of the curriculum.

Mrs. Hodges mentioned her interest in expanding a program for gifted youngsters, but she was not sure that my involvement could be useful. After a pause, we then went over each child on my list of cases. It was gratifying to see her knowledge of each child; her warmth and concern were obvious. Nevertheless, there seemed to be no clear-cut referral process. Nor did there appear to be a consistent procedure for disseminating information to relevant staff members—a question I would want to pursue in subsequent meetings. We approached the end of our first meeting with several specific tasks to accomplish before our next meeting:

1. I was to bring in information on affective programs for Mrs. Hodges to look over.
2. I would introduce myself at the first faculty meeting and explain the consultative way in which I hoped to work with the teachers.
3. I would meet with several teachers individually to discuss specific children and arrange for classroom observation.
4. Sometime in early fall I would give a workshop after school for the teachers on different affective programs.

As we said cordial good-byes, Mrs. Hodges casually mentioned that she was on her way to another meeting with the reading teacher to plan a school-based resource team. Further inquiry revealed that the resource team was one of her objectives for the year. I tried to suppress my dismay at being excluded. When I expressed interest in the team concept, she was rather apologetic and explained that she was under the impression that the psychologist was only to deal with emotional and behavior problems and that other resource specialists would handle learning problems. When I assured her that I had been trained in the assessment and treatment of learning problems and, moreover, was very much interested in working on such a project with her, she readily assented. It was only accidentally, then, that I became involved in a project that did more to further the consultative role than any other activity that year.

The meeting with Ms. Ferguson at Pilgrim Street School was structured in much the same way. We reviewed the consultative way of working I had described in the interview and discussed her objectives for the year. This time, however, the principal had a difficult time thinking of how I fit into her plans. She too mentioned a program for the gifted, but she too seemed dubious about the value of my involvement. She then mentioned a program that had been in effect for several years in which social work interns from a local mental health center made weekly visits to the school for therapeutic play sessions with selected youngsters. When I expressed interest, she looked genuinely surprised. Since the program had been in effect for some time and had run smoothly, it was not evident to her why a psychologist would even want to become involved. I explained that I thought the psychologist's contribution might be useful—both in selecting appropriate children and in working with the interns in order to learn more about the children and to feed this information back to the teachers. Ms. Ferguson assented, but she did not appear entirely convinced. She agreed to inform me when the interns came for their introductory meeting. As before, we also went over a list of children to be followed up, and she added the name of another child who had moved to the community over the summer. Ms. Ferguson too seemed to know quite a bit about each child we discussed, and she had strong opinions about the different characteristics and teaching styles of the teachers. She expressed a desire to have me "work with" a few of the teachers. By the tone and context of her remarks it appeared that she would favor a direct instructional approach, and I was reminded of her comment in the interview about relying on the psychologist to "induce teachers to change." I explained that I very much wanted to work closely with teachers and hoped I could help them make positive changes. For that to happen, though, it would be necessary to build trusting relationships carefully and slowly. As with Mrs. Hodges, we agreed to meet regularly on the day I was in the school and agreed also that I would speak about consultation at the first faculty meeting. Unlike the previous meeting, however, I did not leave with specific tasks to accomplish, a fact that left me slightly uneasy. I was not comfortable with Ms. Ferguson; in fact, I had a vague sensation that we had been engaged in a subtle struggle. I was not at all sure what she thought of me. Here was a woman in firm control of her school who would be, at best, neutral to working with the psychologist in a different way—at least until she could be persuaded that it was useful and suitable to her own leadership style.

Meeting with Teachers

I looked forward to speaking at the first faculty meetings with a mixture of anxiety and excitement. Trying to establish credibility with a group of people, none of whom had fewer than seven years' experience, most of whom were considerably older than I, was a daunting prospect. After being warmly introduced by Mrs. Hodges, I looked around me, took a deep breath, and began. It was not difficult to speak of the respect I hold for teachers; of the constant strain imposed not only by the demands of young children but by their own integrity as well; of my wish to learn more about the difficulties they must contend with in the classroom—and to do so without adding to their already considerable burdens. I explained that I would no doubt be performing many of the same school psychologist's tasks they were used to, such as testing and counseling, but that I was above all looking forward to working with them as a partner. I ended with a request to be invited into their classrooms at their convenience so that I could get acquainted with the children. They responded with warm smiles and invitations to "drop in any time."

The message was the same at Pilgrim Street School, but the context was decidedly different. Ms. Ferguson led the faculty through a lengthy business meeting and recruited reluctant volunteers for various committees. Finally she introduced new staff members and asked them to say a few words. Two teachers and a librarian were welcomed and spoke briefly, and then Ms. Ferguson moved on to the next agenda item. Heart pounding, I raised my hand and reminded her that I too was new to the staff. Ms. Ferguson was appropriately embarrassed and we managed to make a joke of it, raising a laugh from the assembled teachers. Since we had agreed beforehand that I would speak, this "oversight" suggested she might be reluctant to have me establish my own footing with the teachers. My little talk to the teachers contained the same basic message I conveyed to the teachers of Oak Street School. Since the meeting moved quickly to other agenda items, I was unable to assess the impact of my message. I did, however, receive a hastily scrawled note of welcome from the reading teacher and, from the first-grade teacher seated next to me, a whispered invitation to visit her class.

Comparing these initial meetings with principals and staff of two surprisingly different schools, I found it difficult at first not to feel more positive about my plans with the warm, easy-going Mrs. Hodges and the openly welcoming teachers of Oak Street School. The danger in such early impressions is that a less "advanced" consultee may in fact make comparable or even greater gains than a more favored one but may not be credited by the consultant with as significant a success. Alpert, Weiner, and Ludwig (1979) found that the consultee's initial level of functioning is an important factor in the consultant's evaluation of outcome. That is, the consultee who is likeable, easy to work with, and perceived as already functioning at a high level will also be seen as more successful. It was helpful to keep in mind the different "starting points" of the two schools when I was evaluating different outcomes of consultation. By remaining objective, I might eventually conclude that the greatest positive change occurred in the more difficult school.

Following Through

Just as the initial description of consultation at the job interview did not give the principals a clear understanding of my role, a brief explanation at a faculty meeting after school could not be expected to suffice for the teachers. In an evaluation of student consultants by consultees Mann (1973) found that the teachers who actually used consultants were able to give more definitions of the consultant's function that those who did not. The implication, of course, is that a verbal description of consultation is a mere beginning. There must be many experiences if the consultee is to understand the process and use it effectively. The problem of consultee readiness is significant when one is entering a system. Bardon (1977) writes that problems defined as resistance, or as a function of entry, may in fact result from differences in professional preparation for consultation. He then suggests that the value of seeking professional help to resolve complex problems should be inculcated at the preservice level. As in other professions, teachers too should view consultation as a right rather than a sign of weakness. Sandoval, Lambert, and Davis (1977) detail several "categories of understanding" that a consultee must learn in order to benefit from the consultant's skills. These categories include learning how to present relevant information about the problem client, what kind of help to expect from consultation, and what the consultant has to offer. Moreover, the consultee must learn about his or her own style of response and how it may affect a situation.

My first few weeks in the schools showed that following through in the efforts to structure this consultative role would be somewhat like clearing a jungle—a task that would require steady, patient, persistent work with much backtracking and repetition. Certainly there were many misperceptions and projections concerning the psychologist's position. Although they had worked for years with the previous psychologist, who was well versed in learning problems, many at Oak Street School nevertheless thought that the new psychologist was only to work with emotional and behavior problems. At the other extreme, Ms. Ferguson had in the past received complaints from parents who disliked the idea of a psychologist working with their children. The implication was that the psychologist, by definition, must be interested in uncovering all sorts of private information—and, moreover, it would be stigmatizing for their child to be seen with such a person. When I began work at the school, I was dismayed to learn that Ms. Ferguson's solution to this dilemma was to tell parents that there were no emotional problems in her school and that I would be doing only educational as opposed to psychological evaluation. Depending on the school, it looked as though my job could be whittled away from both ends! There were also the usual comments about couches, of course, and suspicion that I was analyzing their conversations.

Caplan has many suggestions for dealing with this problem, including "one-downsmanship" as a response to exaggerated deference. As I spent more time with teachers, certain basic strategies began to emerge from an increased understanding of the realities of their working lives. Although some of these strategies may seem too elementary to deserve mention, the comments I received from teachers suggested that it was just these practical considerations that most enhanced the relationship-building process.

My first realization had to do with time. No adult who

has not spent time in an elementary school can possibly understand what a precious commodity it is. The forty-week school year seems ridiculously inadequate to convey all that a teacher hopes to impart. Especially in traditionally run schools, the day is tightly structured into twenty or forty-minute increments. In addition to the basic subjects, students leave the class for art, music, gym, remedial reading, or other special classes. Each teacher has one planning period in which to grade papers, check homework, run off dittos, telephone a parent, plan a lesson, and perhaps have a cup of coffee. The planning period is the one time during the school day that the psychologist and teacher can talk without being interrupted. The price paid by the teacher, of course, is that all the other tasks normally accomplished during that time must be postponed. Often teachers will attempt a hasty corridor conference with children milling about—or, worse, start discussing a child in the classroom, with the "problem child" inevitably and miserably aware that he is the subject of conversation. When that happened, I tried to support the teacher by acknowledging that her concerns were legitimate and making a specific appointment to discuss them at greater length. Since no significant problem is manageable under such feverish circumstances, my intent was to model a calm and rational approach to difficulties. At the same time, it is necessary to be responsive and meet with the teacher as soon as her schedule permits. One day a week, even in a small school, is not much time and the day can be quickly filled with appointments. A scrupulous attitude about writing down and keeping appointments conveys respect and the message that the teacher's concerns are important.

Another organizing and relationship-building strategy, again a matter of common sense, is to take notes of the day's transactions. A school psychologist deals with so many people that it is hardly possible to remember all the names and details without assistance. Taking brief notes and then reviewing them before entering the school may help the consultant respond with something more intelligent than a blank stare when a teacher asks about a child she mentioned two weeks before. A young kindergarten teacher confided that a psychologist in another district tended to forget the cases they discussed from week to week. She had been insulted by his forgetfulness and felt it implied a lack of involvement with those in the schools.

Yet another practical strategy is simply to follow up. Much can happen in a week, and a suggestion that looked spectacular the previous week can become an obsolete failure within several days. While there are always new cases to occupy one's time, a simple "How is it going?" at the classroom door is enough to show that you care and are available if needed. As the year progressed, my appreciation of teachers deepened when I saw how much they invest in their pupils. In the few situations where handicapped children required special placement, the referring teachers always seemed grateful for periodic information on the child's progress. This keeping in touch was mentioned by several teachers at the end of the year as the factor they appreciated most in the professional relationship. They said that it made them feel someone was on the firing line with them, willing to work for solutions, instead of making the usual set of recommendations and then disappearing.

I believe that these strategies helped to establish my credibility and dispelled some of the sinister associations that accrue to the psychologist's role. Although these efforts were directed toward building relationships with individual teachers, it was the resource team that proved to be particularly effective for consultation.

Resource Teams

My involvement in the development of the resource team at Oak Street School came about accidentally. While the resource team had been one of Mrs. Hodges' building objectives for the year, it also coincided with my own goals of enhancing teamwork in the school and strengthening the school's responsiveness to children in need. Mrs. Hodges had already met with Mr. Thompson, the reading teacher, to work on the team's composition and functions. By the time I entered the process, they had come up with a flowchart indicating the sequence of events leading up to a team meeting. Mrs. Hodges designated funds to pay for substitutes so that teachers could attend meetings during the school day rather than after school. We agreed to rotate responsibility for record keeping among the principal, the reading teacher, and the psychologist. The principal would keep a notebook with a brief referral form filled out by the teacher. The minutes of the discussion, recommendations, and follow-up assignments would be noted on the back of the referral form and, when completed, circulated to staff members working with the child.

Mrs. Hodges had made it clear that she wanted to know who was being seen for special services and why. In talking with teachers about the resource team concept, I soon found that there was some confusion between making a resource team referral and making a psychological referral. We decided to simplify the referral process by having all requests for testing go through the resource team. That way, we could discuss the case thoroughly and, as a group, decide whether or not testing would be appropriate. From past experience, it had been my impression that teachers often ask for testing as a general cry for help—perhaps because they do not know of other types of help a psychologist or team member may provide. I hoped to use the resource team to model a problem-solving approach. As a result of these meetings, teachers would begin to recognize their own capacity to solve problems and rely less on the direct intervention of specialists.

Meanwhile, at Pilgrim Street School, Ms. Ferguson was interested in the progress we were making with the resource team. Although she had conducted occasional "resource team" meetings after school that had been duly recorded by the psychologist, they had not been used consistently. We decided to work together on a flowchart for the Pilgrim Street resource team that would incorporate some of the innovations started at Oak Street School.

Ms. Ferguson and I had had a rocky beginning as we tried to negotiate a contract for my efforts in the school. As an effective administrator who valued direct, decisive action, she was not always sympathetic to the limitations I placed on my efforts. When she asked me to "work with" a teacher, I suspect that she hoped a few well-chosen words from the psychologist would set the teacher straight. I explained that I would indeed make efforts to seek out that teacher; but if our relationship was to be effective, it would have to be purely voluntary, with no hint of coercion or evaluation. It was also necessary to remind her several times that my conversations with teachers, like her conversations with me, would have to be confidential. I think she regarded these conventions as niceties, something of a bother, that must be tolerated as part of the incomprehensible baggage psychologists carry. Although it must have been difficult for her, she always honored the limitations I set.

Perhaps it would be useful here to examine a few of the cases that were referred to the team meetings. These cases illustrate the many varieties of involvement available to school psychologists and the broad range of the consultees' "categories of learning."

At Pilgrim Street School there were seven children on the agenda for the first meeting. I had already spoken briefly to each referring teacher and all had requested testing. Ms. Ferguson had hired a substitute for the afternoon to cover each teacher during his or her allotted time. In some cases, Ms. Ferguson invited the child's teacher from the previous year, an idea that has worked extremely well. Also included in the discussions were the librarian and the reading, art, music, and gym teachers when appropriate. Their inclusion has proved especially useful since they often see strengths in a child that may not be evident in a strictly academic setting—strengths that may form the basis for remedial strategies.

As we worked our way through that first agenda, a certain pattern began to take shape. Taking a problem-solving approach—that is, asking questions about the child's history, past efforts to help, and the context in which the troubling behavior occurred—seemed to stimulate teachers to discover their own solutions. One teacher decided to establish a special time for paying extra attention to a withdrawn girl. Another decided to establish a contract system for a boy who was not doing his homework. Teachers offered to help one another. A fifth-grade teacher having trouble with a volatile boy was advised by the child's fourth-grade teacher that a humorous approach had helped to defuse potential explosions. Later in the year, teachers began offering their classrooms to one another as a place to send a particularly upset or disruptive child for a brief time-out. In addition to structuring the meetings and modeling this problem-solving approach, specific assignments emerged from the discussions. In some cases my assignment was simply to observe in the classroom and consult with the teacher afterward. In others, I was to meet with the parents, sometimes with the teacher present, to gather more information or help them work with the child. In some cases the reading or speech teacher might agree to do an informal assessment. Although a specific date was set for a follow-up meeting to evaluate each child's progress, informal evaluation continued to be an important part of my work at the school. Of the first seven children referred, all were originally thought by the teachers to need testing. Only one was found to warrant a psychological evaluation.

At Oak Street School, things proceeded in a similar manner. At first the teachers seemed hesitant to use this new resource. I was often approached informally about different kinds of behavior, and if a case looked at all worthy of further exploration, I would urge the teacher to put in a referral for a resource team meeting so we could work on it together. Without these informal efforts, perhaps only the most serious problems would have been brought to the team. There was a conscious effort, then, to rewrite the traditional equation that asking for help equals professional weakness.

A first-grade teacher, new to the school, once made creative use of the team by referring her entire class for discussion. At first glance this may seem a dramatic gesture indeed, but I was delighted that she thought the team might be able to help her. She was a highly skilled teacher but, like many, tended to be extremely demanding of herself. Although I had already been in her classroom to help with group discussions on feelings and social problem solving, she continued to be concerned about their "immature and thoughtless" behavior toward each other. When we did exercises to promote listening behavior in the group, for example, she expected better behavior from them

—despite my assurances that the wiggling and occasional talking out were not much worse than I had seen in some fourth-grade classes. At the resource team meeting, several things happened. The reading teacher, who had worked with the same group when they were in kindergarten, recalled that they had been unusually excitable and impulsive. They had improved greatly since last year, he said, and attributed it to the teacher's rewarding of appropriate classroom behavior. The librarian, too, commented that she thought they had matured substantially over the year. The teacher still seemed dubious, but she was beginning to think it over. Hearing the others describe the changes they had seen in her class, she now viewed the situation in a different perspective. Perhaps it was not a badly behaved class but an unusually active group of children who had become more restrained because of her efforts. We then discussed the techniques she had already used. Given a few suggestions, she decided to modify the techniques she was familiar with. By the end of the meeting she appeared more relaxed.

The resource team appeared to meet objectives on several different levels. The principals were pleased with the improved coordination of the referral process, the enhanced teamwork among staff members, and the tightened organization in the provision of special services to children. There were many benefits that accrued specifically to the provision of psychological services as well. Having one major forum in which to discuss children ensured that more children who needed services would get them. When the subject of testing came up, as it nearly always did, I was able to provide information about the process: when and why tests might be used, what to look for in children's responses to different tests, and how tests might be used to develop recommendations. I was able to demystify The Test as a magical solution, and in many cases the teachers themselves could see that testing would not provide useful information in a particular case. And when an evaluation was in fact deemed appropriate, the teachers were now able to make use of the findings afterward. They knew what we would be looking for, why it might be significant, and what teaching strategies they could derive from test findings.

Similarly, whenever I saw a child for counseling, the rationale for the visit had been clarified in the meeting beforehand. I rarely saw a child for more than three sessions, and a major purpose in doing so was to give parent and teacher relevant information to help them meet the child's needs in their respective environments. Maintaining this emphasis on indirect service can be disturbing, however. When a child badly needs someone to talk to but the parents refuse to seek outside help, one is tempted to take the child on for an extended period of time. With such a small amount of time allotted to each school, a psychologist's schedule could easily be filled with such cases and the greater number of children would remain unserved. One way of approaching such a dilemma is to explore the available resources for such a child within the school. In an effectively run team meeting, a number of suggestions can be proposed.

Funneling psychological services through a resource team also allows for efficient setting of priorities. The principal's participation here is especially important, as an individual teacher may see only the urgency of her own case and not the pattern of cases distributed throughout the school. The principal must be concerned with the total picture and can assist the psychologist in developing a realistic timetable for services.

As a means of promoting consultation as the best way of providing psychological services, the resource teams were essential to my efforts. While teachers will always differ in their ability to use the team, some clearly improved their capacity to present a problem, work on it efficiently, and carry out a plan of action. It was my impression that, from the beginning of the school year to the end, there was a gradually decreasing tendency to panic when problems presented themselves. Toward the end of the year teachers were likely to report to me measures they had already taken to deal with the problem—which suggests they had learned to use consultation well. They seemed to be less oriented toward receiving direct service, better able to take a problem-solving approach, and somewhat more likely to reflect on their own style of responding. These changes were subtle, of course, and remain unmeasured by objective means. Sandoval, Lambert, and Davis (1977) have suggested that it takes three to four months of weekly group consultation for a consultee to learn the skills. In our meetings, a teacher usually attended only if she had referred a child. Since most teachers attended only two or three meetings a year, group efforts were supplemented with individual consultation.

In Retrospect

Judging from those I worked with, it was a new and agreeable experience to have the psychologist on the premises for the entire day. Not only did this arrangement enable staff members to discuss their concerns spontaneously as they arose but it also allowed for cooperative efforts such as joint parent conferences and group work in classes. While the consultative role might have resulted in less individual contact with children, my frequent presence in the classroom made it possible to know greater numbers of children. Thus when it was necessary to work individually with a student, the child did not have to leave the class to visit a stranger. As the year progressed, there were more cooperative efforts and increasing trust—in fact, teachers began to refer parents to me "just to talk things over." Consultative work with parents was often effective in defusing situations that in the past might have meant strained relations between parents and school personnel. This was particularly true at Pilgrim Street School. As Ms. Ferguson was able to see positive results from my way of working, she relaxed her efforts to structure my work. And as she learned that I could be unexpectedly helpful in difficult situations, she encouraged an even greater degree of cooperative planning. Despite very different personalities and working styles, we have evolved into an efficient team able to express, negotiate, and even joke about our differences.

Many factors seemed to interfere with the changes I tried to implement. Despite the general concensus that having the psychologist remain in the building for the full day was preferable to an on-call arrangement, the principals wanted to have it both ways. If my regular day at Pilgrim Street School was Wednesday, an important meeting would be "unavoidably" scheduled for Thursday and I would be asked to drop in. Since it is sometimes impossible to get everybody together on a day convenient to all, at times I would rework my schedule and attend. It soon became apparent, though, that I could easily be kept hopping around the district like a grasshopper and the structure so carefully erected would collapse.

No matter how carefully a rational problem-solving approach is developed, there are times when a teacher needs help at once. When other appointments are scheduled for that time, the difficulty lies in distinguishing whether the crisis is real or an overreaction. To be less than fully responsive the first time is not only senseless but damaging to one's credibility. And yet one does not want to called in time after time when there is a pattern of overreaction.

Another problem is particularly acute with beginners: to eagerly accept every involvement that presents itself. Since tasks tend to expand and spawn other projects, it is necessary at times to say no. In my case, the affective project was a time-consuming but worthwhile effort, so I decided against involvement in the program for the gifted. Nevertheless, there must have been times when my efforts to model a rational approach were undermined because I was overcommitted and harried.

These attempts to structure a consultative role in the schools are incomplete and certainly imperfectly realized. To the extent that it was possible to create a different way of delivering psychological services, credit must be given to an administration willing to take a risk and to a system flexible enough to tolerate change. In a larger, more centralized district, such a plan might be beyond consideration. Nevertheless, as Sarason (1971) suggests, school personnel may seriously overestimate the degree to which the system restricts one's role. While he was referring to principals, perhaps his message could be applied to school psychologists as well.

Assessing Problems and Needs in an Elementary School — 2

Judith L. Alpert

Over the last decade I have consulted or supervised consultation in many settings—in public, private, and parochial schools, in daycare centers, in nursery, elementary, junior high, and high schools, in inner city, suburban, and rural schools, and in schools with modern as well as traditional educational philosophies. Although there have been some similarities in our experiences in

Note: Many trainees contributed to the consultative activity in this school and I regret that I cannot acknowledge each of them here. Those who consulted in the school most generously and actively were: Victoria Azara, Lois Berman, Dorothy Dockery, Linda Fodaski, Ann Follansbee, and Joan Silverstein. Those who had consultative contact with the school did not view the process the same way all the time, of course. The views expressed here are mine, and only I am responsible for any inaccuracies in reporting or misinterpreting of events.

schools,[1] there have been major differences regarding what they have taught us, the problems they present, and the ways we have been able to work. Moreover, our relative success has varied from school to school. The learning from one school helped us as we approached the next school. School consultation is a complex business, however, and we continue to learn.

Although there is no such thing as a typical case of school consultation, the case I discuss here is based on my wish to describe certain aspects of the way we work and think about schools. In some ways, we work and think like other consultants; in other ways, we are different. The case presented here illustrates some differences with respect to the diagnostic phase of consultation.[2] Specifically the case shows how we conceptualize the role of school staff and consultants in the diagnostic process, how we use school faculty meetings to diagnose problems and evaluate change, and how we label and relabel schools as a means of helping us to understand their needs. Apart from illustrating what I believe is unique about our approach to diagnosis in schools, the case demonstrates that sometimes consultants consult on issues for which they think they have no training or preparation.

At the outset I should explain that this case is extreme with respect to the style of the principal, the background of the teachers, and the problems experienced by the school. Extreme cases can be useful, however, since processes and characteristics tend to stand out clearly. I have altered names and events somewhat in my presentation to protect the privacy of individuals and the school. Of course, given the limitations of space, memory, and selective perception, the whole story cannot be told. The case study is divided into the following sections: a description of the school, an overview of our relationship with the school, a statement of our contract with the school, a consideration of diagnosis, and a consideration of the intervention, the rediagnosis, and the reintervention.

[1] Throughout the chapter "our" refers to the many students I have struggled and learned with over the years.

[2] For a theoretical consideration of the relationship between the diagnostic process and intervention and evaluation, see Alpert (1977).

The School

At one time this parochial school was associated with a thriving parish. Over time, however, the area surrounding the school changed and the nearby apartment houses were replaced by factories and warehouses. Thus, at the time of consultation, the school was located in a deteriorating section of an inner city. The population too changed significantly. Children from families similar to the teaching staff were replaced by children of immigrants, mostly from Spanish-speaking backgrounds.

At the time of my first visit, the school was composed of grades K–8; there were twenty to thirty-five children in each class. There were seven classes in the school, and grades 1 and 2 and grades 3 and 4 were combined. The lower grades (K–4) were taught by three lay teachers while the upper grades were departmentalized and taught by three religious teachers and one lay teacher, most of whom had taught in the school for at least ten years. With the exception of two lay teachers in their twenties, the all-female full-time staff (five teachers and one principal) were whites ranging in age from their late forties to their middle sixties. The principal was a nun, and she and the religious teachers wore habits and lived in the convent adjacent to the school. Because of the school's diminishing population, it was no longer eligible for governmental services, which had included a remedial reading teacher and an art teacher. Some services (a nurse and a speech therapist for a half-day a week) were provided by the board of education, however.

Since the school looked like a structure from the Middle Ages, some of us nicknamed it "The Monastery." The school had a basement and two floors. The gymnasium and cafeteria were in the basement; the lower grades and the principal's office were on the first floor; the upper grades were on the second. In order to save money, lights and heat were used sparingly. The darkness and cold contributed to the austere and depressing school atmosphere and blended with the impoverishment surrounding the school. Throughout the building were religious statues and signs reminding students and staff about praying, sinning, and being saved. The general feeling conveyed by the physical structure was that of a "no frills and no nonsense" institution—and, as we quickly learned, the structure coincided with the staff's posture.

Relationships

My involvement with the school extended over three years. In the first year, I consulted in the school one half-day a week. I had initiated contact with the school, as I had with several other schools in the area. There was no exchange of money. I wanted to work in the school in order to learn about its problems, to develop relationships with school staff, and to determine whether it would be an appropriate practicum setting for my consultation students. The principal wanted to determine whether consultation could help the staff deal with the difficult population the school served. During that first year, I met with a group of five teachers for six one-hour sessions and discussed their classroom problems. I also observed in some of their classrooms. Most of my time in the school, however, was spent in irregular and informal meetings with the principal. We talked about her school's problems as well as issues related to philosophy (educational trends and the school's response to them); religion (Catholic girls and abortion); pragmatics (the changing population and its effect on the school); and ethics (using the intercom to learn about classroom activity). We even discussed the weekly bingo games. Differences in our values and our way of seeing things became clearer over the year. Sometimes during these talks I thought the principal bore a strong resemblance to a brick wall; sometimes she told me that she felt that way about me. By the end of the year, I felt I had been helpful to the principal and certain teachers and children, but I was not sure that the extent of my help justified the amount of time I spent in the school. On one point, however, I was clear—that I had earned some level of acceptance by the school staff. Although I am not a nun, the principal as well as many of the teachers were calling me "Sister Judie." They had made me a part of their family.

In the second and third year, graduate students from my

consultation course, three each year, consulted in the school for one half-day a week. I too consulted in the school in the last year, albeit irregularly. The focus of the second year was on faculty development; in the third year it was on the future of the school. The case material concerns the last two years.

Contract

Our general contract was similar to that described by Sarason and others (1966). It was developed with the principal and did not involve payment. We would work with the school staff either individually or in groups to sort out the complicated and confusing situations they encountered in the classrooms or in the school, and together we would develop some means of dealing with the problem. Although we would observe children and meet with them, the purpose of the direct contact was to promote consultation with teachers or other school staff. That is, we interacted with children in order to demonstrate or to obtain information for our work with teachers. Thus our focus was on teachers and other school staff; in Caplan's terminology (1970), we were providing client-centered and consultee-centered case consultation and consultee-centered administrative consultation.

What we would do was less clear than what we would not do. We said that we would not test children or refer them to private agencies. We explained that we were not against testing; rather, we were trying to find other means of providing help. At contract time, we made some requests: We wanted a confidential relationship with the person we were working with, and we did not want anyone to feel obligated to work with us. Moreover, we requested a six-week grade period in which to observe classrooms and simply learn about the school.

Diagnosis

There are many methodologies for diagnosing, many aspects of school and classroom functioning that can be diagnosed, and many ways of engaging in the diagnostic process. To provide a framework for our approach to diagnosis, I will begin with a theoretical overview. Next I consider one means we used to learn about the school: analysis of a faculty meeting. Then I want to discuss the school's mental health, and much of my information is based on the analysis of the faculty meeting.

Theoretical Overview. Regarding *how* to diagnose, there are many methods for assessing the problems in a school or classroom. One can observe, interview, administer formal as well as informal questionnaires, or rely on unobtrusive measures such as content analyses of announcements over public address systems or letters to school staff and parents.

Regarding *what* to diagnose, there are many aspects of school and classroom functioning. One can diagnose what needs to be changed, whether there is a readiness for change, what the target of change should be, and which consultant interventions are most likely to succeed.

Regarding *who* should diagnose, there are many ways of engaging in a diagnostic process. Four diagnostic roles will be mentioned at this point: (1) doctor-patient, (2) Ralph Nader, (3) repair, and (4) hired help. Although I present them as discrete roles, the distinctions break down in practice. Determination of the intervention is considered part of the diagnostic process in this discussion since an intervention cannot be determined simply by knowing what the problem is. There must be an assessment of both where to intervene and the type of intervention likely to be most effective. Given different resources and levels of readiness, a comparable problem may call for different interventions in different schools or different classes.

In role 1—doctor-patient—the consultant determines both the diagnosis and the intervention, including identification of the target of change and the type of intervention. Here the consultant is the expert doctor and the school staff is the patient who is examined and receives a recommendation. Role 1, I think, is what most people mean when they use the term *consultation.* That is, they think of an expert giving advice rather than an expert engaging in a process with another whose expertise differs. Although the doctor-patient diagnostic role is appropriate sometimes, it is not always suitable. After all, people do not always change because we tell them to, as Lewin (1958) and Watson (1969) indicate. Moreover, this role results in the consultee's dependence on the consultant and, sometimes, in the giving of values rather than solutions.

In role 2—the Ralph Nader model—the consultant, like Ralph Nader in his consumer activist efforts, makes the diagnosis of the problem while the consultee determines what to do about it. The major problem with this approach is that the teacher or other school staff member may not understand the diagnosis or know what to do about it. When a consumer activist group reported that big cars are safer than small ones, for example, the statement had little effect on behavior since many people felt there was little they could afford to do or wanted to do about the problem. Moreover, this option presents other problems: It is contrary to what we know about change and it perpetuates dependence on the consultant.

In role 3—the repair diagnostic role—the consultee is like a homeowner asking the blue-collar consultant to fix a broken stove. This role works for the mechanic who deals with malfunctioning machines, but school consultants are concerned with more complex phenomena—individuals, the interaction between individuals, and the interaction of individuals with systems. This complexity means that the consultant must get *involved.* In fact, what the consultee identifies as the problem may not be the problem. The consultee, for example, could blame lack of student motivation although the problem lies with the teacher's inability to motivate. Further, since we cannot give a lifetime guarantee, we would like to engage consultees too in the process of conceptualizing interventions. An old proverb is relevant here: If you catch fish for people, they will be grateful to you and dependent on you forever. If you show them how to catch fish, they will catch their own and be proud of themselves.

In role 4—the hired help diagnostic role—the consultant is asked to help school staff do what they want. Here consultation services are bought in order to fill a clear need. If the consultee has correctly identified the problem and the consultant's expertise, has communicated the problem clearly, has thought about the consequences of the implementation, and is aware of all other options, this role works well. This, however, is seldom the case. There are many reasons behind a request for consultative services, and the desire for help is only one of them.

There is, moreover, a fifth diagnostic role—the "joint diagnostic role," which involves both the consultant and the consultee in diagnosing the problem and determining the intervention. It minimizes misdiagnosis, reduces resistance, and promotes the sharing of expertise and the growth of the organization's self-assessment and problem-solving skills. At this point the reader may be thinking that the joint diagnostic role is the right diagnostic role and, indeed, sometimes it is. But sometimes it is not. There are many options with respect to how to diagnose, what to diagnose, and who should diagnose. In practice the how, what, and who of diagnosis depend on the time and the school. Sometimes we answer incorrectly; sometimes we answer quickly without even being aware we have made a decision.

In this case study we used several diagnostic methods and believed we knew a great deal about the school by the beginning of the second year. Our knowledge was based on observations, interviews, and interventions during the first year and on contract negotiation and the first faculty meeting at the beginning of the second year. Perhaps not so surprisingly, the diagnostic information we obtained from one source mirrored or at least complemented that from another source. Regarding the what and who of *diagnosis,* we had contracted to work with the principal and teachers on the complex situations they encountered at school. In essence, then, the what and who were defined as whatever the principal or teachers, either collectively or individually, considered complicated or confusing. We thought, therefore, that they would pinpoint whatever they were ready to change. Regarding the what and who of *intervention,* the diagnosis of both target of change (teacher, child, educational curriculum) and type of intervention (behavioral techniques, tutoring, role modeling) was to be done jointly since our contract indicated that *together* we would find a means of dealing with the problem. Thus, returning to the diagnostic roles, our contract involved a repair role and a hired help role, since the consultee was to determine diagnosis, and a joint role in that consultant and consultee were to determine intervention.

Although the contract indicated that we would work on the issues they identified, obviously we entered the school with well-functioning eyes, ears, and the skills to diagnose child, classroom, and school strengths and problems. Given our diagnostic role, we discovered three potential problems:

1. Consultees might identify problems we did not see.
2. Consultees might not identify problems we saw.
3. Consultants and consultees might not agree on the best way to deal with problems.

In the next section I explain how we used faculty meetings as a means of understanding schools and working in them effectively.

Faculty Meetings. My students and I attend the first faculty meeting of the academic year in all the schools we work with. The reasons for attending meetings and ways of benefiting from them are described in Alpert (1979). Briefly, there are two purposes to our attendance: to learn about the school and to discuss our contract with the school staff. Since I had explained this dual purpose to the principal before the faculty meeting, I was surprised to learn that the meeting had been going for half an hour when my three students and I arrived.

The meeting took place in the convent rather than the school. Immediately we were struck by the spatial arrangements. There was one oblong table around which the teachers sat. Further, the teachers sat in pairs: dyads of religious teachers next to dyads of lay teachers. The principal sat at a desk in front of the room. When we entered, I was told to sit with the principal, at her desk, while the three consultants were given chairs in the back of the room. The seating arrangement indicated separation between lay and religious teachers, line and staff, teachers and consultants. From these spatial relations, we developed hunches about participation in decision making, status hierarchy, and patterns of communication among the staff. We assumed that the principal would be the decision maker. Communication would flow from her to staff; it would then flow between religious teachers and between lay teachers but not between these two groups. We assumed, moreover, that there was a definite relationship between the way the faculty meeting and the classrooms were conducted.

These hunches were supported by our observation of process and content. The principal made a number of unilateral decisions during the meeting, for example, and was the main source of information. We noted too that the principal encouraged communication within—but not between—religious and lay groups; for example, she purchased two subscriptions to one journal, one for religious staff and the other for lay teachers. Given the fiscal crisis at the time, this double purchase seems significant and suggests that there were two groups of teachers, that the two groups seemed to be treated equally, and that this subgrouping was encouraged by the principal. Informal conversations during the staff meeting supported our belief that two subgroups existed.

An analysis of content indicated another hunch that was supported by my knowledge of the school—that teachers were unsophisticated regarding the way children learn and why they behave as they do. "Selfish," "bold," "stupid," "sloppy," "lazy"—these were the words used to describe the children who bought pizza rather than donated to charity, who disrupted the classroom, and who were not learning.

Apart from supporting my impressions of the school culture, our observations raised concerns about how we would consult in the school. Since we had identified three potential problems based on our diagnostic role, we preferred to think that the meeting raised questions rather than more problems. We knew that labels affect perception and approach, and we wanted to label in a way that would lead to a more optimistic outlook. Stated simply, we were determined to work in the school. Too many professionals give up on schools like these, which have few resources but house the most needy children and staff. Further, my consultation experience in the school the first year convinced me that working in this school was difficult but possible.

While we wanted to label in a way that would lead to a

more optimistic outlook, we wanted to be realistic. One reason why professionals give up on needy schools is that after a hard year's work, the school is still needy. At the outset, then, we knew we had to arm ourselves against discouragement. We knew we had to remind ourselves that even if we helped the staff considerably for a year, this school would still have more problems than other less needy schools. After all, it began with more problems. Thus we tried to be realistic about what was possible and what was not.

After the faculty meeting, certain questions emerged:

1. Would teachers view a service sanctioned by the principal as optional, given the principal's role in the school?
2. Could people who related to authority and to each other in such different ways work together?
3. Would teachers who had such limited understanding of learning and behavior identify problems we did not see?
4. Would we see problems the teachers did not? Specifically, we wondered whether school staff would recognize communication patterns as a problem for which they wanted assistance.
5. Could we agree with these teachers regarding the best way to deal with problems?

Our analysis of the faculty meeting pinpointed some questions and sparked discussion among us and with the school staff. While the discussion did not answer all our questions, it enabled us to clarify how we would begin work in the school.

Consultants with different orientations may answer these questions differently. To us it was important to affirm the voluntariness of teacher's participation. This we did a number of times and in many different ways. Moreover, we decided that people who relate to authority and to each other in such different ways could in fact work together. And, since we were entering their system, we were determined to work within their structure. Since decisions originated only from the principal in this school, we knew it was important to work closely with her. While we always check with the principal daily as well as before initiating a project, regardless of the school or organizational structure, we were particularly involved with the principal in this school. We recognized too that the teachers regarded the consultants as students who were low on the totem pole of authority, so the consultants would have to work hard to make their views heard. While the school staff wanted assistance and information about pupil behavior, they had their own ideas about dynamics underlying pupil behavior. Although these ideas were different from ours, it seemed that school staff and consultants could agree on some issues. Basically the teachers were well-intentioned people overwhelmed with the bombardment of learning and behavioral problems they faced daily. Thus both consultants and consultees were intent on alleviating the burdens faced by school staff. There were, however, some goals that we thought they would not identify, and those concerned the organizational health of the school.

Organizational Health. Based on our analysis of the faculty meeting, the school did not seem healthy. We did not think the school staff would care about organizational health, however. We doubted that they would perceive organizational structure, decision making, and communication patterns as important issues that might have an impact on their daily burdens.

While the definition of a healthy individual is murky, it is even harder to define the healthy school. Miles (1965) indicated three task-centered dimensions of organizations (optimal power equalization, communication adequacy, and goal focus); three maintenance needs (resource utilization, cohesiveness, and morale); and four dimensions dealing with growth and change (innovativeness, autonomy, adaptation, and problem-solving adequacy). The task-centered dimension involves the organization's goals and the way decisions are made. According to Miles, in healthy organizations the distribution of power is relatively equitable and subordinates can influence their superiors; clearly this was not the case in our parochial school. Regarding communication adequacy, a healthy school has straightforward communication between teachers, between teachers and principal, and between school staff and parents; in our school, communication seemed to flow from the principal to others and between individuals of the same religious status only. Regarding goal focus in a healthy school, Miles states that goals are reasonably clear, accepted by all, appropriate, and achievable given the available resources; in this respect, our school was organizationally healthy, as the three Rs and good character were goals articulated by all.

Miles' maintenance needs relate to the internal state of the school. We believed that the school did not use its resources as well as it could. Tests to provide diagnostic information about learning were used only to determine promotion, for example, and learning machines and kits that could be used for individual instruction were used only by the entire class. Regarding cohesiveness, the separation between lay and religious teachers suggested that the staff was not attracted to membership in the full organization. Finally, morale was fairly low. Although the staff was relatively constant over the years, it appeared that the low rate of turnover had little to do with the school itself.

Regarding the four dimensions dealing with growth and change, here again the school appeared to suffer. Innovativeness was not its strong suit. Teaching methods were basically those that the teachers themselves had experienced as pupils. Staff, materials, and physical surroundings had changed very little. It was clear that the school had few resources in order to bring in the new. Nevertheless, the fact that we were there indicated a willingness to experiment. The school seemed to have some freedom from parental pressure but little independence from those representing the church. While Miles indicates that autonomy is important, we recognized that we were working within a parochial system where the issue of autonomy was complex indeed. Regarding adaptation, if the environmental demands and the organizational demands do not match, both would adapt in a healthy setting. In this school we saw a lack of adaptation. For example, the population had changed over the years and the new pupils presented school staff with different needs with respect to both pedagogy and ego development. The school staff, however, seemed to respond as it had in the past, teaching and treating the new students as they had their former pupils. The issue of adaptation related to the school's problem-solving ability, which was inadequate also. Although the staff recognized the existence of problems, it seemed unable to invent solutions or cope.

Since there are no operational definitions for the variables identified by Miles, this consideration of the school's mental health can be questioned on measurement grounds. While there are formal instruments that can be used to analyze schools (see Halpin and Croft, 1963, and Walberg, 1974), we did not administer them since organizational health was not a concern identified by the staff. We were concerned about the school's mental health, however, and thought that the school needed help in developing organizational strength. We hoped that by working on issues the staff considered important, we would not only alleviate some of their real stresses but also earn the right to intervene with them on an organizational level. The intervention, we knew, would involve contract renegotiation. We also knew that it might never occur.

Intervention, Rediagnosis, and Reintervention

Intervention took place in the second year; rediagnosis and reintervention took place in the third.

Intervention. Although we thought at length about diagnosis, it did not take long to complete this initial phase. Intervention, however, extended over six months. The consultants met with the teachers informally and individually in an attempt to learn about their concerns. One problem mentioned by all the teachers involved the inability of some children to learn. The teachers wanted to change this situation but did not know how. Although we were not convinced that the children were not learning, most of the teachers were clearly frustrated by the slow rate of learning among some children. Could we help find a means for working with these children?

Our observations indicated that, for the most part, teachers were not individualizing instruction in the classroom. In general, they taught to the average students, and it was these and the more able pupils who did well. The consultants began to talk to the teachers, both individually and in groups, about children with different academic needs and the value of individualization or group instruction. They seemed to think it was impossible. In these discussions the teachers raised three general questions: How do you know what children's academic needs are? What can you do to meet these needs? How can a classroom teacher individualize instruction in a classroom with forty or more pupils? We knew it would take a long time to develop full answers to these questions. We also knew that the answers would have to come from the teachers themselves, since they alone knew what could be done in a classroom.

Few of the teachers had had formal training in education. Most were relatively unsophisticated with respect to teaching methods and cognitive development. The questions they asked were basic, and it was their lack of formal training that enabled these honest and difficult questions to be posed. Our experience, however, indicates that these three questions are common ones for the classroom teachers. Although some are too embarrassed to ask them, others pose them in subtle ways.

We suggested several ways to focus on the first two questions. Most teachers liked the idea of administering a test and considering differences in children's test performance as well as pedagogical implications. For this purpose, we selected the Slingerland Specific Language Disabilities Test, a test for identifying learning-disabled children. At the outset of the project we had two concerns—that the staff might not be realistic about what the test would indicate and that the staff might assume ownership of the project. We dealt with the former by stating realistic goals. We did not expect children to learn magically once we attained test results and developed some ideas about their learning styles. However, we did expect the results to show individual differences in learning and lead to our collectively attempting to develop a solution to the problem. We believed that, in time, this would have some effect on the children's achievement, the teachers' expectations, and the motivation of both. This was a long-term project that would require long-range vision.

The school's ownership of the project became clear when the time came to purchase the tests. Initially, we thought some university funds might be available; when it became clear that this was unlikely, the principal found money for the project. Although we regretted this added burden to an already impoverished school, we were delighted to see they were committed to the project.

Some teachers were more excited about the project than others. Moreover, there were differences in the degree of contact teachers wanted with us. We accepted these individual differences. As the teachers were working toward individualizing instruction, we attempted to recognize their different needs and worked with them on what became known as "The Slingerland Project." Thus some teachers administered and scored the tests themselves, while in some classrooms we did both. We asked, however, that all teachers meet with us as a group in several sessions to discuss protocols and pedagogical implications.

To our surprise, the religious teachers' attendance at the meetings was disappointing. When we talked to them about it, there was always a reason why a meeting had to be missed. One day, while talking to the principal, we found that the religious teachers had been discussing individual protocols in the convent and she wanted to continue these discussions with them. At first, we were reluctant to have two groups—one for the religious teachers with the principal as coordinator and one for the lay teachers with the consultants as coordinators. We were uncomfortable about having separate but equal groups and perpetuating the division in the school. Since we were committed to facilitating the project, however, after some discussion we agreed. As it turned out, the principal's involvement was positive. Certainly it gave the project a visible stamp of approval and seemed to strengthen project commitment. Moreover, the principal was a good coordinator, eager and hardworking. She called me frequently to talk about test results, implications, readings, and the meetings with lay teachers. From these discussions it appeared that the autocratic style evidenced in the initial faculty meeting had been replaced by a more democratic one, at least during the Slingerland Project meetings at the convent. Finally, having the principal run the group resulted in a school-based resource available to the staff on a full-time basis.

Our group meetings with the lay teachers varied from session to session. At first the teachers sat quietly in groups waiting to be "told." While we were prepared to explain the meaning of a low score on a particular subtest and how this deficit might be compensated for, we hoped the teachers would join in the discussion. The teachers, however, were accustomed to a different mode of group interaction, one that had more of a military flair. To engage the group, the consultants therefore used various techniques and simulations. To help them understand the learning-disabled child's experience, teachers were asked to write their name on a piece of paper placed on their forehead. Writing in this way results in a mirror image that surprised and relaxed the teachers. The last sessions of the group contrasted sharply with those at the beginning. There was a sense of camaraderie among the group, and the level of interaction was high. Although it was not our primary goal, we were delighted that this relaxed style seemed to flow into the classroom.

Thus we worked with teachers on the problems that concerned them and began to consider ways of dealing with the learning problems of some children. We began where they were hurting. What was accomplished? As a direct result of our work some teachers began to see why certain children do not learn and began to come up with ideas about dealing with this. Moreover, some of the suggestions generated in the meeting were being evidenced in the classroom. Teachers were beginning to teach some groups of children in different ways than they taught others. In addition to changes in behavior, there were changes in thinking. Some teachers were beginning to think in terms of deficits rather than laziness or bad character.

Most teachers still had questions about the amount of individualization that could be done in a classroom, however. In response, we talked about the possibility of arranging for high school students and parents to work with some pupils and also enlisting the aid of graduate students of reading or learning disabilities. Our hopes were high, our plans were big, and the year ended with good feelings.

At the first faculty meeting of the third year, we could

see an indirect effect of our intervention. The chairs were now arranged in a semicircle, and, in the front of the semicircle, there were chairs reserved for the principal and the consultants. Clearly, this arrangement indicated greater acceptance of the consultants than that of the previous year. Although the separation between lay and religious teachers remained, the meeting was now less formal and the principal encouraged questions from the teachers. She now asked divergent questions and began a discussion of the classroom problems the teachers faced. This discussion revealed how much the teachers' understanding had grown with respect to learning and mental health, and the process indicated a less autocratic group structure. Moreover, we now saw evidence of power equalization, communication, cohesiveness, morale, innovativeness, adaptation, and problem-solving adequacy. Although we had no formal means of assessing these changes and could not be certain of cause and effect, our general impression was one of increased organizational health.

Rediagnosis. Although the third year began on a positive note, it did not stay that way for long. During the first few months of school, it appeared that the teachers were less committed to the Slingerland Project. Their attendance at the group meetings dropped, and some claimed to be too busy to meet with us individually. Further, although the teachers were interested in arranging for a peer or parent tutoring project, they wanted us to make the arrangements. In addition to a general lack of receptivity to us, we noticed a deterioration in school and classroom functioning. School staff now had less time for us and shorter tempers with each other, both in the classroom and in the faculty room. Why the change, we wondered?

One day proved to be a turning point. As I went from one class to another, I observed that every one of the teachers was having a difficult day. Tempers were short, hair was pulled, voices were loud. Eventually I began to wonder whether there might be a school-related cause behind this mood. When I sought out the principal to test my hunch, I found that she too had been affected by whatever it was. Usually the principal had an open door policy and I felt welcome; today she was too busy to meet with me. When I finally saw her, the problem became clear: It was ten days after payday and the principal had not paid the staff their salaries. Given the decreased enrollment, late tuition payments, and an increasingly poor parish, she did not have the money. Although there was not enough money to pay all the teachers, the principal could have paid some of the teachers fully or all the teachers partially. She chose, however, to pay no one and to say nothing. Thus the teachers worried in silence—Would the school close? Would they lose their position? Would they ever be paid?—and the consequences of their worry were evident throughout the school. I told the principal how the lack of communication had affected school life. Then we discussed the need for clarity concerning the school's fiscal situation and the various options for payment. She decided to pay the teachers immediately with the money the school had collected from weekly bingo games, and she would meet with the staff to discuss the fiscal situation. Thus the problem, at least for the present salary period, had been resolved.

Until this crisis, the team of consultants and I had been thinking about differences between the two groups of consultants in the second and third years of the project. Could they account for the difference in teachers' receptivity both to us and the project? There were four issues that might have been relevant. First, in contrast to the second year, two consultants in the third year were less interested in individualization in general and the Slingerland Project in particular. Second, there was a problem of transference. The teachers had certain expectations of consultants and were comparing the consultants they remembered at the end of the school year, who were relatively seasoned at that time, with the new consultants. Moreover, the teachers expected the second group of consultants to have the same strengths as the first group. In some cases they did, but in other cases they had different strengths. Third, there was a problem of countertransference. One of the new consultants had attended parochial schools and appeared to resent her education. As a consequence, she seemed less generous in her relations with the parochial school staff than she might have been in another setting. It became clear to me that I had mismatched consultant and school. Given her knowledge of parochial schools, I had placed this consultant in a school where she could not function to her capacity. Without question, this highly competent person would have been an exceptional consultant elsewhere. While we were focusing on consultant issues in order to account for changes in the teachers' receptivity to us, we had neglected to consider school issues. The salary problem, however, forced us to consider them.

There had been major changes between the two years. First, there were fewer children, which resulted in less tuition money. Second, with less money to pay salaries, there were fewer teachers and, in addition, the principal herself taught a class. Third, the principal had opened a school store and was selling candy and gum during lunch in order to raise more money; she was also holding boxed candy sales after school. Fourth, the school was darker and, as winter progressed, colder. The idea was to minimize use of lights and fuel in order to cut costs. All these signs pointed to increased impoverishment. It became clear that we were trying to help a school grow while in fact it was dying. Stated simply, the school was a terminal case. As the apartment buildings surrounding the school were being replaced by factories, there were fewer schoolchildren, less tuition money, and soon, or so we thought, no need for the school. The school did not have the energy to fight any longer, and perhaps it did not make sense to fight any longer.

Reintervention with the Dying School. While the consultants themselves may have played a role in the teachers' altered level of receptivity, it was clear to us that the lack of resources played a highly significant role. There was a big shift in school finances between the second and third years. Although we recognized the problem in the previous two years, both consultants and staff regarded it as transient. It was as if the school was dying and we, consultants and staff alike, were denying its death.

In some ways it appears that a dying school goes through a similar process as a dying person. Kubler-Ross (1969) labels the stages in the dying process: The first stage is "denial and isolation"; the second, "anger"; the third, "resentment"; the fourth, "depression"; and the fifth, "acceptance." In retrospect it appears that the staff had passed through the first three stages in our first and second years there. Clearly the denial and isolation as well as the anger and resentment over its eventual end were evident during the second year. In some ways, the staff's welcome in our first and second year was a way of bargaining to postpone the closing of the school. We only saw this in retrospect, of course. In our third year at the school, there were greater losses in tuition money, and students and staff faced the consequences of fewer teachers, uncertain salaries, fund-raising efforts, and other cutbacks in resources. It no longer made sense to work toward developing programs such as peer or parent tutoring, which might result in increased individualization. Rather, it was time to help school members prepare for its end. I assumed the major responsibility for helping the school in this regard.

For the most part, the new intervention involved my talking with the principal for a few months during the academic year and throughout the following summer while the other consultants worked with the teachers, mainly on learning and individualized instruction. My talks with the principal progressed as follows. First we acknowledged that the death of the school was imminent. This acknowledgment came only after we had considered some school and community statistics. Although it took a while to accept these statistics, acceptance did come—and with it, I think, relief. Next we began to plan the best conditions possible for all at the time of demise. We talked about when to tell various people about the school's imminent death and what parents, children, and teachers should be told to assist them in their subsequent adjustment. What schools were in the locale? Which schools could meet the needs of various families? Were there different ways of discharging teachers so that the school could function on a smaller scale for a given time? At which point would the school officially end? How might the parish, archdiocese, and community help the school as it was preparing for its end? I had never been trained to help a school and its inhabitants prepare for its end. Although I had few answers to offer the principal, I was guided by my experience around the time of my grandmother's death.

The Meaning of the Case

At the outset of this chapter, I explained why I chose to relate this case. Clearly the school was an unusual one, and the consultation in the last stages was atypical also. Nevertheless, this case illustrates some important concepts:

- Sometimes we consult on issues for which we think we have not been prepared.
- Analogies can be helpful in determining what to do. In this light, labels can be good guides. By labeling a school, we can draw from a different realm of experience—as we did when we labeled "The Dying School." We have labeled schools "St. Sorority" to capture the atmosphere of a Catholic high school, "The Military" to capture the rigidity in other schools, and "The Paranoid School" and "The Obsessive-Compulsive School" to capture the neuroses of those settings.
- While working to bring change to one area, we sometimes effect change in another. In this case we focused on individualized instruction but had an effect on teacher interaction and, we believe, classroom life.

Regarding diagnosis, the case illustrates that:

- Faculty meetings can be helpful in the diagnostic and evaluative process.
- Diagnosis must be repeated again and again. Not only are schools complex settings but situations and people's readiness change, and what may be an appropriate target of change or type of intervention may shift also.
- Diagnosis involves assessment of what to change and how to intervene. Each of these questions can be answered by the consultant, by the consultee, or by the consultant and consultee jointly. The point is that the consultant should be aware of the problems associated with each diagnostic role.

How can I summarize such an involved experience? On the first page of this chapter I made a statement that the reader might see in a new light now: "School consultation is a complex business . . . and we continue to learn."

Working with Elementary School Administrators and Teachers 3

Ruth G. Newman
Claire Bloomberg

This chapter reports on a method developed in the late sixties and used in selected schools within the public school systems of Montgomery County, Maryland, North Haven, Connecticut, and in elementary, junior, and senior high schools in the District of Columbia. The entire consultation experience was reported in Newman (1967). This book, a collection of case histories of schools from the primary grades through high school, is now out of print, but the methods developed there are still in use—by consultants outside the system (often by mental health clinics) and by consultants within the school system (in pupil personnel or psychological services). To my knowledge it continues to be used in various widespread locales.

The System

It is an eclectic and purposely flexible system. The method's cardinal rule is to take an institution where it is, to adapt to the prevailing conditions and atmosphere, and to gauge the leadership (usually the principal) before one enters the area of change. This method demands skillful and sophisticated observation. The consultant must be able to assess the lines of power in order to help the leadership and staff feel secure so that necessary changes can take place without causing more havoc than help. It is of course enormously difficult to adapt to a system that condones practices the consultant judges to be harmful, wrongheaded, or simply poor, but one needs to maintain one's own boundaries without letting value judgments get in the way of the task of helping. While anxiety may be the handmaiden of change, too much of it can be the handmaiden of havoc. The consultant is not unlike an invited guest in a house that is run in quite a different way from one's own. Still, one has no right to move the furniture, make the meals, or rearrange the books. To keep one's standards while creating an atmosphere where needs can be recognized and help can be sought and accepted becomes the crux of the matter.

The story of this method of consultation began in the 1960s through the Child Research Branch of the National Institute of Mental Health. Under the directorship of Dr. Fritz Redl, the project involved the multifaceted total treatment of severely disturbed hyperaggressive boys driven by impulse and without inner controls. A group of these boys were long-term residential patients—the treatment focused on their life milieu, their school and learning, and psychotherapy. As they improved, they could live in an open setting rather than a locked ward, and then, still at the residence, could attend public schools in the area. It was incumbent upon the staff, especially upon me as director of the educational part of their lives, to select appropriate schools for them, work with the principals and teachers involved, and see to it that our NIMH staff (child care workers, residence directors, psychotherapists) worked closely and supportively with the schools.

This collaboration between schools and hospital home was eminently successful. In fact, the principals urged us to help other teachers in their schools with emotionally disturbed children in their classrooms, with the usual problems of management and dynamics, and with the teachers' and administrators' own conflicts about their work and how they were doing it. Out of a desire to elicit cooperation from the schools in handling our most difficult children and to maintain good public relations, a group of us, especially Dr. Redl, Howard Kitchener, and I, found ourselves launched in the school consultation business. The relief and morale created by the collaborative methods impelled us, when the NIMH Child Research project was over, to refine our methods of consultation and apply them to school systems less prosperous and more complex than Montgomery County. Dr. Redl and I asked for and received a three-year grant from NIMH and then a three-year grant from the Eugene Meyer Foundation to try out our methods—largely in the District of Columbia but also, for comparison, in a few schools in other systems as well.

With such a history it becomes clear why our hallmark was flexibility. We had learned to be extremely careful about the sensibilities of our customers: principals, teachers, even parents. At the same time, the iron hand within the velvet glove described our idea of a mentally healthy environment for children. But we tried to enter humbly like good guests—to become part of the everyday school scenery by coming regularly and reliably at least once a week over the school year so that people would regard us not as utter aliens there to scatter wisdom or revolution but rather as sympathetic collaborators in a gigantic task. This task required someone who, along with offering expertise in child mental health and learning, could help staff to develop its own skills without feeling unfairly judged or exploited.

This basic attitude is what we sought to purvey in each school. To do this we had to work closely and evaluate ourselves to ensure that our own values and judgments were not being a burden to the staffs of the schools and that, at the same time, we were not losing our standards. It was essential that we recognize what was unacceptable, what was tolerable but needed work, and what was not only acceptable but deserved encouragement. The *we* I speak of was a small group of consultants from various backgrounds: Claire Bloomberg was an experienced nursery and preschool teacher, administrator, and therapeutic teacher; Howard Kitchener was a social worker with a background of clinical work with children in therapeutic settings; Ruth Emerson, originally a lawyer, was a reading and learning specialist; I was a clinical psychologist with years of experience in working with disturbed children in school settings. Dr. Redl acted as our consultant on his monthly visits. We prepared ourselves to do whatever schools thought they wanted. We gave talks to teachers and PTAs. We observed silently and walked softly. We tried to gauge the power lines of authority—where it was oppressive, where it was nonexistent, where it was effective. We were careful to evaluate our errors and to determine the differences among our own styles and how they fit with the settings we found ourselves in. We learned a great deal.

We discovered there is little use for outside consultants to enter a school if the principal does not want them. Someone within the system may be able to work around that obstacle, but coming from outside it is impossible: One needs at least a pretense at welcome. Success increases in direct ratio to the quality of welcome. We found too that a principal might want one for the wrong reasons—to fight battles with the school system or to get certain teachers fired or hired. The consultant needs to be very sure whether he or she is signing up as a double agent or a consultant. We soon learned how important it is to be able to assess the interests and interactive roles of various groups in the school: cliques of teachers, parents, children, board of education, apparently peripheral (but sometimes central) power figures such as secretaries and custodians. In fact it was this experience that led me to the conviction that the Bion-based study of group actions and interactions is essential in dealing with any school system. (My book *Groups in Schools* is an outgrowth of this belief.)

We learned that an understanding of boundaries is the basic ingredient of consultation. One comes as a consultant to a school as an expert only in what one knows. In our case, we were expert in establishing a milieu to promote the mental health of children so that they could learn and grow. We were not selling ourselves as experts in teaching skills or in any particular subject or in administration or negotiation. Even though, in special circumstances, we might very well deal with any of these subjects by listening, asking, and throwing out ideas, we would not claim expertise. Our boundary was the mental health of the children—which, by virtue of their dependence on adults, meant that we had to be interested in the mental health of their teachers and the settings in which both children and teachers worked.

We found that once this boundary had become completely clear to us in each setting—a hard task—we could break many of the conventional rules of consultation without jeopardy. In a classroom emergency, for example, a consultant can, with skill, take over the class while the teacher gets a hurt child to the nurse. Without losing her role, she will be seen as less an intruder than a genuinely interested person. This intervention is a consultation taboo, of course, but we found it a problem only when everyone, particularly the consultant, is unclear about boundaries. Boundary awareness also saves a consultant from grandiose delusions about what can and cannot be done in consultation one day a week.

We consulted to preschools, junior high schools, and senior high schools as well as to elementary schools and a special school within the elementary school. This was many years ago, but we still subscribe to the value of our methods. We believe that regular consultation once a week is extremely useful. It establishes relationships and offers a familiarity not only with staff members but with the system itself. It indicates patterns of change and places where intervention can pay off. It illuminates areas not visible without a continuing relationship. We came to believe that the covert and overt power of groups within schools can impede or help a consultant do the job. We believe in scheduled opportunities for regular consultants to air their impressions, conflicts, and problems among themselves. And, although we believe in flexibility, we think that the structure of consultation must have clearly defined boundaries that leave room for individual styles.

Those were the positives. We still have the *moral* question of consultation, however. Is the consultation a mere bandage covering a festering sore? Or is it preventative or curative? If it is preventative, it has a great chance of success. If it is curative, the wound has to be examined more closely. Otherwise the consultant can be overwhelmed either with delusions both of ignorance or depression born of despair—both contraindicated for consultation processes.

The following sections describe our experience both in a regular and a special elementary school. The section on Clements Elementary School was contributed by Claire Bloomberg; the sections on Hoover and Lincoln Elementary Schools were prepared by Howard Kitchener. Taken together these selections should offer a taste of consultation in different settings, using the methods we evolved.

Clements Elementary School

The principal of Clements Elementary School was eager for consultation, and because of its social and economic background, the school was of special interest to us. By the time we consulted to Clements Elementary neighborhood, formerly exclusively white, it was composed largely of middle-class black families, along with a recent influx of poorer black families, who were doubling up in order to afford the housing. The heads of the families were mostly government clerks and teachers, but there was a small percentage of doctors and other higher-paid professionals at one end of the economic scale and manual laborers and unskilled workers at the other. There was also a small nucleus of white families who had remained in the area and joined with the blacks to form a chapter of Neighbors Incorporated. This organization was determined to refute some of the myths concerning black occupancy of a new neighborhood, particularly the decline of property values that was said to accompany such an influx. They were successful in keeping the houses attractive and well maintained, but the number of white families was too small to keep the school genuinely integrated. During the year when I worked there as a consultant, the student population was almost entirely black; later it became nearly exclusively so.

Not so the staff. A number of white teachers had remained when the neighborhood changed, along with an almost equal number of young black newcomers. The principal, who was black, was a competent and conscientious woman determined to do a good job of educating the thousand pupils in her school. She had a staff of thirty-two teachers, three of whom were men. The plant itself combined an older building and a brand-new addition, both well kept, and a spacious playground.

As soon as one became acquainted with the neighborhood, it was clear that in nearly all the families in which two parents lived together, each held more than one job. Children were left in the care of relatives or friends during the day. In talking to staff members and getting to know some of the parents, I could see they were determined that the poverty they had known in their youth should not be the lot of their children. In this school the children of even the poorest families were well dressed, extremely clean and neat, and had toys and playthings at home. I had no trouble understanding this fierce upward push on the part of the parents, but I was also disturbed at the unhappy effects of this drive. So much was the specter of poverty to be avoided, so strong was the emphasis on providing material comforts, that these parents often blinded themselves to the loss in warmth their striving caused. The children saw the tension that went along with the overworked lives of their parents; moreover, they felt the continuous demand for academic performance, which was seen as the ladder to eventual success. The results were far more devastating than the parents knew. Although respect for education in the home can be a great asset to a school staff, overemphasis and tension puts pressure on the children, which may create stress and behavior symptoms for many of them. This is especially true when the parents' own aspirations get confused with their children's work and every report card represents future success or failure. Few children seem to thrive in this race to success. Most, even many who are successful in achieving good grades, at least in elementary school, pay the price in physical symptoms and a constant fear that they are not good enough and will lose their parents' love if they fall below parental expectations.

Preliminary Visits. Although I was not to start my regular consultation until the beginning of the school year in September, I made several visits to Clements during the preceding spring. I had arranged them with the principal, Mrs. Tate, who understood my desire to become familiar with the school, the children, the teachers, the schedules, and the physical plant before I began. In a new experience this can prove fruitful, so we tried it whenever possible.

During my first visit I explained to her the background of our project, our objectives, and my qualifications for the job. I stressed that I was not a psychologist, but I outlined the extensive experience I have had with both normal and disturbed children as a psychoeducation teacher. I emphasized my major interest in very young children and suggested that I confine myself to kindergarten and first and second grades in order to find out about the onset and prevention of problems in behavior and learning. Mrs. Tate seemed disappointed at this restriction but agreed to go along. She said she would send around a bulletin explaining what I would be doing, and she gave me a list of the teachers with whom I would be concerned. She mentioned a child in the first grade, bright but nonconforming, and said I would certainly want to observe him. Clearly consultation at Clements would begin, as it usually did everywhere, with the problems of an individual disruptive child.

I thanked Mrs. Tate for her time and told her I would always check with her when I came to the school. She replied that if she was not in her office when I arrived, I should wander around and see what I wanted to see.

On my three subsequent visits to the school that spring, I visited all the classes I would be concerned with the following fall. In addition to the two kindergartens, four first grades, and four second grades, there were a junior primary and a basic primary. The pupils in the junior primary were mostly six-year-olds who had had a year in kindergarten but were considered too immature or too slow to go on to first-grade work. The pupils in the basic primary were older, up to about ten years of age, and extremely slow. The teacher had divided them into groups on about five levels of functioning.

All the teachers were expecting me and all were cordial. It became clear that a few felt no need for special help, others would seek it, and still others would be unwilling or unable to use it, at least at the beginning of the project.

Consultation. According to plan, once I began my visits I was present one day a week for consultation with any teacher of the kindergarten, junior primary, basic primary, first or second grade who wanted to see me. I saw the principal every week except for a few days when she had to be out of the building. Apart from my time with the principal, I had 147 conferences with the teachers in 32 visiting days. Late in the year, when a counselor was assigned to the school, I began to have weekly conferences with her.

In the beginning of the year, as in the other schools in which we worked, conferences with the principal and teachers centered on the problems of individual children and what could be done to help them. Some of these children were brought to my attention by the principal, some by teachers, and some I spotted while observing others in a classroom. Though Mrs. Tate was always welcoming and obviously glad to have extra help, she was by nature reserved, and it took time for us to talk with ease. Moreover, she was kept busy by her duties at the school, meetings with the superintendent, and the fact that she was an officer in a school-connected organization. What really began to break down the reserve between Mrs. Tate and me was the fact that I did not confine myself solely to conferences but allowed her and the teachers to call on me in many ways. Since it was a fundamental tenet of our philosophy to try to meet the needs of the schools as we found them, I stretched the boundaries of my work as much as possible to accommodate special requests.

Special Help. The first request came from Mrs. Tate. A social adjustment teacher had been added to the staff, and she asked me to help her understand her pupils and work out a schedule and curriculum for them. I spent a lot of time trying to find appropriate material and techniques for this teacher, who had not been trained to work with emotionally disturbed children.

There were other ways in which I operated outside the bounds of "consultation." One day when I was observing a child in the first grade, the father of another child suddenly appeared in the room and demanded an immediate conference with the teacher. Since she had been trying to get this man to visit the school, she very much wanted to see him. What was she to do with her class? Seeing her conflict, I offered to take the class until she finished her conference, and she gratefully accepted. This may have been the beginning of genuine confidence in my goodwill and effectiveness on the part of both principal and teachers. It may well be that consultants whose training and background derive from teaching rather than psychology or social work are looked on by principals, and even teachers, with more suspicion than those who come with an additional degree. It is easier to dispel such suspicions if the consultant can demonstrate an ability to cope as well as help.

On other occasions I provided special help by demonstrating techniques, such as the Life Space Interview, helping to get a despairing child started on desk work he did not understand, and sitting in on emergency parent conferences. Moreover, on my own initiative I made contact with special service personnel in the school system, with outside clinics, and with individual psychologists to arrange for referral of several children who needed it. All these efforts were appreciated by Mrs. Tate, and our relationship grew as the year progressed. By the end of the year, I felt free enough to list the children I had observed or discussed with their teachers and make some suggestions for placement in the following year. Mrs. Tate was most receptive—in fact, she later told me she was incorporating my suggestions wherever staff and budget made it possible.

The majority of my time was spent in consultation with teachers. Of the eighteen teachers to whom I was to be available, fourteen used my services during the year, some almost continuously and some only when an emergency arose. In the beginning, most of the requests for help came in relation to one particular child, generally one who was exceptionally aggressive or exceptionally withdrawn. There was no question that the teachers had been trained to recognize problems in children.

The trouble came when they tried to deal with the problem in school and involve the child's parents. I therefore went out of my way to make specific recommendations for classroom handling. I also role-played parent conferences with many of my consultees. Parent conferences were often particularly frightening or frustrating experiences for teachers.

Later, as I became a familiar face at the school, I was asked to help with general classroom atmosphere, staff relationships, and even some personal problems (which I was careful to refer to other sources). As for interpersonal relationships, I felt I had to address myself to these problems when they impinged on teaching, which they almost always did. Fortunately for me, Mrs. Tate was not the kind of person to ask me to spy on a teacher for her, though I can imagine this problem might easily arise in school consultation. In cases of conflict between teachers, or teacher-principal problems, I maintained a neutral stance and encouraged those involved to work it out in the open. Failing that, I tried to help them contain the conflict so that it did not interfere in the classroom.

A Series of Consultations. To show how consultation progressed throughout one case, I want to describe a series of conferences with a new kindergarten teacher. Mrs. Paul had been a playground director before coming to Clements. She is a good-looking woman in her early thirties, married, with children of her own. Being new to the job, she felt insecure, particularly about her ability to maintain order in her class of thirty-four five-year-olds. As a result of this insecurity, as well as her natural orderliness and conscientiousness, she was conducting her class too strictly when I first observed her. This observation was at her request; she had approached me the week before on the playground and asked if I would come and observe a boy in her class who was "driving her crazy." He was indeed disruptive. My notes from this first observation read:

John is really a sad sack. He is always doing something to call attention to himself both from the teacher and the children, and he seems to be rejected by both. In a jumping dance they were doing, he had to jump higher than anyone else and then land on someone's feet or knock over a desk. When another boy was put at the head of the line, he kept trying to usurp his place and made grabbing gestures at some of the others, only to be pushed off with a vengeance. All in all, a most lonely little boy who needs friends badly and doesn't know how to make them.

On this first visit I asked Mrs. Paul to let me see John's record. I went over it and then spent the rest of the time observing. When I left I made a date to discuss him with her the following week at lunchtime. Later she told me what she knew of John's background. He is the youngest child in a family that includes many older children. The father is listed as retired; he presently drives a taxi. He calls for John at school and seems to the teacher to be more dutiful than loving. Other teachers said the mother spoiled this child because "he is darker than the rest of the children and she wants to make it up to him." Mrs. Paul reported she had had to punish him that morning because he had hit another teacher and then went on to detail his other misdeeds in class. I expressed my sympathy and then asked about her legal rights. Did she have to keep the child in class? She thought a child that young *could* be excluded if he disrupted the class, but perhaps his behavior was her fault, perhaps she was handling him badly. I suggested that she watch him during the coming week—particularly his attempts to make friends, to see how he goes about it and how he defeats himself—and think of ways to help him make a place in the group. I emphasized that we were not looking for faults but for ways of helping both her and the child.

When I came into her classroom the following week, Mrs. Paul held up in disgust a few mangled pieces of paper. These, she explained, were John's attempts at making a lantern out of paper. Since it was time to go on the playground, I spoke to her there and found that John was still disruptive—in fact, she was at her wit's end with him. Instead of mentioning her expectation of high performance from an immature and unhappy boy, I told her what I had seen before we came outside: John had made a friend for a few minutes by stirring up trouble between two boys and then coming to the aid of one of them. I pointed out how desperate this maneuver was and stressed again his need of friends. I even offered to help him make a lantern when we went back inside, thinking this might demonstrate something about the way he needed to be handled. Mrs. Paul agreed. I then told John I knew he would feel bad when all the other children left with their lanterns and he had none to take home. Would he like me to help him make one? His response was immediate and pathetic. His whole face lit up and he eagerly said yes. I asked him if he knew how to make the lantern, and he proceeded to do it—immediately and perfectly. Then he put his lantern on the teacher's desk next to those of the other children and quietly joined the group who were listening to a story. From time to time he would tiptoe to the desk to touch his lantern, and the teacher would stop the story to say, "You're very proud of that, John, aren't you?"

Any encouragement I might have felt about this development was quickly dissipated when I entered the classroom the following week. The class was in an uproar. There was Halloween all over the place, the principal had just been in to observe, and there was a mother in the room on some business concerned with library books. I was about to withdraw quietly when Mrs. Paul grabbed me. "Please don't leave," she said. "John has been in a snit all day. He's full of tales about a family fight and has been in trouble again and again. Now he's in the bathroom and I can't get him to come out—maybe you can." My notes for that day tell what ensued:

> I opened the bathroom door and there was John, huddled on the floor with his head cradled on his arms, looking completely forlorn. How long he had been there I don't know and didn't ask, because Mrs. Paul seems to feel at once so guilty and so angry with this child. I just sat down on the floor next to him, put my arms around him, and said, 'Tell me about it, John.' He launched into a long account of a big fight at the breakfast table with his mother and father mad at him and his older sister because they wouldn't eat their cereal and the milk was sour. They were also mad at his older sister because she didn't do any work, and he, John, always did his work. He has two bedrooms to keep clean. He shouldn't have to do any work

today but the bug man was coming and he had to clean them up. Mixed in with all this was a tale about his father burning him with a cigarette. By gentle questioning I found that this had happened on another day when the father had to go to the dentist and had taken John along. John knew it was an accident, but in his present state the burning and his father's anger of the morning were all one—he showed me the scar. All the time this was going on he was racked by internal sobs; he wouldn't let himself actually cry.

At one point I reminded him that I was the lady who had helped him with his lantern the week before and he corrected me. 'You didn't help me. You just sat next to me and I did the work.' I said he was quite right—he had done a good job all by himself and I bet he did a good job of cleaning the bedrooms, too. I asked if he didn't want to go out and hear the story, and he said no, so I held him for five minutes more without saying anything. Then I said he would feel better if he went back outside. When I said I would go too and sit next to him, he came along. Twice during the story John talked out loud to me. When I whispered in his ear that he was interrupting the story and should save it until later, he pulled away, but not so far that I couldn't reach him to pat him. Finally, I whispered that I had to leave but would be back next week. Mrs. Paul interrupted her story to come outside and ask me what had happened. When I told her, tears came to her eyes. I looked at her and said, 'I know, he makes me feel that way, too.' She asked if he had mentioned how he felt about her, and I said he hadn't and promised to come back and talk to her about the whole thing at lunchtime.

At lunch it was apparent that Mrs. Paul was in great conflict about John. She was sensitive to his suffering and wished she could help him, but at the same time his disruptive demands for attention were making it impossible for her to conduct her class and making her angry. We talked about this ambivalent feeling, and I kept reminding her that she had a large class to deal with, was new on the job, and should not feel so guilty. I then suggested using a child in the group to help John. I outlined a plan whereby she could enlist one of her most reliable children to sit next to John at story time and remind him not to interrupt. She smiled when I said this and pointed to a textbook on group dynamics. Although she was taking a course in the subject, she had not thought of using the group itself to help John. The conference broke up on a note of hope. From this time on, Mrs. Paul backed and filled in her relationship with John, according to her feelings of encouragement and hope or guilt and despair about him. These feelings were reflected in her relationship with me, as the following episodes show.

November 6: Mrs. Paul tried to use another child to help John, but this maneuver failed. She feels he is somewhat better, mostly because she had been tough with him. I noted that "any attempt to use the group to help John will fail until Mrs. Paul is herself convinced that John can conform—otherwise her feelings of despair about him will be transmitted to the other children."

November 13: Mrs. Paul told me at lunchtime that John was much better in class. When he hit another child in the hall, Mrs. Paul had winked at the teacher of the other child and taken John's part in the battle. "Poor little kid," she said, "I had to take his side sometime." Perhaps she was supporting the child at the wrong time for the right reason because she felt I was lined up with John against her. Perhaps this was an attempt to please me, which was certainly not the point. I was beginning to think I had become too involved with John and his problems. I resolved to keep my relationship with him casual while showing Mrs. Paul that I could identify with her and her problems.

November 20: Because of my resolve, I did not visit Mrs. Paul's room during the morning. As a result she came up to me at lunchtime and asked if I had deserted her and John. She said he had been a mess again, and I agreed to come and observe again the next week.

November 28: Observation in Mrs. Paul's room: "John is quite a changed boy—he is playing with the others, goes out of his way not to bump into the blocks of others, listens quietly during story time. Mrs. Paul goes out of her way to give him a chance to respond to questions about the story, which he does correctly in a loud, clear voice. He ignores me for the first fifteen minutes of observation, then goes to his desk and gets his lunch bag, from which he draws a cookie and offers it to me. It is as if he senses that I must not become too involved with him but realizes I have something to do with the improved relationship between him and his teacher. I am not entirely sure what has happened."

December 5: "John is busily working. Mrs. Paul reports that he is much better, though he has acted up several times during the past week. When he does act up he retreats to the bathroom for a while but then returns to the group and tries to control her with his anger. I get the impression she has been able to handle this–refusing to be controlled by the anger but letting him know he may retreat if he needs to. When I remarked that he did not seem to be bothering her as he had at first, Mrs. Paul replied that she had been new to the job and worried about establishing herself as a teacher.

Although this was our last scheduled consultation about John, we continued to chat about his progress in the lunch room. From time to time Mrs. Paul would stop me in the hall and talk about her family or herself.

On January 28, when I had occasion to observe another child in her class, Mrs. Paul had a long discussion with me about her teaching. Since she was concerned that perhaps she was too rigid with her kindergarten children, we explored the ways in which scheduling provided a framework of security for some children and the ways in which a teacher could be flexible within that framework. On February 25, Mrs. Paul interrupted a conference with another teacher in the lunch room to tell me that John was doing so well she wanted me to visit her class that afternoon. Since I was not free then, I made arrangements to come the following week. After that observation I made some notes:

I stopped in Mrs. Paul's room to see my old friend John, and what a joy it was! He is a big shot in the class, liked by the kids and teacher. He raised his hand for everything and recited well. When he forgot something he didn't go into a fit, but waited and learned the right answer. He waved to me when I entered, but he obviously didn't need me. Mrs. Paul is proud of him and what she has done with him. When I congratulated her, she said she couldn't have done it without my help. But this child is now too compliant, too much the teacher's pet. What will happen with another teacher next year, I don't know. I wish I were going to be around to see.

Clearly, consultation had been of help to Mrs. Paul, even though we had both made mistakes along the way. The fact that she had perhaps gone too far in helping John become a leader in the group was a natural human reaction after all the guilt and self-questioning she had gone through.

The whole course of consultation with Mrs. Paul emphasizes the pressing need of new teachers for help and support as they start their careers. The function of a consultant is to help new teachers trust themselves, to see what is happening with individual children, to know how to tailor classroom activities to help them along with the group, and, above all, to get comfortable in the teaching role. There is never enough time to follow through as thoroughly as one would like. There is no question in my mind that consultation about a particular child should last more than a year if one is truly to help him and his teachers. Here is my final comment to this effect in my notes: "John has learned how to get along in a classroom and how to accommodate himself to the personality of one teacher. It is quite probable that he will have further difficulties with different teachers, and I made it clear to Mrs. Paul that she might help his new teacher by passing on her insights."

There were many other series of consultations with teachers about individual children and other problems. However, one unique result of consultation with teachers and principal grew out of a major crisis during the school year.

An Experiment in Consultation. Mrs. May, the social adjustment teacher, was about to leave the school to have her baby. This caused conflict and turmoil for Mrs. Tate, principal of Clements Elementary School and Mrs. May—and, indeed, affected the whole school. Though the school had funds to pay a social adjustment teacher at the beginning of the year, no such teacher had been available. There were six severely disturbed and disruptive boys in the school who needed special placement, and the principal and I had had many conferences to work out ways of keeping them in school. Then about the middle of October, Mrs. May had been hired and a social adjustment class had been set up for these troublesome boys. We had worked together long and hard. Now she found she would have to leave, since she was a temporary teacher and school rules forbade her remaining on the job after the fourth month of pregnancy. Once again we were faced with the problem of placing these boys, and a three-way conference was called to see what we could do.

My feelings at the conference were somewhat mixed. Mrs. May was a sensitive and intelligent woman, and I hated to see her leave. On the other hand, though she had tried valiantly, it was becoming clear that these six boys did not mix well. They had been acting as catalytic agents for each other's acting out rather than as reinforcements for improvement. In a large school the budget provides for a social adjustment class within the confines of one school building, regardless of the pathology of the children and their individual needs. I had felt from the beginning that our inability to select the members of the class on the basis of good grouping was a serious handicap, but since our consultative method stresses not trying to change what cannot be changed and meeting the needs of the schools as we find them, I had tried to help within the existing situation.

Though the boys had not been functioning together as a group, each one had established good personal relations with Mrs. May, and it was clear that this relationship was helping the child to progress. I suggested during the conference that Mrs. May continue to tutor the boys individually in a special room but recommended that they be placed immediately in regular classrooms with carefully selected teachers. During the time Mrs. May remained in the school, she would give them special assignments on their academic level, which they would work on in the regular classroom. Moreover, she would use her room as a sanctuary for the boys when they could not cope with the pressures of the larger class. Mrs. Tate and Mrs. May agreed with my plan and began to work out the details. But what would happen after Mrs. May left? The boys would still need the one-to-one relationship she had been providing. I thought of all the "big brother" projects I had heard of, and then I had an idea. There was a high school adjacent to Clements—why not use the high school pupils as helpers to our younger boys? It seemed to me that the age of the high school pupils would work in our favor. The younger boys reacted with defiance toward adults, conveyors of the culture in which they found themselves lost and unacceptable. Adolescents would be old enough to be respected but not so old that they could not be trusted.

Mrs. Tate liked the idea and called the principal of the high school to enlist his support. In response to her request, he circulated a school bulletin asking for volunteers to work with our boys. The response was immediate and gratifying. Just before the Christmas holidays we had our first orientation meeting for the volunteers—eight boys willing to work with troubled elementary school children. Seven of them were seniors and one a sophomore. Later in the year this sophomore brought over another volunteer, a girl, just at the point when we needed a girl to work with a certain boy in the school. As had been expected, the volunteers consisted of those who were outstanding in school as well as those who had problems of their own. The successful ones were more numerous; the troubled ones were only mildly so, mostly because of academic problems, and proved quite able to help the younger boys. All the volunteers were either members of the school band or friends of members. Consequently, they were used to working together and brought to the group a camaraderie that included a lot of joking and horseplay. The volunteer group was half white and half black; the younger boys with whom they worked were all black.

At the orientation meeting I explained the plan to them. They were ostensibly there to help the younger boys with homework, but the important thing was to build a relationship of trust if the younger boys were to make any progress. Any academic work they did with their young charges was to be supervised by the child's homeroom teacher. They would come to Clements as often as time allowed—during free periods, lunchtime, or after school. I cautioned them against signing up for more time than they could spare. If they had to withdraw in the future, the younger boys would assume that, once again, they themselves had failed.

Mrs. Tate arranged to have the homeroom teachers at the meeting, and the younger boys waited in another room. I then gave a thumbnail sketch of each boy—his classroom behavior, his academic difficulties, and as much of his home background as seemed consistent with confidentiality. As each high school volunteer heard the description of a child who appealed to him, he raised his hand and was taken by the homeroom teacher to meet his new charge and arrange to visit him at Clements. When all had been paired off, I described the plan, stressing that the most important part of the work would be the relationship with the younger child. I set up a weekly seminar at which the older boys could bring up problems. The meeting ended with cookies and soft drinks. We arranged to meet the following week for our first seminar, and I made a mental note that refreshments must always be part of the meetings.

The seminars got under way just after the Christmas holidays and continued until the end of May, at which time the seniors became so busy with exams and graduation that we had to stop. All in all, there were twenty-two hours of seminar work with the group that year. A few of the topics that arose during the year can be listed here.

First: the process of maturing in an individual. One high school boy said the child with whom he worked did not seem much in need of help. Although he was unable to share attention and affection, that seemed natural. This comment triggered a long discussion of the need to share in everyday life. I pointed out that it is impossible to share without the basic experience of individual attention and affection we were trying to provide.

Second: the belittling effect of having everything made easy. One of the elementary school boys had a mother who never demanded that he live up to his potential, never made him face the consequences of his refusal to work—and, in fact, had sent him to North Carolina to avoid having to repeat a grade at Clements. When this child tried to make Fred, his "big brother," react to him in the same way, Fred firmly let him know that he expected the child to do his best. He was afraid, however, that perhaps he had demanded too much. When other boys in the group gave examples of having had too little expected of them, Fred was reinforced in his intuitive handling of the child.

Third: the meaning of separation to a young child. This question arose when Mrs. May left and several of the younger boys acted out their feelings about her departure. Later in the year one of the young boys anxiously asked when his high school boy would have to stop coming. As the end of the year approached and the seniors had to cut down on visits because of exams and graduation, all the younger boys reacted adversely in one way or another. I equated these reactions to the feelings of the older boys as they faced the end of high school, going to work, or leaving home for college or jobs. Their response was immediate and clearly showed how the feelings of the older boys had enabled them to identify with the younger ones.

Fourth: the curative value of a relationship. This question was discussed often in relation to the work of Carolyn with Bertie—a shy boy who caused no trouble in the classroom but was indulging in sex play with other boys in the lavatory. Since his mother had been in a mental institution, we felt he needed a warm relationship with a female. Almost from the first he acted out with Carolyn his feelings toward women: shying away from her, then becoming openly hostile, and at the same time beginning to hit girls in his class. When Carolyn was too accepting of his acting out and invited him to hit her, I pointed out the need to accept his feelings while stopping the hitting in order to prevent the buildup of guilt. As the end of the year approached he began to act out all his fears of separation from Carolyn, and there was much discussion of how to help him with this.

Not all the time was spent in serious discussions; there were many occasions for other satisfactions, including humor. The older boys reported how the younger ones phoned them at home or called to them across the street. Homeroom teachers reported how the elementary school boys talked about their big brothers in the classroom and at home. The identification with the younger boys was clear from expressions of resentment when the older boys thought a teacher had mishandled their young charge or failed to teach him well. As the year ended, several of them made summer plans for the young boys to go to camp where they would be counselors. One tried to arrange music lessons for a younger boy who had begun to show an interest in the violin. Carolyn had a plan to keep in touch with Bertie through weekly postcards. There were many occasions for laughter—as when Richard, who had shied away from arithmetic with Gordon because of his own lack of skill, admitted that he and Gordon were doing arithmetic after all, and Gordon, who was good with figures, had shown him a few things. On April 24 the whole group received an award from B'nai Brith for community service.

To help me evaluate the project I had final interviews with the participants of the seminar. All said they would repeat the experiment again if given the chance. They felt they had learned things about themselves that would help them in their later lives, particularly when they became parents. Some felt they had learned things that would help them in later job choices. Carolyn in particular, who had been certain she wanted to be a veterinarian, was no longer sure—she felt she might like to work with children. All had experienced satisfaction in doing something for others. Two expressed appreciation for the relaxed atmosphere of the seminars and the respect shown for their judgment.

It is difficult to evaluate the effects of the project on the elementary school boys. They were so disturbed to start with, and came from backgrounds so difficult to change, that no claims for lasting gains can be made for any of them. Further, the project began late in the year and finished by the end of May, so there was not a great deal of time to work with them. All of them did remain in school and made the difficult adjustment to large classrooms. Two showed marked improvement in work habits and some academic gain; one showed no change; and one, though he did not deteriorate in the classroom, felt humiliated by being singled out for help. All the rest felt that having an older person visit them was a status symbol and boasted about it in the classroom. We learned a lot about the pairing off of younger and older participants. The best endorsement of the experiment was the fact that Mrs. Tate conducted another such project without my services the following year. The original high school participants rounded up twenty-five volunteers for it, and our one sophomore boy and his friend Carolyn continued their participation.

Our experiment was successful not only in this one school, however, for other schools set up similar programs. It was reported at the meetings of the Group Psychotherapy Association in January 1964 and in the January 1964 issue of the *NEA Journal.* Moreover, it has influenced programs in community attacks on poverty in which college youth were enlisted to help high school students.

The Lessons of Clements. I was fortunate in having been invited to consult at Clements, since I had a chance to work with a principal who was open to new ideas and willing to try them. The racial and economic background of the school was such that we learned a great deal about the aspirations of middle-class black parents. I was not surprised to find that they exert the same pressure for academic achievement on their children as do the white middle-class parents with whom I have worked. In this case the pressures are exacerbated because the status of the black is improving. Since these parents see education as the golden key to a place in the sun for their children, they push all the harder. On the basis of contacts with a small sample of poor black parents, it seems to me that they share the same aspirations. Thus, in addition to the ordinary burden of growing up and those imposed by membership in a minority group, the children at Clements showed problems in response to these pressures too. I think our method of on-the-spot consultation—that is, making weekly visits and accepting things as they are—was successful in alleviating some pressures that handicapped learning in this elementary school. Several factors contributed to this success. One of these was direct intervention. Perhaps the way I functioned at Clements might be regarded dubiously by social workers and psychotherapists committed to a nondirective approach in helping other people. And yet I am quite sure that I came to be accepted by the principal and teachers simply because I took over a class from time to time, or held a conference with a parent, or spent time with a child in need. One teacher expressed this to me on the last day of school. "We are going to miss you," she said. "You aren't just doing a job or gathering data for research—you really care about us and the children." Perhaps it is because my background is in teaching that this eclectic, sometimes direct, sometimes nondirective, approach worked for me. Different backgrounds offer different styles of consultation, of course, and there may be more than one road that leads to Rome.

Hoover Elementary School

Suddenly there was a dramatic shift in the tone of the meeting. The teacher of a low-IQ class, sitting in an isolated spot down the table, interrupted the flow of conversation to ask in a loud voice: "Mr. Kitchener, I've been wondering, just what is it you're going to do here?" The general chatter stopped and all the teachers looked expectantly at me for an answer. It was as if all the lively talk had been politely screening this question for each of them.

The teachers asked if they would have to keep anecdotal notes on various children. I told them that it was not our job to prove anything to anyone and that we were free to find the methods of communication most useful to us. I added that we might find anecdotal notes useful in some situations, but our purpose was to make their life less, not more, burdensome. There were sighs of relief.

Discussion then developed about the extent of teacher involvement in some classroom problems, and finally Mrs. G. raised the question directly: "Aren't you trying to treat the teachers?" I answered that this was not our purpose. Our focus was really on the child, and if we succeeded in relieving some of the stress, it should enable teachers to work more effectively.

There was a noticeable reduction of anxiety in the group as this point was clarified, and later, when the meeting broke up, Mrs. G. said, "What we were most concerned about has been answered to our satisfaction." It was clear to me that she was referring to the issue of treating the teachers. After the teachers' fears and questions about the consultant's presence had been allayed, requests for consultation and observation increased at a remarkable rate.

Reaching a Principal. On many occasions I observed that when a child was having a talk with the principal, Mrs. Adams, and started to express negative feelings, she shut the child off with such phrases as "Oh, no, you don't feel that way at all; you just have nice feelings about that boy." One day when she asked a small boy why he had misbehaved, the child answered that sometimes he "just felt all black and hate inside." Mrs. Adams denied that the child could have such a feeling and told him he must be mistaken because he was really a very nice boy. The point is that psychotherapists, and many teachers, work for hours to get a child to acknowledge negative feelings so that he can accept himself and behave more healthily. Mrs. Adams could understand in general that children are not all bad and that they need to feel self-acceptance, but her denial of their negative feelings prevented her from helping children make use of their awareness.

After I had been at Hoover several months I began to realize how frequently Mrs. Adams was missing our regularly scheduled conferences. She was often out to lunch with a colleague or busy with chores about the building. One day I suggested that we meet at a nearby restaurant for lunch. Mrs. Adams was delighted with the idea, and our talk turned out to be one of the most productive discussions we had.

While waiting for lunch Mrs. Adams made some comment about the difficulty of talking in her office, where there are frequent interruptions or the call of other duties. I mentioned that her job made unusual demands on her and it was sometimes hard to know where to focus attention. Then she began to talk about a recent argument between two teachers over the transfer of a child. The child was moved from a young teacher's room to a brighter group under an older teacher's charge. When the older teacher said the child could never measure up to the performance of the brighter group, however, the young teacher got quite upset and asked to see the principal. Mrs. Adams had handled this nicely. She told her that this older teacher had standards too exacting for many children, that she should not be concerned about implied criticism because the principal was the one to do the evaluating, and that she was well satisfied with the young teacher's performance. Mrs. Adams went on to tell me that although this young teacher drives herself with great expectation, she does not have the kind of children who will show dramatic results.

She then began to discuss her own failure to communicate with another teacher. She seemed to be criticizing herself in much the same way as the young teacher had criticized herself. I carefully asked her how she could so effectively help the young teacher see that success did not depend on reaching all the children but could not allow herself the same latitude with her teachers. Mrs. Adams saw my point, but then the characteristic denial took over. She said, "Oh, I don't feel inadequate in any way; I have a good relationship with all the teachers. We have our little conflicts now and then. But who doesn't?" I told her we all felt inadequate in one way or another. When there seemed to be blocks in my communication with her, I said, I felt responsible and despaired of resolving the difficulty.

A little later Mrs. Adams was much more relaxed and talked about her long struggle with one of the older teachers in the school, a woman who had been there before she came. This teacher was too strict and tried to run the school. The department wanted to transfer her, but Mrs. Adams had asked for a chance to work out their difficulties. When a supervisor visited the school recently, he was astonished by the transformation in this teacher. Mrs. Adams had carefully assigned her functions that would enhance her status, and this treatment showed quick results.

Here we see some of the sympathy and awareness the principal brought to bear, despite her tendency to deny the problems around her. She was aware of the personality conflicts between some members of her staff and was willing to make allowances for what could not be changed immediately. Since a transfer would have been a devastating blow to the older teacher, Mrs. Adams had given her managerial status. The teacher then began to relax her rigid attitudes about managing children. The supervisor, impressed with the teacher's performance, was also impressed with the principal's manner of bringing it about.

A Teacher Asks for Help. After our luncheon conversation, there was a noticeable change in the way Mrs. Adams began to use my services. A few weeks later she said she wanted to discuss some difficulties she was having with one of her special teachers. She told me she regretted that she was unable to spend more time with these teachers. They had different, and sometimes harder, problems than the regular classroom teachers. The supervisor who evaluated Miss Z. (who had a mixed class of low-IQ and emotionally disturbed children) wanted to give her a lower rating than the principal thought she deserved. I had observed some of the children in class and was able to support Mrs. Adams's contention that the teacher possessed reasonable capacity, but there was no question that she needed additional help in understanding the children. Miss Z. seemed to be caught between the need to express her distress to the principal and the fear of exposing her shortcomings. She was certain that exposure would only substantiate the supervisor's evaluation. Mrs. Adams asked me if I would concentrate on this teacher and hold regular conferences in an effort to help her.

This manner of referral was entirely different from that in force at the beginning of the program: Mrs. Adams had insisted on scheduling conferences only for teachers referred by herself. At that time there was no indication that the teachers understood or wanted such conferences with me; and since referral by the principal would have been resented, my effort would probably have been negated. Now, since Miss Z. had already asked me to observe her class and discuss her problems, it was easy to see that the severity and number of problems in her room would require regular conferences. Mrs. Adams arranged to have a room mother cover the class while Miss Z. attended the conferences, and she said she would occasionally cover the class herself if necessary.

Lincoln: A Special Elementary School

During my initial tour of Lincoln, an elementary school for special problems, it was apparent that the teachers and children were accustomed to having the principal, Mr. Graham, drop in on them for unobtrusive observation. In most classrooms, they simply continued a class discussion until there was a convenient point for the teacher to interrupt. She might pause to explain the context of the discussion or invite Mr. Graham to comment or participate as he wished. Other teachers simply proceeded without interruption unless Mr. Graham indicated that he needed their attention. In classrooms where desk work was in progress, the teachers came over to meet me and chat briefly. In each room it was apparent that Mr. Graham was allowing the teacher to determine the opportune moment for interruption. This respect for the autonomy of the teacher was striking and seemed to characterize his relationship with his staff. Some classes were quiet and some noisy; some were involved in highly organized activity while in other rooms diffuse individual activities were in progress. Whatever the activity, noise level, or organizational style, none of the teachers seemed defensive or needed to explain why they were working in the particular way they had chosen. The atmosphere of easy communication and implied trust between Mr. Graham and his teachers became even more noticeable during the lunch period.

As the noon-hour bell rang, we stopped in at the teachers' room. This was a shrewd move on Mr. Graham's part since the informality provided a chance to chat with the teachers at ease. The first ones to enter were quite uneasy, however, as they thought they were interrupting a conference between their principal and me. They accepted Mr. Graham's invitation to join us, and there was lively talk as the teachers tried to figure out who I was. When told that I would be around to help solve their problems with children, they enthusiastically related recent experiences in their classrooms—some disturbing, others humorous. They were sharing their reactions in a way I suppose they ordinarily did with Mr. Graham, but now some of the conversation was addressed to me. One of the teachers, Mrs. K., related an anecdote about a large, rough girl in her class. Before explaining what she had done with the girl, however, she turned to Mr. Graham and asked, "Is it all right to tell him?" He answered, "Sure, you can tell him anything. He's going to be one of us." At this point I began to relax.

One day when I was eating lunch with the teachers, two of them started comparing notes on the composition of their respective groups. One commented that she had the scrapings from three other fifth grades while Mrs. X. had a "regular" fifth grade. When I asked how the regulars were selected for a school like Lincoln, she implied that they were the undesirables and the misfits. Mrs. X. remarked that some of these children were not academic or behavior problems but their parents were particularly difficult, which might have been the reason they were screened to attend Lincoln. I then asked them to compare Lincoln's flexible program with that of the other elementary schools. While accepting the staff's lament that Lincoln often got more than its share of the difficult children because of its flexibility, I suggested that it also got regular ones who would do better with this kind of program. Several of the teachers agreed and gave examples of children who did much better here than they would have done in another school.

Mrs. X. spoke of some of her former pupils, who were extremely deprived and yet had more zest for learning than some of their more fortunate classmates, and gradually built up to her greatest success in all her years of teaching. She described a boy whom "the school had salvaged from a rat's nest—a bright boy with an IQ of over 140." She went on about the glories of this boy's attainments: "He became a jet pilot, married into one of the best families, and now he's right up there reaching for the stars." This was a moving moment in the lunch room discussion. There were eight or nine teachers in the room, and it seemed to me that they all identified with Mrs. X.'s satisfaction and longed for a similar success in their own work.

I commented on the satisfaction we would all derive from such striking measures of success but wondered how to measure success when you have a child with an IQ of 70 and are trying to help him function at his capacity. They all pounced on this question, and there was a half-hour's lively discussion about sources of replenishment for the teachers of children who are never going to touch the stars. Some spoke of former pupils who now hold a steady if menial job in the community; others cited former students who still visit Lincoln although they are married and working. One teacher suggested that some of her former pupils are now better parents than their own parents were—at least they now come regularly to PTA meetings.

One could readily feel the sense of worth the teachers experienced in this discussion. Although they were five or ten minutes late to their afternoon classes, they all seemed reluctant to leave. When I stopped in to tell the secretary I was leaving, she remarked, "It must have been a good discussion today—some of them stopped in here on the way to classes, and you could tell they'd had a good meeting."

Establishing a Mental Health Team in a Middle School

4

Rhona S. Weinstein

Over a period of two years, as an external consultant, I was involved in the inception and growth of a collaborative mental health team within the confines of a school. The primary objective of the team was to explore innovative ways of helping problem children within the school setting while relying on the school's own resources. As plans became translated into action, the team faced an evolving set of institutional constraints. The organization and its members resisted new relationships and new behavior. Conflict grew out of the fact that the collaborative team concept violated the prevailing norms of the school system.

Note: The contributions of Seymour B. Sarason, I. Ira Goldenberg, and Kate McGraw in creating a stimulating and supportive environment for growth are gratefully acknowledged. Certain details and names in this case history have been disguised to protect the identity of the participants.

Both the composition of the team and its behavioral commitment to collaborative solutions made inevitable the resultant confrontation with organizational values and priorities.

This chapter addresses the evolution of the team in the face of these institutional constraints and examines phases in the team's development. These phases reflected anticipatory as well as reactive problem solving vis-à-vis obstacles met in the course of implementation. In response to these constraints, modifications were made in the team's structure and its strategies of implementation. The characteristics of these accommodations are of interest because they provide insight into the factors affecting the development of a new organizational structure. Further, an examination of the natural history of group development in a responsive social environment can generate new knowledge about the use of group processes to facilitate organizational change.

Thus, drawing upon a single case history, this chapter describes the development of the group consultation model and its implementation in a middle school. By analyzing the stages of group development, I hope to reveal implications for the study of organizational change.

The Consultation Model

The impetus for this team approach grew out of frustration with earlier interventions focused on consultation with individual teachers. What was achieved in the classroom was often short-lived as new approaches received no reinforcement from the organization. The consultant working at an individual level was frequently forced into serving as a feedback mechanism between teachers and administration while the school's response to behavior problems never really changed. Studies of the school culture (Sarason, 1971), the course of educational innovation (McLaughlin, 1976), and the implementation of behavior modification in natural settings (Tharp and Wetzel, 1969) similarly highlight the role of institutional influences in controlling new programs in the classroom.

Further, analyses of the school as an organization suggest several structural features that have specific implications for the ways in which services are defined and delivered to students and for the pathways for spreading innovative programs. These analyses underscore the school's simple and loose internal structure, which is framed around the autonomy of classrooms where individual solutions are stressed and relationships between staff are minimized (Bidwell, 1965; Meyer and Rowan, 1978; Weick, 1976).

Since school norms encourage individual problem solving, school staff members typically undertake the problems of students on their own. Their problem-solving activities most frequently occur in sequence, following upon the failures of the helpers who preceded them. Referrals most often occur at crisis points—sharpening negative feelings, limiting productive energy, and often reducing the range of appropriate interventions. Once referrals are made, most teachers feel that they have exhausted their intervention repertoire. Ready to pass the problem to others, they frequently adopt a hands-off policy toward the problem student (Sarason and others, 1966). Such referral patterns (from teacher to principal or from teacher to special services) tend to encourage the use of labeling. Moreover, they limit the range of problem-solving strategies developed and underutilize the potential resources of the school.

Given the absence of structural interdependence between organizational units within schools, few pathways are available for transmitting and sustaining new ideas (Miles, 1967). Large-scale evaluations of the impact of federal funds on school functioning support this observation in their failure to document enduring innovation (Berman and McLaughlin, 1974). Hence new programs are not easily nurtured or spread in school settings.

Consultation methods with individual teachers often maintain these organizational features of school culture. The implementation of new ideas becomes an individual decision, with little systemic support for the development or continuation of new approaches. If the intent of consultation is to improve the capacity of schools to handle problem children, then clearly very different components have to be built into the consultation model in order to facilitate organizational support for new interventions.

Group consultation methods (Altrocchi, Spielberger, and

Eisdorfer, 1965) provide an appealing framework for intervention in that these methods directly channel peer influence and peer support. However, group consultation with just any array of school staff members would not afford the necessary leverage at an organizational level to support new approaches in work with problem children. Lessons learned from the implementation and evaluation of organization-development approaches in the schools (for example, as reviewed by Fullan, Miles, and Taylor, 1980) suggest the critical importance of the principal's involvement, a school-based follow-through, and a focus on the task at hand.

Thus, drawing from both mental health and organizational consultation, a group consultation approach was developed that involved the creation of a mental health team in the schools. By design, the team included the following components: a cross section of school staff as members, principal membership, consultant leadership, continuity in scheduling (in this case, a weekly meeting throughout the school year), a meeting site in the school, and a focus on school-referred problems. This approach placed program development in the hands of the staff that would be implementing the changes. The problems addressed and the solutions proposed could then be unique to the setting and its needs. The cross-sectional composition of the group ensured that a broad array of information about a problem could be gathered, that varied resources could be made available for planning interventions, and that the opportunity was provided to forge and legitimize new policy. Moreover, the regularized base of the team within the school would permit contributions from parents, from community resources, and from other schools in the district as well as facilitate a process from which innovative programs could emerge and be sustained.

A Case Example

This group consultation model was first implemented in a middle school of a small lower-middle-class industrial community. Consultation began in the opening year of this school. The school system was experimenting with its first middle or junior high school, and seventh and eighth-grade students from all the elementary schools in the district (365 students) were moved into the old high school building. Twelve teachers were selected from the elementary schools for this new program on the basis of their interest in this age group, and one of them was appointed principal. By September, the mood was one of anticipation and excitement.

At the time, the Yale University Psycho-Educational Clinic was providing consultation services to this small school district and I, along with another consultant, approached the superintendent and the principal of the new middle school with a proposal for services. We explained that our primary interest as consultants lay in exploring new ways for schools to use their own resources in resolving the varied difficulties they face in the handling of problem children. We suggested that a group consultation approach rather than individual consultation with teachers might provide a better structure for innovative solutions. We proposed to organize a group of interested individuals–the principal, the guidance counselor, the school nurse, and volunteer teachers–to explore collaborative solutions to classroom problems. We were pleased to find both the superintendent and the principal receptive to our plan and also eager to have the middle school participate.

After an introductory meeting with the entire school faculty, in which we gathered a number of interested participants, we began our group. During the first year, the regular membership consisted of nine people–the principal, the guidance counselor (sole special services personnel), the school nurse, four teachers, and my colleague and I. We agreed on a format of weekly two-hour meetings to be held during the last forty minutes of the school day and after school (with release time for teachers available through the use of parent aides and preparatory periods). These meetings were to continue throughout the academic year. The group flourished and continued its meetings throughout a second year with minor changes in composition. My colleague left and a departing teacher was replaced by another member of the teaching staff who joined the group at the start of its second year.

Phases in the Growth of Collaboration

During the two-year life of the group, there appeared to be five distinct stages of group development. These stages reflected shifts in the nature of the problems confronted by the group as its members addressed the needs of the children presented for discussion. The phases involved (1) establishing group cohesion, (2) enabling task accomplishment, (3) facilitating alternative solutions, (4) monitoring rebellion, and (5) supporting reformation. I will describe them as they were revealed in the handling of successive cases by the group.

"Not Free to Talk": Establishing Group Cohesion. Every new group is confronted with similar tasks. As described by Yalom (1970), group members must first decide on a method of achieving the group's mission and then address the aspects of social relationships that interfere with that task's accomplishment.

The group began its work by exploring the nature of the task and defining the rules under which they would work. The role of the consultant in the early meetings focused on developing a safe and supportive structure for problem solving and encouraging problem identification. The group chose a case-conference format in which they would address the problems of children referred for discussion by group members. With strong principal support in terms of partial release time for teachers, a two-hour weekly meeting was assured.

Although the team members had all volunteered and the organization had supported the idea, much stood in the way of the comfortable sharing of problems. Members came to the group representing their various roles in the organization. Since the group was embedded in its natural environment and continued over a period of time, group members went back and forth between the group life and their life in the school. This meant that, early on, group members presented themselves largely in terms of their roles in the organization, continually bombarding the group with system norms and procedures.

The variety of roles represented in the group underscored differences in language, perspective, and status. Hence early meetings of the group were marked by suspicion and mistrust. An example of how contrary role expectations interfered with productive communication emerged in the very first group meeting:

Example 1: At the first meeting of the group, during an exciting point in the discussion, the principal tore himself away from the meeting. We learned, upon his return, that he had left in order to ring the bell for dismissal. At issue here was the now explicit status difference between the principal and the other staff. To the extent that the principal was free to come and go as he pleased in order to attend to other responsibilities, he would be unable to assume true membership in the group. This question was resolved when the principal volunteered to delegate responsibility for dismissal on the days of our meetings.

The discussion of role expectations and status differences also revealed the threat inherent in collaboration. By sharing problems and feelings, group members exposed themselves to others and risked evaluation. This threat was heightened by the presence of the principal in the group, since evaluation by the principal was indeed a fact of life for teachers. Inertia was a common response in the early meetings as teachers were reluctant to present problem cases. It was only by exploring these feelings and assessing the stigma attached to owning up to problems that trust could develop. By focusing on these constraints, the group members began to share their feelings and support each other despite different perspectives.

"Not Free to Act": Enabling Task Accomplishment. Problems and problem-solving strategies became accessible only as the group members began to trust each other. One example of how role definitions stood in the way of potential interventions with children is illustrated in the following episode from the treatment of Angelina:

Example 2: In the first few weeks of school, Angelina, a thirteen-year-old "flower child" who presented problems to all her teachers, came up for discussion at our group meeting. Having recently moved here from New York with her mother and brothers, Angelina was having difficulty adjusting to, as she termed it, "the highly unsophisticated" town, the school, and its young people. This difficulty was further complicated by severe kidney problems that often kept her away from school. When present, she was forced to leave the classroom continually in order to urinate and therefore became further isolated from her new situation.

Angelina had been absent for the entire week, and since she had no close relationships in the school, it seemed highly unlikely that there was much here to bring her back. It became clear in discussion that the school had to keep in touch with her in order to facilitate her return to school. Numerous suggestions were offered by the group, such as homebound instruction or daily visits by the guidance counselor who appeared to know Angelina best. Although suggestions flowed freely, so did the rules that prevented their application. Apparently there existed a school system ruling that homebound instruction may only begin after three consecutive weeks of absence. Teachers could take it upon themselves to tutor a student at home before three weeks had passed but would not be reimbursed for their efforts. Further, guidance counselors were not permitted to make home visits—this was the domain of the social worker.

This dilemma was not resolved until two weeks later when, faced with a second absence, the guidance counselor made three consecutive visits to Angelina's home. This experimentation with role definition involved a certain amount of risk. It was clearly easier to refrain from action and accept the immutability of the rule network. Further, there were few organizational rewards for such action. At this early point in the development of the team, risk taking was a highly personal decision—one that took the guidance counselor two weeks to make. However, rewards for such actions appeared in the group itself. As individuals began to function outside their roles, they gained new information and opened new pathways for intervention. Sharing the information the guidance counselor had learned about Angelina and her family through home visits brought the group much closer to an understanding of the girl's predicament. Thus the risk taker became instrumental in developing programs of assistance for the group.

Struggles concerning the nature of each role ensued throughout the life of the group. How much leeway did exist in the definition of roles? The requirements were never clear. The fact that individuals with different roles and different functions in the school committed themselves to a yearlong collaboration made inevitable the continual questioning of the school structure even though their primary goal was the welfare of individual children.

"Supportive Action": Facilitating Alternative Solutions. Gradually, role constraints on action diminished in the group. The following case illustrates that when the group began to focus on the task at hand rather than on prescribed roles, the solutions they proposed reflected greater collaborative responsibility and greater role interchangeability. Solutions were becoming more creative and the group members became more supportive of each other.

Example 3: With time, two things became clear about Angelina. When she did attend school, she came primed for a good day or a bad day—one could tell by the state of her hair-do. The guidance counselor would see her every morning for a talk before classes. Angelina seemed to respond to this opportunity, and bad days were often halted right there. She felt comfortable with only two teachers, both of them male. With the others, all women, she had difficult relationships. Bad days meant confrontations with those teachers by blatantly disobeying the rules governing conduct, such as eating an apple in class, spitting at a teacher, or talking back. The teachers threw up their hands in despair and continually sent Angelina to the principal for discipline. The principal therefore faced Angelina in the worst of situations, and these confrontations ended in suspension. As he explained to the group, "You dumped Angelina on me when you couldn't cope with her any longer." The principal, alone in his role without support, had little alternative but to climb the prescribed disciplinary stepladder.

Angelina by her very actions was asking for suspension. Her power to create that outcome frightened her and consequently she acted out more intensely. Furthermore, home was not the place for her. The group set up a collaborative plan that committed every member to share responsibility for Angelina.

First, she would attend school only half-days. (Because of her kidney ailment, a day seemed too long—half-days might reduce her absences.) Second, she would attend only the classes she negotiated without major incident (the two male teachers). Third, the principal would tutor her one period a day to work on the subjects she was missing. Fourth, the guidance counselor would continue seeing her daily before classes. The plan proceeded smoothly—Angelina's attendance improved and she was learning. The principal obtained a great deal of satisfaction from the tutoring.

At this time, the principal received notification that the superintendent had called a meeting with Angelina's mother in order to issue a warning of possible expulsion. Expulsion could result in residential placement for the girl. The group reacted to the news with a wave of depression—a sense that all was lost and no alternatives remained. In reality, however, the group had more information about the girl than did the superintendent, and a warning to her parent at this point was premature in light of our recent success. Further, it became clear that the superintendent did not know much about our program and, moreover, this was hardly the time for him to be receptive to our plea for more time. Not to have involved him in our activities before a crisis occurred was a glaring oversight on our part. After much deliberation and with the group's support, the principal volunteered to approach the superintendent with the history of our work with Angelina and explain that a meeting with her mother at present was premature. The superintendent agreed to cancel the meeting.

This episode illustrates quite explicitly that a consideration of alternative behavior rests on some measure of support. Earlier the principal had felt alone in his role as administrator and relied heavily on strategies that defined his role sharply—that is, suspension. However, increased support from a group of concerned individuals and the sharing of responsibility allowed him to act on his beliefs regarding the girl and to take a stand against the superintendent's decision. The increased support seemed to come from greater role interchangeability in handling problems. The principal exchanged his disciplinary role for that of a teacher when he began tutoring Angelina; the other teachers shared the principal's role of disciplining Angelina. As a result, the bond between group members deepened.

Although the group was able to extend role definitions, participate in greater role interchangeability, share decision-making power, and reinterpret rules, these changes also occurred in an arena outside of the group and thus had an impact on other teachers, higher levels of the administration, and the community. For example, there were repercussions from the principal's halting of the meeting between the superintendent and Angelina's parent. Shortly thereafter, the principal was asked to tighten his school policies—the superintendent had voiced concern with how the school was running. The message appeared to express the intensity of the threat the collaborative team posed for the superintendent. Cancellation of the meeting with Angelina's mother represented a weakening of the superintendent's authority. Instead of suspensions passing through the regular channels into his ultimate responsibility, a group of teachers and one of his principals took matters into their own hands. It should be noted, however, that the principal's head, not the group's, was on the chopping block.

The root of the problem appeared to lie in an ever increasing divergence between the superintendent's perspective and that of the group. As a result of our collaboration, we had begun to think differently about how to approach a problem child. The superintendent, who had not shared our experience, perceived situations in vastly different ways, as illustrated by another incident. Upon seeing Angelina appear at school dressed inappropriately, the superintendent ordered her to go home and change her clothes whereas our own experience with the student had taught us to place priority on regular attendance at school rather than on infractions of the rules. By viewing problems differently and engaging in alternative actions, group members faced repercussions from the system at large. Although a new set of norms had been created within the group, outside this protected setting the culture and its solutions had remained the same. The locus of constraints upon action had shifted from within the group to outside.

"Acting in the Face of Institutional Constraints": Moni-

toring Rebellion. The growing conflict between the superintendent and the group is further illustrated by our work on another case:

Example 4: Twelve-year-old Anthony, because of his earnestness and love for school, won everyone's heart at the middle school. He was in the special class for retarded children. One day he pulled a knife taken from the home economics room on his beloved teacher. She was able to calm him down. His teacher, a member of our group, was less frightened than concerned. She felt that simple hunger was at the root of this outburst. Not only was he rarely fed at home but he possessed only one set of foul-smelling clothing, which he wore every day. The teacher had been supplying him with her lunch, but clearly it was less than adequate. Our group met with the welfare worker assigned to Anthony's family and together we explored the family situation by making a home visit. What we encountered was a highly disorganized home environment—a helpless mother with many children, a virtually absent father and paycheck, an empty refrigerator and filthy surroundings.

First we addressed ourselves to what the school could do for Anthony. We attempted to set up a program to provide food for the child daily. This plan was vetoed by the superintendent as extending beyond the responsibility of the school. Thus we set up subsidiary programs, handled by individual teachers, providing food, clothing, and washing opportunities. And we placed all our energy into working with the family to help them accept the services of a homemaker.

The superintendent's veto was regarded by the group as a clear warning to return to the school's previous method of dealing with behavior problems—that is, referral through the principal to the guidance counselor or an outside agency. All final decisions would then be reviewed by the superintendent. The refusal of the superintendent to support our program for the boy led the group to bypass the organization in order to ensure the resolution of the case.

The decision to work around the veto represented the beginning of a period of open rebellion by group members. Although the group continued to take action in the face of these institutional constraints, all were left with a feeling of uneasiness about these accomplishments and their lack of acceptance by the school system. What the group desperately wanted was approval for their activities. Instead, they were threatened—particularly the principal, who in every case was on the firing line. This feeling of vulnerability was expressed in a number of ways. In a humorous vein, the group asked to be paid for the extra time spent in collaborative efforts. They complained about the teachers who were not involved in our program and suggested compulsory attendance for "the undedicated." And there was a growing fear that the principal's job was in danger. Yet at the same time that the group members were frightened by the superintendent's veto of the food plan, they were enraged by the apparent insensitivity of the school system to the needs of its troubled students.

"Pressuring for Institutional Change": Supporting Reformation. Anticipating additional reactions to innovative problem-solving strategies, the group began to address the issue of involving other teachers, community services, parents, and the superintendent in order to stop the growing divergence between the new generation (the group members) and the established one as well as to collaborate further in shared plans of action. This plan was only agreed upon by the group members as they developed sufficient trust among themselves, as they began to take risks in a responding environment, and as they felt forced to circumvent existing policy. The uneasy experience of rebellion, coupled with the group's apparent success in helping children with problems, resulted in the articulation of a new mission for the group. We committed ourselves to the goal of legitimizing the collaborative problem-solving method.

The extension began informally through invitations to those who cared about the problems discussed and would be affected by their resolution. And with it came increased feelings of vulnerability and more obstacles to consider.

Given that most of the conflict at this point had emanated from the higher levels of administration, we began by inviting the superintendent to the next group meeting with the assumption that observing and learning more about our efforts might enlist his aid. The consultants and the principal met with the superintendent before the meeting to familiarize him with both the case under discussion and the format of the group.

Example 5: The case we discussed was that of Fred, a twelve-year-old boy who did not return to school following the Christmas vacation. His mother reported that he did not wish to come to school at all. All efforts to get the mother to school to talk with the staff had failed. After three weeks of the boy's continuous absence, the principal visited the home and forcibly brought Fred to school. Fred returned on his own for only two consecutive days. The principal reported that Fred's father collected guns and a number of rifles were hanging over Fred's bed. The superintendent remarked that the principal had broken the law by going to the boy's home—and, further, the standard procedure for handling such children was to call the police (who in this town serve as truant officers) to pick up the boy each morning. With that, he left our meeting in order to attend another.

All the group members felt intimidated by the superintendent's remarks. His physical presence in the school (his office was in the middle school) exacerbated our fears of conflict if we could not facilitate Fred's immediate return to school. During that week, the principal called the police to pick up Fred. It took them forty minutes to get him out of the house, all the while the mother suggesting they put a straitjacket on him. The next day Fred came on his own, but for one day only. The principal received definite pressure from the superintendent to resolve the case or it would be taken out of the hands of the group.

The group decided to explore the resources in the family to determine whether anyone in that family was strong enough to take responsibility for getting the boy to school. Our group met with Fred's parent, his seventeen-year-old sister, and his 21-year-old sister and her husband. We were prepared to meet as often as necessary. We put our cards on the table—and explained as bluntly as possible the serious nature of the problem and what we had done to help. We could not get Fred here on our own. The son-in-law emerged as the strongest member of the family and volunteered to appear daily at his in-laws' home to take the boy to school. It took five very difficult mornings, but after that Fred appeared at school on a regular basis. The school had prepared for his arrival—he had been placed in a new class where students were less aware of his predicament.

For the superintendent to learn about the group's way of thinking and for the group members to become aware of his pressures from the community did not prove to be an easy task. As the example describes, the same role expectations that first pulled the principal from the meeting to ring the dismissal bell interfered with the superintendent's involvement in the group. A context for reexamining the case, looking beyond the blinders of existing role definitions, could not be established. The group was both frightened and challenged by the implicit time limit imposed on their work. That, coupled with the exciting and highly successful solution to Fred's problem, left the group members feeling victorious, much like comrades in battle. A trade-off had been won—the collaborative risk taking had brought with it a sense of increasing vulnerability, but it paid off in the opportunity to influence decisions about the welfare of the students. The quality of group life had changed sharply as a result of that victory. There was a cause to support—the institution of our concept of collaborative problem solving on a systematic basis—and great determination to achieve this goal without compromise to its essential ideas.

After adjourning for the summer, the composition of the collaborative team in the second year was altered by the loss of one of its consultants and one of its teachers (transferred to another school) and by the addition of a new teacher. In the second year, the group began to function like a pressure group in the planning of strategies. The thorniest problem we confronted was that this group, as a result of its experiences, had come to think differently about handling problems. Our goals differed from those of the superintendent and the teachers who had not been involved in our teamwork. And despite our extended invitations, their participation had been fragmentary. In examining past incidents that reflected the divergence of values and priorities, the group began to consider that shared knowledge was not enough—mutual responsibility for both the decision and its consequences was needed as well.

This insight led to a change in strategies. Our informal outreach became more formal through regular weekly meetings between the principal and the superintendent—meetings that allowed continual feedback from the administrative office as well as updates on interventions planned by the team. As a liaison between the superintendent and the team's activities, the principal sent weekly reports of the group meeting to the superintendent and then reported the superintendent's position to the group. In this way, our team became informed about the constraints of the superintendent, his perspectives, and his concerns in the planning of interventions with students. Further, the superintendent became better acquainted with the thinking of the team.

One case the group addressed during its second year illustrates how the team and the superintendent negotiated a mutual plan of action that satisfied both the goals of the group and the administrative concerns of the district.

Example 6: Our concern was Stanley, a highly anxious and compulsive boy who had never had any friends. Stanley had an overprotective mother who waited daily outside the school in order to escort him home. Since the father was virtually absent from the home, Stanley was the focus of his mother's life. His home and his school were all the boy knew. An attempt to help Stanley would bring little success unless we could reach a highly alienated family. Our proposed intervention was to offer the mother a job in the school with the goal of getting her out of the home each day, bolstering her self-confidence (she would be paid), and encouraging her to take an interest in herself. Further, she would become more accessible to help. Such a proposal needed the superintendent's support for both financial and strategic reasons. It was a difficult maneuver to hire someone for a school job that had not been posted in the community. The superintendent, who had been involved in the case since we began, supported the proposed program of assistance if the middle school would take responsibility for public relations and half the cost.

Thus, with mutual responsibility for the consequences, the team and the administration became better able to negotiate acceptable and productive intervention strategies for students.

Until now, the group had addressed relatively few children; instead, our emphasis was on the development of new approaches to problem children. The team recognized the importance of reaching more children and encouraging other teachers to join the collaborative efforts. By now, all the teachers in the school had been invited to attend at least one group meeting. Although all of them were by now familiar with the collaboration and its format, they hesitated to involve themselves with the group. Only one new teacher appeared able to make a commitment to join. One consequence of a "battle-scarred" group was that it appeared to alienate teachers. Although our meetings were always open and teachers had been asked to attend and share information about certain children, the aura of an in-group remained. To interest more teachers, and in response to dissatisfaction with how slowly our work had gone, a number of group members wanted to reorganize the format of our collaborative efforts. They suggested that each group member take more initiative in gathering information and formulating programs of assistance. The proposal involved selecting a coordinator in the school for each case that came up and using the weekly group meetings as a resource. The realignment had the potential of involving more teachers on a less formal basis. Teachers who had been unable to commit themselves to the collaborative team might become involved in the informal sessions with the case coordinator. All would be free to join the weekly meeting for support and stimulation of ideas.

The shift in format helped change the leadership patterns of the group. The principal began to play a greater role in directing the discussion, and the consultant gradually withdrew from a facilitative function. This change in leadership was welcomed. Not only were the group members familiar with the process but the consultant planned to leave at the end of the school year. The idea evolved of broadening the collaborative effort to include the neighboring elementary school, which in the following year would have as its principal a member of our team. Both principals planned to serve as leaders of a joint team meeting that would include interested teachers from the two schools, the nurse, and the guidance counselor. The group's particular concern had been to follow up the children who left our programs and, until now, the problem had been difficult to resolve because of limited resources. A joint group involving a representative staff from both schools would provide the means of instituting an effective follow-up program. An added implication of the joint meetings was that the power balance would be affected —two principals in the school system would then be involved in collaborative methods.

Implications

From the perspective of the consultant, an examination of the group's accomplishments suggests change at several levels. From the perspective of the individual client, a number of students were helped over the course of the two-year project. The interventions we planned alleviated the problem behavior of these students and reintegrated them into the classroom. Further, help was given in ways that strengthened rather than severed teacher-student relationships.

Regarding changes in the consultees, group members learned to extend their role definitions and to engage in greater role interchangeability in their work with problem children, thus opening up a wider range of possible interventions. School staff, regardless of title, began to use home visits as a means of reaching students who had alienated themselves from school. These changes in role possibilities were enlivening to the school staff. The added challenge of new ways of working with students along with the provision of group support seemed to lessen the opportunity for burnout. School staff became willing to work harder and longer with a broader array of the problems that students presented in classrooms.

At an organization level, the mental health team concept had gained substantial legitimacy in the school system. Appropriate referrals were being made to the team. Student problems became the shared responsibility of the staff regardless of role. Intervention plans received the support of the central office. And interventions extended the reach of the school in the community by involving staff in interventions with families regarding parenting skills and school problems and in coordinating outside resources such as homemaker services in the development of plans of assistance.

Clearly, these observations of change are limited by their self-reported nature, by the single vantage point of assessment, and by the absence of follow-up information after the termination of consultation services. Each of these additional perspectives would have enhanced our understanding of the events presented here. Yet, at the very least, these observations do suggest that during this two-year period, the mental health team concept became implanted in the organization in ways consistent with the underlying goals of intervention. Hence the essential idea of collaborative problem solving was not distorted in purpose or practice despite the fact that modifications occurred during implementation in response to the constraints of the social setting.

Constraints against change are an inevitable fact of organizational life. These constraints are both functional in their support of the continuity of social systems and dysfunctional in their resistance to new and potentially productive alternatives. The important question is not how to avoid these constraints but how to resolve the problems they present.

The anecdotal literature that chronicles the ups and downs of a wide variety of consultation efforts provides numerous examples of structural resistance or even sabotage encountered in the course of intervention. The sources of resistance have been extensively analyzed but primarily with a focus on organizational conditions. Less attention has been paid to the acceptance of system participants during the period of implementation (Gross, Giacquinta, and Bernstein, 1971). That the source and nature of resistance can change during the course of implementation—and hence might require shifts in implementation strategies—has been less clearly described in the literature.

Thus the case example affords a view of the implementation history of a group consultation model where adjustments in response to local conditions have been scrutinized. This history reflects what Berman (1980) has described as an adaptive mode of implementation in contrast to a programmed approach.

The adjustments included (1) the opening of group boundaries to enable the occasional participation of new members, (2) the inclusion of a higher level of the school system hierarchy (the superintendent) in the functioning of the team, (3) a change in leadership patterns with the principal assuming more group leadership and the teachers more case leadership, and (4) changes in the functional goals of the group meeting.

In the early stages of implementation, the team's primary focus concerned group development. The team began as an array of individuals who, because of role constraints, felt free neither to talk nor to act. These obstacles had to be surmounted in order to build a cohesive working group. In a loose social system like the school, collaborative problem solving in the service of student needs cannot be easily mandated—for example, as intended by Public Law 94-142—but must be learned and nurtured with strong system support. Once a solid working group had been established, other system constraints appeared in response to the team's new behavior. Although these obstacles precipitated a wave of fear and rebellion in group members, the issues stimulated reform in the group.

Thus, nurtured by the response of the school organization to team programs, the mental health team added a new purpose to its agenda and became an active pressure group in the system. The innovators built a supportive constituency—a powerful force that pressured the organizational structure to change. The broadened base of pressure stemmed from three crucial developments: the weekly exchange between principal and superintendent regarding the group's activities; the new format, which involved more teachers; and the fact that in the future two principals would be involved in collaborative problem solving. In this way, institutional constraints became instrumental in the group's development. The growth that did take place—that is, a commitment beyond individual change to the goal of legitimizing the collaborative concept—occurred in the context of the social system's response to the interventions. The collaborative team owed its growth as a pressure group to its presence in the school, a presence that guaranteed continuing conflict with the prevailing norms of the institution. Yet throughout these adaptations in the implementation of the mental health team, the integrity of its conceptualization had been preserved.

What factors proved critical in resolving the institutional constraints? First, the representative nature of group membership forced continual discussion of the differing role pressures and role constraints of staff members as they grappled with the problems of students. Such representation brought into the group discussion the precise problems that needed to be addressed in order to examine new avenues for intervention. Further, the representative membership enabled the team to function as a pressure group in the social system.

Second, the existence of a structure (the weekly group meeting) for coordinating, monitoring, and planning responses to system feedback ensured the resolution of institutional constraints. The regularity of the school meeting allowed thoughtful analyses of these obstacles and provided a forum for evaluating the outcomes of any adaptations introduced in the model.

Third, the sense of group identity encouraged the consideration of alternative courses of action and the taking of risks. Group support also cushioned team members against the hazards of their risk-taking behavior. Further, the willingness to open group boundaries in order to gain broader access to feedback about proposed interventions and their consequences became a possibility only because of the team's solidarity.

Fourth, the presence of leadership from an outside consultant enabled the group to study itself as well as its organizational context. The consultant facilitated the development of trust among group members, thereby creating a context in which both the intragroup and the extragroup reality could be examined. The consultant also encouraged diagnostic inquiry into individual and system problems. Through modeling, active intervention, and interpretation, the consultant played a large role in guiding the impact of the mental health team on the school at large. These four features of the group consultation model—its representative membership, group identity, external leadership, and structural commitment to monitoring the effects of application—facilitated the development of creative responses to the institutional obstacles we encountered in the course of implementation.

One final question concerns the generalizability of this example. To what extent do local conditions affect the implementation of this mental health team model? Are some schools more responsive or less responsive to this group consultation approach? In this particular case, the collaborative team was implemented in an organizational structure (the junior high school) where teachers were subject specialists and thus taught the same pupils. Hence the team began with a common focus of concern that facilitated group cohesion. Further, the collaborative team was embedded in a new school with a new leader where excitement and commitment were extraordinarily high. Hence the engagement of a core group and the involvement of the principal were easily assured. The relatively brief history of school relationships also meant a rapid resolution of intragroup role conflicts.

On the other hand, the project was implemented in a small school in a small school system. Further, the superintendent's office was located in the middle school building, thereby increasing the frequency of interaction between levels of administration. Given these characteristics, there appeared to be many more systemwide constraints to consider and more fear about the new leader's vulnerability. In response, the team experienced greater difficulty in dealing with extragroup obstacles and extending boundaries.

Implementation of the mental health team model in other school settings suggests great differences between schools in the locus of perceived constraints on action (Weinstein, 1979). Thus, for the consultant, predicting the locus of institutional constraints becomes an important goal of preliminary assessment. Greater knowledge of the obstacles to collaborative problem solving in a school may lead to different definitions of representative membership. From what levels of the hierarchy should the group's members be drawn? The answer is of significant concern.

This account of the implementation of a school-based

mental health team suggests several structural features that may resolve institutional constraints in ways that respond to the school's concerns while preserving the essence of the innovation. Such features are more likely to ensure that real rather than manifest changes are incorporated in the system (Rappaport, Seidman, and Davidson, 1979). Further, group consultation appears particularly suited to creating the conditions that can address system constraints in the implementation of innovations.

Involving Students in Organizational Change in a High School

5

Cary Cherniss
Edison J. Trickett
Michael D'Antonio
Katy Tracy

This chapter describes the experiences of two consultants, advanced graduate students in clinical/community psychology, who initiated psychological consultation in a New England high school. The specific focus is on one aspect of their consultation —the inception and development of a student group called the Student School Effectiveness Committee (SSEC). The report covers the two-year period when the graduate students were involved as creators of the group and consultants and is written from extensive notes. The value of the case-study format cannot be overemphasized. While the general literature in consultation is increasing dramatically (see Grady, Gibson, and Trickett,

1981), much of it remains narrow, technical, and uneven in quality. Case studies, while embodying their own methodological weaknesses, are often embellished with rich details that can stimulate deeper, more precise thinking about consultation.

The material in this chapter is not organized around a formal model of consultation. In our judgment, no adequate framework for such a presentation has been developed. Rather, it is designed to illuminate the processes involved in this particular consultation, the questions the consultants asked and could have asked, and the assumptions and beliefs the consultants brought to their tasks. Learning to do consultation involves far more than the acquisition of techniques—it involves the evolution of a unique social role that links specific skills to the social context where the consultation takes place. Not only is it important to understand what types of consultative interventions exist, but one must ask *why* they exist and *how* their existence influences and is influenced by the setting.

Based on these general assumptions, two sets of factors provided us with particularly useful ways to approach the reporting of the consultation. The first set involves an understanding of the host environment. Consultation does not occur in an environmental void. The environment defines the problems, contains the resources, and, through its norms, values, and policies, channels the nature and direction of the consultation.[1] How the consultant conceptualizes the setting is therefore a central aspect of the consultation itself. Embedded in this perspective are such questions as how the setting defines its problems, what the possible range of interventions are, and how the interventions mesh with the ongoing life of the setting. In our reporting of the case study, then, attention is paid to the social environment of the school where it occurs.

The second set of factors focuses on how consultants develop the consultative role within the constraints of the setting. For example, the negotiation of the contract and the decision

[1] See Trickett, Kelly, and Todd (1972), Trickett and Todd (1972), and Trickett, Kelly, and Vincent (in press) for one example of how ecological concepts can illuminate an understanding of the local context.

to adopt a certain intervention are "choice points" that define the consultative role. Such choices are influenced both by the nature of the setting and by the values, assumptions, and general consultation perspective of the consultant. Thus our interest is in how the consultant translates values and assumptions into the consultative role. We are less interested in specific skills or techniques than in describing the dilemmas, processes, and decisions the consultants engaged in as they designed and implemented their intervention.

Because we did not use a well-developed conceptual framework to organize our observations, it is difficult to present a compelling case for our methodology. To what degree did our personal philosophies affect not only our consultative decisions but our selection of case-study materials? How did we choose what to report on and what to omit? What assumptions about consultation, schools, and change influenced the data? Although our orientation was based on an understanding of the school environment and the definition of the consultative role, there are no clear answers to these questions. We may, however, specify the intent that guided our efforts. We have attempted to distinguish between our descriptions of events and our interpretation of those events. We have further attempted, wherever possible, to state not only what we did but why we did it. Above all, our intent in presenting such a detailed case report is to encourage the reader to examine alternative interpretations of both the content of our report and the processes implicit in the development of the SSEC and our presentation of it.

Town and School: A Brief Sketch

The town of Altamont is one of a cluster of "valley towns" in New England. On the banks of the river running through them is much of the small industry that has historically provided employment for the work force of the town. Politics, especially ethnic politics, is taken seriously and pervades all aspects of the town, including the public schools. Though Altamont is less than fifteen miles from a major city, the primary identification of its citizens is with The Valley. Not only is it the largest of the towns with a population of 25,000, it is also the most heterogeneous. Twenty-six different churches—many of them Catholic—serve the predominantly Italian, Polish, and Lithuanian community. Moreover, Altamont is the only valley town with a significant black population; at the time of the consultation, 10 percent of the students in the high school were black. While there is some integrated housing, de facto segregation is prominent and many blacks live in housing projects at one end of town.

Altamont High School is the only public high school serving this community. Built in the 1930s and reflecting the educational ideology and size requirements of that time, the high school is a three-sided, two-story brick building with a self-contained auditorium and undersized gymnasium. Originally built for 750 students, the school now serves over 1,100 students per year. Offices have been subdivided, and every nook and cranny of available space is utilized during the academic year. For several periods during each school day, there is no free classroom or office in the entire building—a fact of obvious consequence not only for the privacy of individual students and faculty but for the psychological consultant as well. The auditorium is sufficiently close to several classrooms to provide intrusive music when the school band is rehearsing. A second building, about a block away, serves as the vocational wing of the school and houses the administration of the entire school system. Students walk back and forth to their classes in the vocational wing. Outdoor areas for gym are limited to a one-acre plot behind the high school; the athletic field for varsity competition is over a mile away. The neighborhood in which the school is located is residential.

Public educators in Altamont have long been dissatisfied with the antiquated buildings. The old library has been converted into a "media center," though lack of appropriate space and money makes the media center more a semantic innovation than an educational redefinition. Laboratories for the science program are badly needed, according to the science coordinator, as are adequate visual aids. Four times in recent years the town has voted on a referendum to construct a new high school and four times the referendum has been defeated.

The faculty and administration of the high school reflect

a somewhat inbred character, since more than 75 percent of the faculty either had gone to the high school as students or grew up in or around the valley. The principal and assistant principal are also local men, both with long service in the high school, first as teachers and then as administrators. This faculty and administration composition lends an "all in the family" air to the school. Some teachers have *their* old teachers as department chairpersons and have brothers, sisters, and children of their high school classmates as students.

Until the year the consultation began, psychological services for students at the high school were meager. Five guidance counselors, only one of whom had any formal training, were responsible for the learning difficulties and behavior problems of the 1,100 students. A local hospital with a psychiatric unit served as the sole outside mental health resource, and its relationship to the high school, because of inadequate resources, was limited to letters and phone calls about students. Waiting lists prevented the clinic from giving immediate attention to students referred from the school, thus increasing its irrelevance in the eyes of school personnel. The school had no social worker or psychologist on a full or part-time basis, though a part-time nurse was employed.

Informally, several teachers, coaches, and at least one administrator provided sympathy and support to students, but several expressed concern over the limitations of their own training. Moreover, for the 10 percent of the students who were black, there were no black faculty or administrators to turn to, although one of the white guidance counselors was identified closely with the black students.

The Consultation Relationship

The consultation relationship with the public schools in Altamont had a one-year history in the elementary schools before consultants were asked to enter the high school. In both instances, the assistant superintendent, not individual school administrators, initiated the request. Because the negotiations were between the assistant superintendent and the director of the clinic, the individual consultants—graduate students working in the clinic—were not part of the original discussions. Thus when the consultants began their work in the high school, a year of contact between clinic and school had transpired and a working agreement for the following year had been reached.

At the beginning of the school year, the consultants met first with the superintendent and assistant superintendent of schools to get acquainted and talk specifically about the high school. The superintendent had recently come from a small community in a neighboring state, so the assistant superintendent did much of the talking. He explained that the guidance department at the high school could not cope with students' numerous problems. He also expressed concern that students were apathetic and that absentee rates were too high and cutting too frequent. The consultants then told the assistant superintendent and superintendent about their background and experience with adolescents and schools; they suggested that the next step would be to meet the new high school principal and his assistant. Further, they suggested that before agreeing to provide specific services it would be important to spend time in the school talking with teachers, guidance counselors, and students in order to understand the culture, needs, and resources of the school. The consultants emerged from that meeting with a general sense of the problems that concerned the assistant superintendent but with no clear mandate to pursue a specific problem at the high school. There was more a feeling of scouting out the situation before deciding on a role or function.

The ensuing meeting with the principal and his assistant, though positive, was equally vague. The principal had only recently been informed of the availability of consultants by the assistant superintendent and had not thought about what use they could be other than "helping with the problems." The conversation was congenial, and again the consultants suggested a period of getting to know the school. Plans were made to talk with faculty, student homeroom representatives, and guidance counselors. Moreover, plans were made to continue meeting with the administration and, less often, with the superintendent and assistant superintendent of schools. The one function consultants stressed was indirect service to students through consultation with teachers and guidance personnel. It was also emphasized, however, that this effort would not preempt other services in the future, should the principal request them.

Thus the consultation relationship was, in the beginning, defined ambiguously by both the school system and the consultants. Neither the administrators of the school system nor the principal of the school had clearly defined needs, goals, or functions they wished consultants to fill. On the other hand, the consultants did not approach the high school with a clear conception of what they should provide or the boundaries of their role. Communication gaps existed on both sides. On the consultee side, the assistant superintendent determined the advisability of consultation in the high school without input from the new principal; on the consultant side, there was no discussion of the clinic's relationship with the school system or the nature of the conversations leading to the decision to have consultants in the high school. The open-endedness of the consultant-consultee relationship created an ambiguous "contract" that made constant negotiation and redefinition inevitable. The involvement of one of the consultants in the Student School Effectiveness Committee typified that process.

The Student School Effectiveness Committee

Origins and Rationale. After meeting with various groups, the consultants began assessing the school more extensively while school members, inevitably, began assessing the consultants. Psychological consultants had never been available before, and much time was spent discussing "shrinks" and feeling out the consultants as professionals and as people. Many of these informal meetings took place in one of the teachers' rooms, where the small number of people and the informal atmosphere encouraged information sharing. Moreover, meetings were held with guidance counselors as well as continued discussions with the administrators. While each group had its own set of agendas, needs, and gripes, there was agreement to structure consultation around students who needed, but in the past had been unable to receive, assistance. Groups also agreed that the school had more pervasive problems: student apathy, poor attendance, increasing misconduct, and general student disaffection.

During this initial period, the consultants also began to know the school itself. The most immediate impression was that of a loose, amorphous, rather confusing and chaotic place. The noise level in the building was high, and students often roamed the halls during class time. Class schedules had somehow been delayed or printed incorrectly, and many students spent considerable time trying to correct them. Moreover, several teachers complained that announcements from the administration over the public address system were not saved for a special part of the day but would randomly interrupt classes. Further, there was considerable ambiguity over rules and procedures for dealing with student misconduct.

Although the principal and the assistant principal were new at their jobs, they had both been teaching in the high school for many years. The principal had a wide range of support from his colleagues, and the opening weeks of school were a kind of honeymoon period with his faculty. Many teachers referred to his concern, fairness, and accessibility. They did not know what kind of a leader he would be, but there was general agreement that he was a "nice guy." Soon, however, he was caught up in the larger organizational ambiguities of the school's structure and policies. During this initial period, which lasted several weeks, the administration's major goal was keeping up with momentary crises—crises made more frequent and prominent by the lack of articulated plans for accomplishing the organizational tasks of the school. Indeed, several meetings of the consultants with school personnel were abruptly broken off by unforeseen school problems. While teachers in general felt positively about the principal, they expressed concern over this organizational unpredictability and their conversations were often tinged with sarcasm about the quality of life in the school.

Four groups seemed to constitute the majority of the student culture: the athletes, cheerleaders, and club members, socially aware and involved in the formal offering of the school; the "heads" and radicals; the black students; and the quiet "poor whites." Informally, students seemed to organize themselves by grade, and most social interactions occurred among students in the same grade. Formally, there were two governing units: the student council (thirty-two students elected at large by grade and the three class presidents) and the class officers (president, vice-president, secretary, and treasurer). Class officers planned class social activities, while the council dealt with all other issues.

As this rather general organizational structure was emerging through observations and conversations with students and school personnel, sporadic meetings with the superintendent were also being held. At a meeting with the superintendent about six weeks after school began, he mentioned, among other possibilities, the idea of creating a student committee modeled on the School Effectiveness Committee of the local teachers' union. The latter consisted of a small group of teachers in the school system who gathered, on behalf of the union, faculty opinions about current policies and proposed policy changes. The group was new and its effectiveness unknown, but the idea seemed promising in light of what the consultants were learning about the school. Such a student group might introduce some purposeful planning in troublesome areas such as discipline—and if stúdents were given an organized voice in planning and decision making, their commitment to the school might grow.

The consultant asked the superintendent if the student council could serve this function. The superintendent expressed the belief that its potential was not promising. Its functions were more organizational (arranging for the prom and running student elections) than innovative, and its real influence had been waning through apathy. Its unwieldy size (thirty-five students), its unrepresentative character, and its history of not dealing with issues of personal and educational relevance to students made it an unlikely candidate. The consultant expressed concern that regardless of whether or not a new group was formed, the student council was the elected student representative body and, as such, should be consulted about any idea like a new student committee. If a new group was successful, he suggested, it might even goad the council toward more effective functioning.

The accountability and responsibility of a new student committee was also discussed with the superintendent. The consensus was that the committee should report to the student council, the high school principal, and the superintendent; its mandate should be to articulate student concerns and proposals for change. Moreover, it was clear that any of these guidelines could be modified if circumstances changed. The meeting concluded with the consultant agreeing to explore the idea further. The next steps were to discuss these proposals with the principal of the high school and the student council.

Formation. Shortly after the meeting with the superintendent, the consultant met with the principal. He discussed the prior meeting with the superintendent and the proposals they had developed. The principal, at first, showed limited enthusiasm for the idea, wondering if such a committee was necessary. Already overworked from the daily demands of his new job, he expressed concern that this would be an additional time-consuming activity. The consultant concurred but suggested that such a committee might open channels of communication between students and the administration and serve as a sounding board for student opinion. The principal agreed with the potential benefit of the group and decided to give it a try. The principal's acquiescent style and the superintendent's sponsorship of the committee seemed to be the primary factors involved in his acceptance of the proposal. If such a committee were formed, the principal said, he would release committee members from class for weekly meetings—a clear demonstration of the school's legitimization of the committee.

The principal also stressed the importance of the student council in forming the committee and agreed to call a council meeting for the consultant to discuss the proposal. Failure to act through the student council, he stressed, would antagonize a group whose support was needed. More important, the student council constituted the most extensive, stable student organization in the school, it was known to the student body, and its influence, however limited, was critical to the development of any new student committee.

A fundamental issue raised by the proposed student committee dealt with student governance in the school. The student council, while reportedly ineffective in the areas defined by the new committee, was still designated to deal with such questions. The proposed committee would, understandably, be seen as encroaching on student council turf, and the precise relationship between the old and the new would synthesize into a more responsive student government that increased student participation and sparked student interest in school issues. Before such a synthesis was possible, however, the committee would have to be organized, gain student support, serve as a forum for student concerns, and demonstrate that it could help articulate student opinions.

The consultant approached the student council meeting as an advocate for a smaller, more representative student committee, but he defended no position about who should comprise it or how it should function. The meeting was attended by most council members, the consultant, the principal, and the guidance counselor who served as faculty advisor to the council. After forty-five minutes of council business, the principal introduced the consultant. The consultant discussed the possible creation of the Student School Effectiveness Committee. He explained the rationale behind the committee—to give students a greater voice in school policy and to rekindle student interest in the school. He commented, moreover, on the promising outlook for the committee—a new principal and a new superintendent who valued student opinion and desired change in the school system. Anticipating some of the concerns the student council might voice, the consultant stressed the need for a committee that was small and diverse with respect to students' grade, sex, race, academic track, and interests.

Reaction to the presentation was mixed; most council members seemed uninterested or skeptical. Students had a number of questions. Some asked why the consultant favored a new committee rather than improving the council. The consultant agreed that improving the council was an appropriate concern, but that the council's large size and select membership were not well suited to the function of the proposed committee. When asked about the committee's purpose, the consultant summarized the earlier discussions with the superintendent and principal and replied that the general mandate would be to consider student proposals to improve both the education and the quality of life in the school. One student wanted to know precisely what was being asked of the council. The consultant answered that he was asking support to plan and implement the committee, including discussion of such issues as the selection of members. Some students expressed their conviction that the committee would not accomplish anything. Others felt more hopeful about its prospects. After a half-hour of discussion, it became clear that there was not enough time to consider the matter fully at that meeting. The consultant suggested that discussion be continued the following week, and the council agreed.

At the student council's next meeting, much of the discussion took the same form, although one new major point was raised. Several members of the council said they had few significant school-related problems and did not know any students who might have such concerns. Was the Student School Effectiveness Committee really necessary for the majority of students? The consultant attempted to clarify the assumptions underlying this position (that the school was effective for all but a few problem students) and asked about the other issues such as student apathy, discipline, and absenteeism that might affect a larger segment of the school. Some members, at this point, proposed an open meeting of the student body to determine student needs and concerns. The council approved the suggestion.

At the open meeting two weeks later, some fifty students, about half of them from the student council, attended. The consultant was introduced by the assistant principal. He and the president of the council presented the SSEC proposal, explained the reasons for the present assembly, and opened the meeting to the floor. The consultant limited his role to asking students for clarification of points and to summarizing the discussion at the end of the meeting. The bulk of the discussion concerned lack of school spirit. Often students ascribed these conditions to the community ethos, where, as students put it, nothing ever happens. Students at the meeting did not see much hope for the SSEC because they regarded the school and community as set in their ways. They cited the small attendance at the open meeting as an instance of noninvolvement. At the end of the meeting, the consultant and student council president agreed that the consultant would meet with the council again.

The next student council meeting was attended only by council members and the consultant. The absence of school personnel and the growing trust between students and consultant seemed to encourage candor. At this meeting the students reversed their position about having no concerns and launched into an emotional catalogue of complaints. They attacked school personnel, courses, disciplinary procedures, and the generally bland school atmosphere. When the proposal to create the SSEC was raised, support was positive. A few students enthusiastically endorsed the idea; most were willing to try it on the grounds that it would not do any harm and might do some good. The student council moved that the SSEC should be composed of twelve students—half from the student council and half from groups not represented by council members. Student council members would take responsibility for talking with other students about the SSEC, and an additional meeting was planned to determine SSEC membership.

Composition and Procedure. The first meeting of the SSEC, held in mid-February, began haltingly and uncomfortably. Students were unclear about the mission of the group. After they had spent fifteen minutes addressing topics and quickly discarding them, the consultant commented that the group did not know where to begin. He suggested that it start by examining itself. Since no black students were included in the meeting, he raised the possibility that their absence might reflect school conditions. This comment launched the group into two interwined discussions: one on the composition of the group, the other on race relations in the school.

In forming the group, each council member selected for the SSEC had been charged with the task of recruiting another SSEC member who would diversify the committee. Informal social structure and the method of recruitment, it was decided, resulted in the absence of blacks. Student opinions about race relations were diverse. Some felt that blacks were treated leniently and whites were discriminated against. Others believed that blacks were not being treated fairly. Some agreed that blacks and whites formed two unequal school societies, but they felt incompetent to deal with the problem. Still others did not think difficulties existed and could not understand students who believed there was a problem. After considerable discussion, one member suggested that black students be invited to join the SSEC. When the group favored this suggestion, the president of the student council (an SSEC member) and another influential student agreed to recruit black members.

The final portion of the initial meeting was spent on procedural detail involving such issues as release time from class and a decision to rotate the meeting times throughout the day so that students would not miss the same classes each week. Meetings were set for one or two class periods a week, depending on tasks to be accomplished.

Phase One: Setting Priorities. During the three or four meetings following the inauguration of the SSEC, the committee openly discussed school issues. Although the consultant's role in these meetings varied, he was, in most cases, an active leader. When ignorant or unsure of some point raised in discussion, he asked for clarification. Often he would prod students to explore the implications, ramifications, or assumptions of points; at other times he would stress the theme implicit in the discussions. He also attempted to solicit the opinions of students who had not expressed themselves on issues they seemed concerned about.

After a number of weeks, the consultant felt it was appropriate to discuss a change in the focus of the meetings. Unless the deliberations moved toward concrete action, the SSEC might continue discussions that, however cathartic, would have little impact on the school. His proposal to take action met with committee approval, and members decided to establish the priority of problems and begin developing strategies to resolve them. The following issues were designated as salient: inadequate and incompetent teaching; a restrictive dress code; the need for additional modern language courses; the ethnocentrism and racial bias of the history curriculum; the lack of institutionalized rewards for competent, sensitive teachers; dual standards of treatment for black and white students; student apathy; excessive drug use; the current irrelevance of the Student Honor Society; and the lack of community support for educational improvement.

The discussion then turned to various strategies for addressing these issues. The following three seemed promising: proposals to the school administration; direct action in the community via school board meetings and local media; direct action in the student body. At this point, the number of problems and strategies threatened to overwhelm the committee with too many options. After the consultant pointed out the need to establish priorities for the proposed issues, the SSEC decided to emphasize the following topics: the dress code, additions to the modern language curriculum, change in the history curriculum, and the absence of institutionalized rewards for good teaching. The choice of issues reflected not only the magnitude of student concerns but the pragmatics of what the committee thought it could influence.

Phase Two: Proposals and Consequences. The first issues the SSEC took action on were the history and modern language curricula. Prompted by black students and those of other ethnic minorities on the committee, the SSEC explored the racist and ethnocentric nature of the American history course and the perceived irrelevance of the school's black history course, which focused on African and Asian history to the exclusion of Black American history. The committee also discussed the importance of offering German for students whose career choices required the language. After a couple of weeks of discussion, the consultant suggested that a subcommittee draft a proposal outlining the desired changes and their rationale. A subcommittee of two wrote the proposal and submitted it to the SSEC for final consideration. Once it was agreed upon, a copy of the proposal was submitted to the principal.

The principal appeared at a later SSEC meeting to discuss the proposals. He indicated that the suggestions were under consideration, but, because of budgetary constraints, it was unlikely that German could be offered. The history course proposals, he said, had been passed on to the chairperson of the history department.

Although students on the SSEC regarded the meeting with the principal as generally positive, its outcome was uncertain. The principal had not explicitly agreed to follow through on any specific proposals. Moreover, a few members of the history department were irritated by the SSEC proposal, which they viewed as interference in departmental affairs. As a consequence, both the consultant and the SSEC realized the need to confer with those affected by their proposals before they were finally decided on.

The second major issue the SSEC addressed was the school dress code. Although the dress code was not particularly restrictive in comparison to neighboring schools, some students felt its ambiguities led to capricious enforcement. Others thought student dress was not a legitimate school concern unless it affected health and order. Strategies for changing the dress code paralleled those for improving the curricula. After a subcommittee drew up a proposal to abolish the school dress code, it was submitted to the principal and superintendent. The superintendent placed the proposal on the school board agenda for the following meeting, and the SSEC sent representatives to the meeting to argue for the document. The board decided to place responsibility for the decision on the principal and superintendent, and, after meeting with the SSEC, the administrators agreed to abolish the dress code on a trial basis. While students reacted positively to the policy change, it also reawakened the dormant rivalry between the student council and the SSEC. Significantly, and unfortunately, the consultant made no effort to help student council members deal with the feelings of rivalry they expressed. As was the case with the history department, the consultant and the SSEC failed to anticipate the impact of this success on other groups.

While the preceding issues were the only ones the SSEC dealt with formally in the spring semester, the group also served as a resource and sounding board for future events. Committee members met twice with the superintendent, at his behest, to apprise him of student concerns and viewpoints. Moreover, the SSEC spent two meetings with the consultant discussing the possibilities of implementing a drug education program the following year. Topics included student reaction to the current drug program, potential program improvements, and the nomination of student-oriented teachers who might become involved in the project.

The First Year: Ambivalence

The consultant's function varied with different phases of the formation and operation of the SSEC. Ambivalence and uncertainty about the role were often present. Initially, it was unclear how and when leadership might emerge from the group. Should attempts be made to foster student leadership by creating a leadership role? Should the president of the Student Council be asked to take charge? Or should the consultant model leadership initially and then promote gradual student involvement? On the one hand, the consultant wished to give students maximum freedom to plan the goals and strategies of the SSEC; on the other hand, he felt that clear leadership was needed to transform ideas into action. The consultant decided to be an active leader. When students touched on important issues, he encouraged the group to explore them. At times, he presented his own views—less to influence than to model the process of thinking through an issue. While the consultant was aware that active leadership might make students dependent on him, a primary aim was to increase the group's confidence by helping it create changes. The assumption was that student leadership would take over once the SSEC became functional, but time constraints and the consultant's decision to be an active leader interfered with this process.

At the end of the first year the SSEC was in an ambiguous position. Initially attendance had been consistently high and morale was good. Students believed the school could be changed, and, at the final meeting of the year, several members said the SSEC had been the most exciting educational experience they had had. In terms of its impact on the school, however, the SSEC appeared less successful. Its only clear contribution was the abolition of the dress code, and its relationship with some of the faculty and the student council was strained. Further, the SSEC was still not well known to students, nor were there yet well-developed procedures for students to inform the SSEC about their concerns.

Transition to the Second Year

The issue of the group's continuation was clouded by ambiguities about group logistics and the future availability of the consultant. Although the superintendent, principal, and SSEC members agreed the committee should continue, no concrete plans had been made for *how* it would be reconstructed the following year—no criteria had been set for selecting members or for deciding whether older members who were not graduating should remain on the committee. Moreover, while a consulting relationship with the school was assured, it was not clear who the consultant would be or how he or she would approach the job. Thus, at the end of the first year, the SSEC was a permanent committee without a permanent structure or philosophy.

Before the first year's consultant left the area, he met with the new consultant. The old consultant described the steps involved in setting up the SSEC and defined its scope in conjunction with administrators, teachers, and the student council. He emphasized the unfinished task of making the group known to the rest of the school and the need to deal with other groups in a way that fostered goodwill rather than antagonism.

While a great deal of time was spent discussing the SSEC in terms of the school, the SSEC as a group was hardly mentioned. How the committee approached the school was emphasized; how the old consultant approached the committee was almost ignored. Leadership style, degree of engagement, group process, internal organization—these issues were overridden by such topics as the group's relation to the rest of the school. One unfortunate consequence of this emphasis was uncertainty on the part of the second consultant about a *modus operandi* for the next year's group.

The Second Year: Reorganization

At the beginning of the second year, the new consultant met with the superintendent to discuss the SSEC. After the superintendent expressed pleasure with its previous performance, the formal decision to form the SSEC for a second year was made.

Soon after their discussion, the consultant met with the student council. The proposal to reconstitute the SSEC met with considerable opposition. Several council members felt the SSEC was doing the council's job; if the council was ineffective, they said, it should be reformed rather than abandoned. The consultant recognized the validity of the students' comments and added that he would willingly help the council. At the same time, however, he expressed his belief in the need for *both* the SSEC and the council. His position was supported by a few council members who had been part of the SSEC the previous year. The informal quality and frequency of SSEC meetings and the diverse composition of the group, they said, encouraged effective functioning.

After the consultant had presented his views, the council voted to reestablish the SSEC. To his embarrassment, however, some students remarked on the ineffectiveness of the council's current adviser and requested that the consultant take over the position. Concerned about the possibility of a rift between himself and the student council adviser, the consultant arranged a meeting with him. Their conversation was brief and cordial; the adviser had not in fact been offended. For the rest of the year, the adviser remained distant but pleasant and rarely discussed the council or the SSEC with the consultant.

It took several weeks for the council to select the new SSEC. Volunteers were recruited via bulletin and public address system. The consultant, along with the council officers, devised methods to ensure that the committee represented a cross section of the student body. Each class president met with the class officers and selected three students from those who had volunteered from the class. There were few volunteers from the lower classes, and in a few cases potential members from these classes had to be approached and invited to join. The first meeting was held in mid-November.

Phase One: "Redefining Mandates." The first phase of the SSEC's second year paralleled, in many ways, the first year's experience. The consultant planned to begin in an informal, unstructured, nondirective way by allowing committee members to air their views of the school. This passive, clinical approach was predicated on several assumptions. One was the belief that an informal atmosphere would encourage group communication and interaction and, consequently, foster individual commitment and committee cohesiveness. Moreover, through an extended period of open-ended discussion the group could explore issues and reach consensus on actions and strategies. Further, excessive participation by the consultant could create nonadaptive dependency. And, finally, a less active stance would decrease the possibility that the consultant, consciously or otherwise, might manipulate the group to fulfill his own hidden agendas.

From mid-November to February, SSEC members randomly discussed a variety of school-related topics. As frustration and apathy grew and attendance dwindled, the consultant became increasingly concerned about the SSEC and his role in it. Part of the problem seemed to be the unique ecology of the school. Organizational chaos, accompanied by low morale, frustration, and faculty pessimism, characterized much of the school's atmosphere. The principal, in his first year, had proved himself to be eminently humane but a person whose ability to make decisions was, in the words of one teacher, "wishy-washy." Certainly the principal's behavior toward the SSEC seems to have fit this administrative style. In brief, the principal agreed to the SSEC but did not actively care about it. Although the committee meeting took place on the same day each week, for example, the principal rarely remembered the time and place without a phone call from the consultant.

In addition to a lack of active support from the principal, the SSEC was hampered by limited space. Each meeting was held in a different location—a classroom, the cafeteria, the auditorium stage—which added to the diffuse quality of the group. Congruent with a student norm of noninvolvement, some SSEC students began to drop out psychologically and even miss committee meetings in the same way they might cut an unrewarding class. In general, the SSEC meetings bore a remarkable resemblance to the school's social system, and, as we discovered later, paralleled the problems of many other student and faculty committees.

Important as these ecological considerations were, however, the initial phase of the SSEC was also a direct result of the consultant's assumptions about group leadership. By being passive, the consultant did not transfer leadership to group members; he only failed to make explicit his implicit role as organizer. Without someone to organize, plan, and mobilize resources and support, a clearly defined agenda did not emerge. In this school and with this group, the lesson was clear: Nothing happens unless you make it happen.

Phase Two: Transition to a "Work Group." The consultant decided to become a more active group leader. He shared his frustrations about the superficial, aimless discussions with the SSEC and stated that a major problem seemed to be a lack of time concentrating on each topic. He further suggested that the following week the group select a specific topic and stick to it. The group agreed with the consultant's suggestion and decided to focus on disciplinary problems at the next meeting. This was the first time the consultant took initiative to set an agenda for the meeting, and there was a feeble but real stir of interest in the group.

As planned, the next meeting focused on discipline. It quickly became apparent that discipline problems in the school were related to problems of race relations. Many white students and teachers felt that blacks were punished less often and less stringently for rule infractions than whites. Some white SSEC students thought this treatment was due to the administration's fear of blacks. The three black students on the committee remained silent during most of the discussion. The consultant decided to place the discipline issue in a larger perspective. Although he had on occasion seen partiality shown toward blacks in his other work in the school, the consultant hoped whites and blacks would think about the problem as more complex than "preferential treatment." Launching into a didactic presentation of institutional racism, the consultant attempted to explain that blacks were treated differently at the high school in diverse ways—sometimes to their benefit but often to their detriment. Discipline problems were at least in part a manifestation of institutional racism, he continued, and such discrimination hurt both races.

While some students found the content of this impromptu lecture difficult to grasp, they did respond to the consultant's changed stance. He was actively participating by introducing new ideas and stating viewpoints. The students became more energized and decided to invite the principal to the next meeting to discuss some of the issues raised. Although they did not delineate in any detail the specific agenda for the meeting, the consultant agreed to ask the principal to meet with the group.

The principal accepted the invitation to join the group, but the meeting was disappointing for all concerned. The principal became defensive and argumentative. He attempted to discredit most of what the students said about discipline procedures and, in a few instances, was clearly condescending. His behavior, however, was not totally unjustified. Given only a vague outline of the agenda, the principal was not prepared for a discussion of the specific topics raised at the meeting. He was not anticipating the kind of questions and, sometimes, accusations the students presented him with. On their part, students had not always studied the issues and sometimes lodged accusations they could not subsequently defend. When the meeting ended, students, principal, and consultant were disappointed. Students were angry about the principal's negativism and lack of sensitivity to their concerns; the principal was upset at being the butt of accusations he felt were unfair; the consultant was frustrated at not being able to control the meeting sufficiently for substantive issues to be discussed. The SSEC decided to analyze what had happened at the next meeting.

Only one student was absent from the next meeting. The consultant structured the gathering by stating his general reactions to the previous meeting with the principal. He stressed the importance of viewing it as a learning experience, underscoring the need to understand what had happened and why. The consultant raised two important points about why the group was ineffective: They lacked hard documentation of certain points, and some of the comments were phrased in negative, unconstructive ways. He further stressed that the meeting had demonstrated a real need for the committee to start working on positive proposals and critiques. Agreeing that organized, specific action was imperative, the students listed issues according to priority and created subcommittees to investigate them. The flavor of the group experience had become distinctly different. Adrenalin was flowing and minds were working fast. The SSEC had become actively involved and strongly committed.

Phase Three: Committee Action. For the next two and a half months, the committee was consumed by activity. Weekly meetings were task-oriented—subcommittee proposals were presented, issues were discussed, and reports were submitted. During this period, the SSEC concentrated on two major activities: creating proposals that addressed major student concerns and involving the group more directly in daily school life.

From February to May, the following proposals were written and submitted to the appropriate people: creating special study halls to legitimate the talking that was already going on; repairing school buildings and fixtures (one student undertook an admirably detailed survey of school dilapidation); allowing greater flexibility in curriculum programming; installing a soda machine; eliminating lunch periods to shorten the school day; allowing students who have first or last period study hall to come to school late or leave early; and a lengthy proposal for modifying student government procedures.

Apart from proposing a variety of changes, SSEC members increased their involvement in daily school activities by publishing a bulletin outlining committee activities, sponsoring an information table during lunch periods to solicit student opinions and suggestions, evaluating the effectiveness of a new hall pass system instituted by the teachers' discipline committee, writing a letter to the editor of the local paper discrediting some pejorative rumors about school events and asking for more objective news coverage—and, finally, meeting with the teachers' disciplinary committee, the superintendent, and the board of education.

What were the consequences of this prolific and energetic activity? All proposals were taken under advisement by the principal or superintendent. Study hall rules were changed to allow talking and the principal sent the list of needed repairs to the superintendent for action. As consequence of these proposals, the board of education initiated a meeting with the SSEC.

The students presented their thoughts and, to their surprise, the board expressed interest in some of the substantive issues such as shortening the school day by eliminating lunch. The board, while reacting favorably to the proposal, needed time to study it. By late fall, however, a junior high school had closed and the high school was forced to switch to double sessions. Periods were shortened and, as a result, lunch became optional. What might have happened otherwise is unknown.

While the meeting with the board of education was a positive experience for the students, the meeting with the teachers' discipline committee went poorly. As in the meeting with the principal, the teachers reacted defensively to the students who made irresponsible claims and inarticulate proposals. The situation was worsened by one of the assistant principals, the school's main disciplinarian, who seemed especially belligerent and intractable. His role made him unpopular with students, and their bias antagonized an already tense situation.

Efforts to become more involved in school activities caused mixed reactions. The principal, for example, appreciated the work done on the hall pass system. The students demonstrated great interest in the suggestion table and responded, for the most part, thoughtfully. Not all of the faculty, however, was as gracious. Many teachers were still unclear about the mission of the SSEC, and some resented that students were being excused from class for the council. One older teacher, known for his conservatism, came up to the SSEC table during lunch and told the representative he thought the group was composed of "a bunch of kooks and radicals." A better name for the group, he suggested, might be "Seeds of Sedition."

Although this teacher's response was far from representative, some of the faculty did resent not so much the SSEC itself but the fact that they were not being informed about school events and issues. Communication was haphazard between administration and faculty, and often teachers were interrupted in the classrooms by surprise announcements over the public address system or told of decisions via memo—the decision, for example, that faculty should punch in to ensure they arrived on time in the morning. The SSEC, like the administration, had been too consumed by its own tasks to keep the faculty informed about its activities. The committee thus became one of a long list of school programs about which faculty felt uninformed.

During this period of increased activity, the group's perspective began to narrow. The development of proposals became ends rather than means. It was a period of excessive activity and insufficient reflection on consequences. The SSEC's conflicts with faculty and student council members, along with its failure to follow up on submitted proposals, typified the consequences of proposal mania. Although proposals were considered by the administration and in some instances implemented, more could have been accomplished if the group had closely evaluated faculty, administrative, and council reactions to the suggestions and considered alternatives for further action.

The Question of Perpetuation

By the beginning of May, the SSEC was ready to complete the year and discuss the question of perpetuation. There were two primary reasons the consultant initiated the topic: First, he believed that self-perpetuation as an end in itself was potentially destructive; second, he wanted the SSEC to analyze itself and, if continuation seemed warranted, discuss strategies for future implementation.

At first the students gave somewhat automatic and uncritical reasons for maintaining the group. In their initial reaction the group ignored their struggles earlier in the year and their conflicts with other groups in the school. Eventually, however, these issues were confronted. Students conceded that the committee's accomplishments, although unprecedented, had not been as successful as possible. While they admitted the group had difficulties, they felt that maintaining a diverse group to represent a broad range of students was important and the group should continue as constituted. Also important, they decided, were the informality and frequency of meetings.

Once the decision was made to perpetuate the SSEC, a plan was drawn up for the following year to deal with some past problems. One set of proposals dealt with group size and the selection process. Students thought the committee should be smaller to increase informality and individual participation. Representatives should be selected from all classes, but there should not be a fixed number from any class. To give the group continuity, some members of the present SSEC should be retained, and, finally, new SSEC candidates should be selected by present members and screened carefully to ensure energy and commitment.

With respect to the recurrent student council problem, no specific resolutions beyond the desire for increased communication were formulated. The committee took refuge in the knowledge that one of its most influential members—a junior—had just been elected president of the senior class, a position that placed him automatically on the student council. They were assured of his support and interest, and he had campaigned on a pledge to make student government more effective. Although a wait and see attitude was adopted, the potential conflict with the council was considered more deliberately than in previous semesters.

A final decision, and an important one, was to select a faculty sponsor to assume the present functions of the consultant. Several lines of reasoning led to this decision. First, a faculty sponsor would be available daily to deal with crises or offer guidance, whereas the consultant was at the school one day a week. Second, the consultant had achieved his goal—the group had been established and its character developed. It was time to encourage the committee to run on the school's own resources. As Levine (1969, p. 220) said of community psychology practice, "The form of help should have the potential for being established on a systematic basis, using the natural resources of the setting, or through introducing resources which can become institutionalized as part of the setting." The third major reason dealt with setting an important precedent: the right of student groups to recruit their own advisers. In the past the student council, school newspaper, and other student groups had always been assigned a faculty adviser. The frequent result was an adviser with little commitment who was not particularly effective in making the activity a learning experience for students. The SSEC had discussed this issue with regard to the student council and, in attempting to select its own adviser, hoped that a precedent for other groups might be established.

The SSEC ended the year with a series of mixed successes but with a distinct agenda for the following year and a plan for reconstituting in the fall. The consultant attempted to arrange a meeting of the SSEC with the person who would be replacing him, but scheduling problems disrupted the plans. The consultant did talk to the SSEC about the fall and the fact that someone would be there to help the transition. All agreed that finding and getting to know the faculty sponsor would be important tasks for the SSEC and next year's consultant.

The SSEC's Meaning

We introduced this report with two sets of questions that provide useful ways of thinking about psychological consultation. The first set stresses the importance of understanding the host environment and its impact on consultation; the second set stresses the development of the consultant's role in terms of values and assumptions and how they become translated into the intervention itself. In the following discussion we consider both sets of questions as they relate to the evolution of the Student School Effectiveness Committee. Specifically, we examine the initial proposal and the way the school's ecology affected its implementation; how the consultants' assumptions about change and the school's culture influenced this process; and the interdependence between the consultant, the SSEC, and the school's culture. Finally, we draw on the case-study material to discuss general implications for the theory and practice of school consultation.

The Initial Proposal. Many writers have suggested that the way a new program is conceived and implemented significantly affects its development (Sarason, 1972; Cherniss, 1972; Goldenberg, 1971). In this case, deciding how the problem should be defined, who should define it, and how, based on these processes, the intervention should be created set the precedent for the program's evolution. Because our assumptions about problems and their resolution are templates for later decisions, the implicit structure of an intervention often exists before the intervention itself has been designed. Many issues the consultants confronted while promoting the SSEC can be traced to the way initial decisions to create the committee were made.

During the early diagnostic period when the consultants were learning about the school's culture, they concluded that student apathy—reflected in absenteeism, tardiness, misconduct, and noninvolvement in school activities—was a concern shared by several school groups. When the superintendent suggested the formation of a student group, the problems in promoting that suggestion became the consultant's main concern. At the time the decision was made to set up the committee, however, the consultant knew little about the school's history, traditions, and current climate, the real causes of student apathy, and student and faculty attitudes about this problem. It is thus fair to say that inadequate attention had been paid to assessing the school environment *before* deciding that a new student committee would be the best way of dealing with student apathy.

Implicit in the ideas of creating the SSEC were a number of unarticulated assumptions about the nature of the problem and the nature of the solution. With respect to the nature of the problem was the belief that student apathy and discipline were widely shared concerns in the school, even though proof was meager. With respect to the solution, it was assumed that the existing governing structure, the student council, was ineffective because of its size, composition, and traditions. Further, the consultant, in agreeing with the idea of a smaller, more diverse group, demonstrated a commitment both to participatory structures and to the use of small groups as agents of change in the school. The point is not that these assumptions were necessarily wrong; rather, because they were implicit aspects of the consultant's thinking, they foreclosed the possibility of considering alternative strategies. Indeed, in adopting the role of advocate for the creation of the SSEC, the consultant consolidated his commitment to all those assumptions. He was not entering the meetings with the principal and student council to learn about student apathy; his purpose was to persuade, advocate, and gain sanction for the creation of the SSEC.

The decision to advocate for a new student group did set the stage for inevitable conflict—as Sarason (1971) has pointed out, the creation of new settings always implies criticism of the old. In like manner, the creation of the SSEC implied a belief that the student council was ineffective, a point not lost on the student council members who objected to the formation of the SSEC because it was doing what the council was supposed to do. Thus it was predictable, perhaps inevitable, that relations between the SSEC and student council were strained, even though efforts were made to include the council in the structuring of the SSEC.

Yet there was another group whose inclusion in the process of creating the SSEC may have been useful: the teachers. While individual teachers and consultants had discussed school problems, the teachers, as a group, were neither involved in the decision to create the SSEC nor specifically informed about the group's purpose after its creation. Teachers faced student apathy daily, would eventually become aware of the SSEC, and could conceivably be significantly affected by it. Laying the foundation for communication between faculty and committee members, however, was not considered a central aspect of the intervention. That such a link was important was underscored later in the year when the SSEC proposed a change in the social studies curriculum. The social studies faculty resented the SSEC not only because of the committee's proposal to change American history but because, like other teachers, they had not been consulted about the creation of the committee itself.

Two other issues are relevant to the creation of the SSEC: the composition of the group and the allocation of resources. Assuming that a truly representative student group would be more perceptive and influential than the student council, the consultant selected students from each subgroup and grade level in the student culture. Community organizers such as Alinsky (1946) have argued that representative coalitions offer the most effective way of mobilizing support and increasing participation in a community. For such a coalition to be effective, however, it must include the true leadership of the groups represented. Attempting this strategy with the SSEC would have necessitated, first, assessing the informal social structure of the student body to ascertain what groups existed and second, selecting leaders from these groups for membership in the committee. The SSEC was not organized around this basic principle. There was no explicit effort to involve natural leaders. While some leaders did end up on the committee, and while they proved to be active and constructive participants, their selection was more fortuitous than planned.

The final issue we wish to mention is the allocation of resources. Two important resource questions were never raised: What resources (time and energy) would be necessary for the SSEC to meet its goals? And what resources were in fact available to the group? In creating the SSEC, the consultant assumed that he and a heterogeneous group of students could make progress by meeting once a week with no time allocated specifically for planning and coordination. Student time too was limited by the demands of school. The important point to stress is that the human resource requirements of the proposed intervention were not prominent in the consultant's thinking when the committee was being planned. Because these issues were not part of the initial planning, there were contradictions between the committee's aspirations and the resources available to achieve them.[2]

While various themes of consultation may be seen in the idea and creation of the SSEC, two seem of central importance. First, at the outset the consultants accepted a number of assumptions about intervention, the school environment, and the process of change. Thus, before any direct consultation work was begun, their implicit theories and values determined the content of consultation. Second, many of these assumptions

[2]The resource problem is closely related to the fact that the program's creators were unfamiliar with the school culture. If the consultants had known more about the climate and structure of the school when they set out to form the SSEC, they would have realized how difficult it was to find space and time for meetings during the school day. Similarly, familiarity with the school would have indicated that for many students, the SSEC could present distractions and conflicting commitments.

concerned group, organization, and community process—assumptions deriving from theories of community organization, participatory structures, and the use of groups as agents for organizational change.

The SSEC and School Culture. Several writers concerned with the problems of organizational change have observed that organizations have an institutional character—a coherent set of values, purposes, and norms perceived as central to its mission and identity. Sarason (1971), for example, suggests that a school can be seen as a culture—that is, as a pattern of traditions, values, and behavior that inevitably govern the interventions introduced into the school. Thus knowledge of the setting plays a critical role in designing interventions that can protect themselves from the noxious aspects of the environment while generating sufficient support to be sustained by the setting. The history of the Student School Effectiveness Committee provides clear evidence of the pervasive effect school culture can have on a program's evolution.

Altamont High School was described as having an amorphous, often chaotic, atmosphere. Students roamed the halls during class time, classes were frequently interrupted by announcements, discipline was inconsistent, and the building was overcrowded. In this setting, well-organized, goal-directed activity was traditionally difficult to establish. According to teachers, many programs, groups, and administrative procedures had, after a short life, decayed in confusion and disorder. Many interactions between the consultants, the SSEC, and the principal, faculty, and student council can be usefully viewed within this larger context.

Teachers at Altamont High characterized their principal as congenial but not an active organizer of school life. Although his leadership style undoubtedly influenced his relationship with the consultants, his meager support of the SSEC was also a result of the amorphous school culture. The decision to create the SSEC was made not by the principal but by the superintendent, who was ambiguous about his reasons for requesting consultation. Once the principal inherited the responsibility for this vague proposal, he had to decide how much time to invest in the project. Given his task of orchestrating this chaotic high school, it is not surprising that he chose a passive role.

The SSEC's tenuous relationships with some of the faculty and the student council were another result of pressures generated in the school environment. A common complaint of teachers, for example, was that requirements and meetings were sprung on them without adequate warning by the administration. In like manner, the SSEC was created without warning and without their participation in the process. Thus it was viewed, at least partially, as yet another nasty surprise. In like manner the relationship of the SSEC to the student council reflected the general school environment. The council, like many other groups in the school, did not act with strength. Several council members themselves doubted the possibility of change and felt left out of important school matters. This feeling helped set the tone for the interaction between the council and the SSEC as one of competition and strengthened the belief that the SSEC would not accomplish anything. Both groups thus felt powerless to influence their milieu—and by not involving them more intimately in the development of the SSEC, the consultants highlighted the powerlessness they felt in this environment.

When the consultants set out to form a student group designed to channel student sentiment into organized thought and action, they encountered the same pressures that eat away at other well-intentioned efforts. Indeed, many meetings of the group mirrored the random quality found in the environment at large. It is tempting to consider this phenomenon—reported by each consultant during the first part of each year's group—as primarily a function of the group leadership approach of the consultants. Clearly this played a role. But the broader setting was teaching students that activity burns out, that programs have short lives, and that meetings often get canceled at the last minute. When the consultants stated that nothing happens unless you make it happen, they were in a sense saying this: Adapting an active advocacy role is the best way of not being swept away by forces in the school environment. Consultation as a reflective exercise would have been futile.

Nevertheless, the school culture did allow such a group to

be created. The principal supported the group sufficiently to attend meetings and respond to certain issues, as did the superintendent. The dress code was changed as a result of their efforts, and students in the SSEC reported great satisfaction in their participation. The amorphous environment permitted a great deal of self-initiated activity that did not have to pass under the administrative scrutiny of more regimented schools. In these and other ways the setting not only provided constraints but yielded unique opportunities for a group such as the SSEC to live as an experiment.

The SSEC in Perspective

We have examined several factors that seemed important in the design and implementation of a high school student advocacy committee. Despite certain unique aspects of the project, we believe our case study of the SSEC contains general implications for the theory and practice of school consultation.

The first implication is that effective action requires intensive study of the setting. Specifically, a consultant who wants to catalyze organizational change must first examine the organization's structure, power distribution, norms, and traditions. Premature action—action initiated before one understands the social milieu—is unlikely to accomplish its goals. Implicit in this principle is the notion that effective consultative strategies are designed to mesh with a certain setting. Only then can the consultant design interventions that will tap a setting's resources, circumvent its limitations, and become integrated into the daily life of the organization.

A second implication involves the degree to which consultants are aware of the values behind their consultative decisions and their assumptions about the social structure. The present case study outlines the many unstated assumptions underlying the consultant's decision to advocate the creation of the SSEC. It further stresses how the consultant's values and theories of change affect his decisions. Consultative decisions are often the result of complex factors. Who was asked to define the problem and propose ways to resolve it? Who was excluded from this process and on what grounds? Even before interventions are designed, their structure, their processes, and, in a sense, their outcome can be strongly influenced by the implicit values and assumptions of the consultants. To understand the evolution of their role, consultants must attend to the fundamental values they bring to the situation.

To have enduring impact, change must be supported by enduring structures. Creating these structures is often a primary task of the consultant. What are some of the conditions that facilitate this goal? This brings us to a third implication of the case study—that the development of legitimacy, trust, and a constituency in the host environment are the consultant's primary tasks. Consultants, by definition, are outsiders marginal to the ongoing life of the setting. Outsiders, as Hefferlin (1969) and others have argued, may be particularly effective agents of change because they bring new ideas and a fresh perspective. If outsiders do not develop a legitimized role in the system, however, and gain the trust of those who are respected in the setting, their chances of developing enduring structures are diminished. Thus the development of legitimacy, trust, and a constituency are basic to the consultant's ability to influence the setting.

A fourth implication is that creating and sustaining programs requires substantial resources. Thus a primary task for the consultant is to assess the resources that are needed and the resources that are available. Resources not only refer to time, energy, money, and equipment; they can include existing programs, influential persons, and value systems. It is critical that consultants evaluate available resources and plan strategies that will use resources wisely. Given limited resources, how can they be allocated most effectively? How can additional resources be developed? What are the points of diminishing return for the various resources? In other words, at what point do propositions become impositions? How do consultants decide who the most useful resources are? Although there are no formal models to answer these questions, consultants must learn to view the implications of their intervention in terms of resources.

Our final proposition is one we introduced at the beginning of the chapter: We still know very little about the way people actually consult and effect change in school settings. Not only are there no universal consultation models, but few consultation reports are comprehensive. This work represents one attempt to describe what happened when a group of consultants created a student advocacy group in a high school setting. To the degree this case has stimulated thought about the intricacies of consultation, it has broadened our understanding of this complex and challenging field.

Improving Discipline in a High School

6

Frederic J. Medway
Richard J. Nagle

Despite the growing literature on school consultation (Curtis and Zins, 1981; Meyers, Parsons, and Martin, 1979), little has been written on the practice of consultation at the high school level. Certainly the mental health professions have not neglected the adolescent, having devoted considerable attention to research and intervention on such questions as adolescent crime and delinquency, teenage pregnancy and sex education, vocational preparation, and adolescent drug and alcohol abuse. Nevertheless, on the whole, the number of articles written about the school-related problems of elementary and middle school children has been reported to exceed the number of articles written about the school-related problems of high school students by as much as a nine-to-one ratio (Kramer and Nagle, 1980). Furthermore, much of the literature on mental health interventions in high school deals with individual short-term programs, typically of a direct-service nature, which are generally designed by people outside the school system who fail to describe how school consultants can function as integrated members of the high school environment.

School psychologists and guidance personnel have not written widely of their experiences in high schools, presumably because most psychological services are directed toward the elementary school students. We believe that this current emphasis on the younger child can be traced to at least three factors. First, this emphasis is consistent with the importance placed on the prevention and early detection of intellectual and emotional disorders in children. Consultation and education have historically been viewed as the primary strategies for assessing the mental health needs of schools and communities and for mobilizing resources to meet those needs. Second, our understanding of early childhood development exceeds our knowledge of adolescent development, thus making it more difficult to discover the principles underlying effective mental health services for adolescents. And finally, programs and courses of study on school consultation tend to provide only meager exposure to work in high schools.

This lack of systematic involvement of school consultants at the high school level becomes even more difficult to understand when one considers the overwhelming documentation of the numerous personality problems confronting adolescents and young adults. As a brief illustration consider that over a million adolescents run away from home each year, that 20 percent of the babies born in the United States are born to teenagers including a million children born out of wedlock (Finkel and Finkel, 1978), that one in seven high school seniors becomes intoxicated at least once a week (Brickman, 1974), that 40 percent of all serious crimes are committed by individuals under eighteen years of age, and, finally, that adolescents are particularly vulnerable to loneliness, depression, and suicide. These and other problems can often be triggered by school variables such as academic failure, entrance into a new school, and problems with peer relationships in school (Green, 1979). Further, the increases in truancy, delinquency, vandalism, and racial conflict within the confines of the high school attest to the problems facing high school administrators.

In the pages to follow we detail our approach to high

school consultation and describe two of our experiences: consultation with regard to discipline problems in a high school and our attempts to coordinate high school and community resources. In our work we have recognized the importance of viewing high schools from an ecological perspective as suggested by Trickett, Kelly, and Todd (1972). This orientation requires an awareness of the high school environment and its relation to the community in addition to information regarding the individual characteristics and roles of students and faculty. From this perspective we have found several elements that are unique to high school settings and differentiate consulting at this educational level from consulting in elementary school settings. Accordingly, in our high school consultation work we attempt to take these various factors into consideration in deciding how to deal with a situation and in anticipating the future results of our actions. We list these factors here so that the reader will be able to see how they relate to the experiences we will be describing.

The Key Variables

Physical Environment. High schools differ from elementary schools in terms of size, layout, and complexity. The National Council on Schoolhouse Construction recommends that high schools be at least 30 percent larger than junior high schools. Accompanying this size increase, however, is a greater need for special facilities: auditorium, gym, shop, and industrial arts areas. Thus, compared to elementary schools, high schools are more often perceived as being overcrowded. The layout of the building typically stresses compartmentalization—for example, administrative areas, teaching areas, research areas, and recreational areas are often located in separate and sometimes distant parts of the building. In many high schools it is difficult to get from one part of the building to another in a short time so that literally as well as socially some students can get lost in the system. It is also difficult to monitor student activity in restrooms, stairwells, and parking lots. In certain areas such as large study halls and the cafeteria, discipline problems are particularly prevalent.

High school teachers tend to have less contact with their

colleagues since they usually work in one part of the building. The loneliness of the classroom described by Sarason (1971) is particularly acute. The sheer size and physical complexity of high schools tend to block communication, increase interpersonal distance, and add to a general sense of powerlessness.

Organizational Structure. High schools differ from elementary schools in terms of organizational complexity, personnel size and specialization, and institutional requirements. High schools are administered by a principal and one or more assistant principals. Principals generally spend most of their time in their offices dealing with issues of administration and districtwide policy implementation, staff orientation and management, and organizational coordination. They generally have limited time to devote to curriculum, discipline, and guidance. Discipline problems are generally relegated to an assistant principal—an arrangement that occasionally raises problems in consistency between what the principal says and what the assistant principal says.

There are a greater number of teachers with generally more specialized knowledge in a high school than elementary school. High school teachers are typically assigned to departments based on their expertise (rather than grade), and each department is usually administered by a department head. Since the roles and expertise of many of these educators are often complementary, the consultant can serve an important function as coordinator and resource linker. Coordination of personnel for special projects tends to be more difficult here than at the elementary level, however, since with increasing specialization comes the possibility that staff may view their roles and functions somewhat narrowly. Moreover, it must be recognized that competition among departments for material resources and student enrollment is not uncommon in some high schools.

Finally, most high schools have a student council as part of their administrative plan. The council usually has some influence, which varies from school to school, in terms of making policy recommendations. The student council may make various use of student opinion, which is often shaped by the student newspaper. The considerable diversity of personnel and complexity of the high school administrative system requires the consultant to be visible and accessible, to make ample use of procedures to assess the need for change and readiness to change among the various school subgroups, to coordinate the different subgroups, and to intervene simultaneously at various levels of the high school system.

Student Population. Not only are high school student populations larger than those in elementary schools, but the populations are more diverse in terms of background, aptitudes, interests, and values, creating a need for differential programs. Many ninth-grade students are more academically and emotionally mature than their twelfth-grade counterparts.

Compared to younger children, high school students are more verbal, more influenced by peers, and more socially and vocationally aware. They also tend to have more insight into their own behavior and experience problems and situations specific to the adolescent stage of development. Progressively less time is spent at home and less interest is shown in parents and teachers.

Most adolescents view the high school as a social rather than an academic institution (Coleman, 1961). Their socialization is often limited by the requirement that they change classes on the hour and thus interact with different teachers and peers each period. For the student who has trouble socially, this changing of classes tends to increase anonymity.

Although adults expect high school students to take responsibility for their learning and education, the emphasis on didactic education in high schools keeps students intellectually dependent on their teachers. Few schools have definite mechanisms for students to make suggestions or register complaints. Students who have negative feelings toward school and school policies will find it hard to accommodate their behavior to the demands of the district. Many students see little connection between what they are required to do in high school (like secure a pass to go to the nurse) and what they will be required to do as adults. Thus student powerlessness and frustration are common.

Relations with the Community. During adolescence, social, vocational, and civic interests are expanding—creating a need for diverse recreational and employment opportunities. The high school and surrounding community are intimately linked in terms of athletic programs, work study programs, mental health services, and general acceptance of the high school student as consumer and citizen. Social changes in the community are seen in microcosm in the high school, and the high school is an important socializing agent for the community (Trickett, Kelly, and Todd, 1972). High school consultants will need to build upon school-community relationships and should be aware of the population characteristics, the attitudes toward youth and youth problems, the geographic setting, and the sources of power and influence in the community.

In our view, then, high school consultation necessitates an involvement with the total school, with high-risk as well as normal adolescents, and with the surrounding community. Although both individually as well as jointly we have consulted in various high schools over the years, some of our most rewarding experiences were at Central High School. In the pages to follow we attempt to capture some of our excitement and a little of our frustration, to analyze what we did and why, and finally to relate our experiences to the basic principles of high school consultation we have just described.

Consulting at Central High: A Case Analysis

The Setting. Central is the only high school in the town of York, a suburban area of 19,500 lower-middle to middle-class residents located near a metropolitan city of over 210,000 inhabitants. York is directly across a river from the metropolitan area and faces the city's light industrial area on one side and borders the metropolitan airport on the other. The four-lane highway from the city to the airport cuts directly through the center of York and is crammed with small businesses, fast food restaurants, professional offices, and small manufacturing plants that employ most of the residents. Most of York's adult population has grown up in the town, attended Central High and possibly one of the local colleges, and then married high school sweethearts when in their late teens or early twenties. Only about a fifth of the residents have lived in other states, and most of these people are affiliated with the large military base just to the east of York and north of the city. York has a rather low employment rate but a rather high divorce rate. One out of three children live with single parents or stepparents. York is a very religious community; nearly thirty churches in the town sponsor various youth fellowship programs. The recreational facilities include a number of parks, public swimming pools, and tennis courts in town. The major cultural facilities are in the city and include a zoo, science museum, state library, and major university.

When we began our consultation at Central, the York school district had a total enrollment of approximately 3,600 students. Some 400 children were enrolled in each of the four K-6 elementary schools; 900 students were enrolled in the grade 6-8 middle school; and 1,100 students were enrolled in Central, which housed grades 9 through 12. Approximately 30 percent of Central's seniors go on to college, and another 30 percent go on to technical schools.

We became school consultants at Central High because of our affiliation with the neighboring university. At the time, we were both assistant professors of school psychology in our early thirties. As a result of a formal agreement between the university and the school district, we spent two or three days a week in the York schools providing psychological consultation and supervising school psychology interns who served as in-house psychologists to those schools. Two years earlier our university had departed from a traditional, one-year external internship and contracted with the school districts of several towns whereby faculty would serve as consultants to the schools and supervise interns. All cases involving psychological assessment were handled by the student interns. For this service, the York School District paid the university $3,000, the bulk of which went for intern support and a small portion of which went to offset faculty travel expenses. Thus, although we were not full-time, salaried employees of the York School District, we were not wholly outside the system either, since we spent several days a week in the schools, usually over a three-to-four-year period. Moreover, we did not have to negotiate formal entry into the system, since our entry was inherent in the agreement established between the school district and university. On the other hand, our formal entry was only at the level of district administration. The personnel at Central, though used to having university psychologists in the school, were still unfamiliar with us personally. Clearly we would have to introduce ourselves.

Entree: Our Introduction to Central High. We drove out to Central on a hot, muggy morning in late August awaiting our scheduled get-acquainted interview with Mr. Sands, the school principal, with a combination of enthusiasm, uncertainty, and apprehension. Shortly we got our first glimpse of the school, a sprawling two-story brick structure located at the intersection of four residential streets. Directly in front of the main entrance was a small parking lot for administrators and visitors. To the east was the teachers' parking lot and a small park with wooden picnic benches; to the south was a large student parking lot and the athletic fields; and to the west, across a small road, were a number of small red brick cottages and a small convenience store on the corner.

The time was 7:45 A.M., fifteen minutes before the start of homeroom period, and as we approached the main entrance, we passed by a number of students lounging on the small front lawn awaiting the bell. Black and white students readily intermingled, and student dress and appearance were casual. Later we would learn that there was no official dress policy since the school had difficulty administering one fairly and impartially.

The main hallway, like the rest of the school, was painted a dull, light green color. As we walked toward the administration area, we passed a number of identical-looking classrooms, each neatly arranged with one large desk at the front of the room facing twenty-five or so stationary chairs. The hall walls were lined with pictures of past school presidents, cases filled with sports memorabilia, and row on row of lockers.

In preparation for this day we had spoken to several teachers at Central, parents who sent their children there, and the previous school psychologist to get a feel for the organization of the school day and school policies. The school day at

Central runs from 8:00 A.M. to 2:30 P.M. for students and from 7:30 A.M. to 2:45 P.M. for teachers. The day is divided into seven 45-minute periods not including homeroom. Most students ride the bus to school, and all are required to remain on the school grounds during school and to have a pass when they are not in their assigned classes.

Central has had the same principal, Mr. Sands, for the past ten years. We had heard that he was well liked by the teachers and respected in the community where he is active in civic and religious affairs; we had also heard that students found him somewhat aloof and difficult to talk to. Central has one assistant principal, Mr. Hill, who handles student discipline, coordinates student activities such as clubs and social activities, and spends some time in teacher evaluation. Central's eighty-five teachers are divided into twelve subject areas, each with a department chair. There are three special education teachers, two for students diagnosed as learning disabled and one for students diagnosed as educable mentally retarded. Equivalent to the teachers in terms of status in the organizational hierarchy are the pupil personnel workers—four full-time guidance counselors, a school nurse, and part-time speech therapist and social worker. Counting the thirty-eight support personnel who serve as secretaries, aides, janitors, and cafeteria workers, the total staff numbers 131. The building itself consists of three wings. One wing houses classrooms for academic instruction, a second wing houses classrooms and shops for commercial and industrial arts, and a third wing houses the gym, auditorium, and library. The administrative offices are located at the central junction of the three wings.

Although we tried to prepare ourselves for our initial introduction to the school and the principal, we did not have a consultation plan or purpose in mind. The bell for homeroom period had just rung when we entered the main office. Suddenly the halls were alive with students, some moving quickly and briskly, others moving slowly and somewhat aimlessly. Walking up to the long plastic counter that separated the administrative staff from the general student body, we introduced ourselves to Mr. Sands' secretary and told her we were there for our 8:15

meeting. As we were somewhat early, we waited a few minutes until Mr. Sands finished leading the pledge of allegiance and making a few announcements concerning changes in the day's scheduled routine. In high schools, in particular, the school routine is frequently broken by special assemblies, meetings, trips, movies, and teacher in-service days.

It was not until 8:25 that we were actually escorted into Mr. Sands' office, and our meeting turned out to be much briefer than we anticipated. It lasted only about fifteen minutes. Mr. Sands, an athletic-looking man in his early fifties, opened the meeting by telling us his philosophy of high school leadership. He characterized his leadership style as "laissez faire," by which he apparently meant that he believed in minimal staff supervision. And yet, while he endorsed the importance of staff contributions to the school's decision-making process, he did not mention any way in which this was actually carried out in practice. In what was left of the meeting, Mr. Sands asked us a few brief questions about our background, high school experience, and, near the end of the meeting, our opinion of a study he was contemplating for his doctoral dissertation in educational administration. Only tangentially did we touch upon issues of a psychological or professional nature.

Mr. Sands, though seemingly burdened with administrative duties and paperwork, did offer to assist us in whatever way he could. Given this opening, we immediately suggested that we would like to learn more about the school and then meet with a small group of school personnel to discuss how our services could best be used. Mr. Sands was receptive to both these ideas and, at the conclusion of our meeting, had his secretary summon to the office three senior boys (honor students, we learned later) and asked them to take us on a tour of the school. The meeting we suggested was tentatively set for a week later, and we were to inform Mr. Sands within the next few days who we wanted to attend.

We were introduced to the three seniors as two new psychologists who would be working at the school and wanted to see what it was like. Our escorts appeared both flattered that the principal had selected them for this duty and amused by the request itself. For the next three hours we proceeded up and down each wing of the building, occasionally stopping to chat with the teachers and students who resided there. Each wing appeared to have its own identity and unique form of educational philosophy. In the wings that housed most of the academic instruction, for example, teachers could be seen lecturing, questioning, collecting homework, and handing out ditto assignments. Many of these teachers seemed barely able to control their classes; few did more than nod as we stuck our heads in the classroom. By contrast, the art, music, science, and shop rooms we visited were alive with activity and the teachers were performing supervisory functions. Many more of these teachers appeared to have time to pause and chat.

One of our last stops on the tour was the guidance department. This suite of six small offices was located in a corner of the academic wing, up a flight of four small steps. The mere physical location of the offices suggested that guidance activities were not a high priority at Central.

Central had four guidance counselors. Two of them, Ms. Loren and Ms. Lutz, were in their late twenties and had worked at Central for about two years. The third counselor, Mr. Bryan, was in his early thirties and had been at Central about five years. The fourth counselor, Ms. Gregory, a woman in her late forties, served as head counselor. When we first learned we would be consulting at Central, we had called Ms. Gregory and introduced ourselves over the phone. She was familiar with the university-school district arrangement, having had some contact with previous psychologists and university personnel who had worked at Central. We had not met her until this morning.

Our three escorts took us into the guidance wing where Ms. Gregory was making changes in the master schedule. She immediately stopped what she was doing, as if relieved that she could take a break from her clerical duties. We began talking about the present guidance services and the relationship between the counselors and psychologists. Ms. Gregory seemed quite willing to tell us about her frustrations—among them her bitterness over having to spend a great deal of time scheduling and giving information while having little time for counseling or consultation. At this point we merely listened to Ms. Gregory and occasionally reflected her feelings. Her tone of voice and lack of responsiveness to what little we said made us feel she resented our freedom to do work more meaningful in her eyes than that which the principal assigned her.

Possibly because of her attitude, there had apparently been little collaboration between the guidance staff and the psychological consultants in the past. Ms. Gregory was explaining that she regarded the psychologists as mere testers or therapists when the bell rang for another period and she was called away for another meeting. By this time, Ms. Loren and Ms. Lutz were back in their offices and with the departure of Ms. Gregory we introduced ourselves to them. They too mirrored some of the sentiment of Ms. Gregory. Most of their time, they said, was taken up in scheduling, vocational and career advisement, and group achievement testing, and although both of them had strong interests in consultation, and graduate training in group work, neither could find the time to consult without some assistance. They seemed quite willing to work with us, however, and encouraged us to let them know our thoughts. We left thinking that at least we had two allies in the guidance department and intended to invite them to the meeting scheduled next week.

Informal Assessment of the School Culture. The purpose of our first formal meeting was to meet more of the people we would be working with, to delve deeper into the workings of Central, and to outline a working consultation arrangement. The meeting was held in the principal's office during school hours and scheduled for one period. Although we had usually found two hours to be necessary for initial consultation meetings in our work with other community agencies, in schools it is often difficult to keep people from their other responsibilities for more than a period, especially if one wishes to leave the meeting on good terms.

As we entered Mr. Sands' office we could see that everyone we had invited was there. In addition to Mr. Sands, who sat at the head of a long conference table, there was Mr. Hill, the assistant principal, Ms. Gregory and Ms. Loren (Ms. Lutz could not make it), and two popular and respected teachers we had met in the past week, Ms. Horn and Mr. Updyke. We had specifically tried to get some people at the meeting who could provide us with administrative support, some who valued consultation services, and some who might help us gather resources and meet the staff and students.

Mr. Sands opened the meeting with some brief remarks concerning the importance of the psychologist in high schools and how the rest of the group should listen to what we had to say. Then, much to our surprise, he dismissed himself, saying that he had an emergency meeting with the superintendent. Although this situation made us somewhat anxious, we tried to remain composed. Nagle began with a brief introduction, but before Medway could make a similar introduction, the assistant principal, Mr. Hill, immediately asked us if we would continue the direct-service activities that had been offered in the past such as group counseling and lecturing in the psychology class. By this remark, it was apparent that Mr. Hill (and perhaps others at the meeting) already had expectations concerning our capacities. Mr. Hill's tone and expression implied that we should not only be providing direct services. Our response to Mr. Hill was to outline the role we envisioned for ourselves. We were waiting until later in the meeting to explain our proposed role fully once we thought the group understood our orientation and was willing to work with us in the manner we had described.

It did not take long for the group to mention some general areas where psychological consultation was needed. Mr. Hill and Ms. Gregory mentioned discipline. Both were concerned with a lack of values, discipline, and respect in the school—a situation they blamed on changing times, broken families, and students who did not care about their education. Mr. Hill, who served as the school's disciplinarian, was stern and rigid in his attitude, saying that physical violence was the only way to reach certain students. This statement seemed to bother, but not shock, everyone else.

Although there appeared to be general consensus that discipline was a problem at Central, most members of the group did not want to pursue this issue. Consequently, it was not difficult to redirect the conversation to a discussion of consultation

—in particular its advantages over direct-service activities. We were both careful to point out that we would feel uncomfortable tackling any problem without intimate knowledge of the school and its organization. We mentioned some of our successful high school experiences but stressed that we were not there to impose a particular project on the school. Considering that we did not have the freedom to reject consulting with Central (as an outside consultant might have been able to do) in light of the university-school district agreement, we did not rule out direct-service activities but tried to point out the value of our consultation approach.

With this groundwork laid and our position seemingly understood by all, we spent the last half-hour of the meeting trying to get people's impressions of the flexibility of the school's organizational structure, the clarity of the norms and written policies, and the sources of informal and formal power and influence. Here the guidance counselors were particularly helpful because of their intimate knowledge of the school's functioning and their familiarity with the current programs in the school and in the community at large. Further, it was apparent that in terms of interests, training, and professional values, we had a great deal in common with the guidance counselors, particularly Loren, Lutz, and Bryan.

Over the following week we formally set up shop at Central. Ms. Gregory was instrumental in getting us an office in the guidance suite, and although we were generally in classrooms or in the halls talking to students and teachers, it was gratifying to have a place to store materials, use the telephone, and generally feel part of the school. We posted our schedule of the days we would be at Central in the main office, in each of the departmental work areas, and in the guidance office, and at the next faculty meeting we introduced ourselves to the whole staff. We noticed at that meeting that teachers tended to sit with other teachers in their department. There was not a great deal of socialization between departments.

To introduce ourselves to the student body, we arranged to have an article written in the school newspaper about our interests, background, and training (and how they differed from traditional clinical psychologists and guidance counselors), our hours at the school, and location of our office. We also addressed a student council meeting, attended school social events, and ate in the cafeteria. Immediately teachers began to seek us out for classroom management assistance and information on adolescent development. Students also stopped us in the halls or dropped by our office, especially if they had other business in the guidance suite. Most students came more out of curiosity than for any specific psychological problem.

It took us well over a month to make our presence known at Central, meet the staff and students, and conclude the entry process. We spent most of this time observing in different settings and learning about the myriad rules and regulations such as needing a pass to walk in the halls or a permit to park in the student lot. A picture began to emerge of Central as a school where both teachers and students felt there were many unnecessary rules and policies they were obliged to follow. Teachers believed they had little to say about the content of courses and scheduling. Moreover, they did not have the time, nor were they given the incentive, to work with students with special needs. They felt they had little control over what the students learned and how they behaved, particularly students with academic and social problems. They complained about the lack of a clear discipline policy, problems with current disciplinary procedures, the failure of the administrators, particularly Mr Hill, to back them up in a dispute with a student or parent, and the school's high truancy rate. Many teachers had given up trying to make their opinions known to an administration that seemed to act either very slowly or not at all.

A similar situation seemed to prevail with respect to student opinion. Students complained that they were given little choice of course offerings, that there was little recognition for academic accomplishments compared to athletic accomplishments, and that teachers and administrators looked down on them.

Formal Needs Assessment of the School. By the beginning of October we had a pretty good idea of the problems facing the students and faculty at Central. Our assessment of the situation had been very informal, however, and it was possible that our conclusions might be colored by our high regard for shared decision making and open communication. Furthermore, even if we had diagnosed the situation correctly, would the staff and administration accept our analysis? We knew that before we acted we had to evaluate Central's problems objectively and involve school personnel in this process.

Accordingly, we thought that a formal needs assessment survey (Siegel, Attkisson, and Carson, 1978) would be of value and, further, that this survey should be developed, distributed, analyzed, and disseminated by people within the system. We first discussed the idea informally with the guidance staff. They were enthusiastic, and Ms. Loren and Mr. Bryan agreed to work with us. Our next contact was made with Mr. Hill, who endorsed the idea in principle but wondered whether the results would be worth the time and effort. Nevertheless, he did agree to work on the project. Next we enlisted the help of the two interested social studies teachers, one of whom had worked part-time for a survey research institute. And, finally, we enlisted the aid of three students willing to help with the survey. The students were given independent study credit in their history and psychology courses for their participation.

It took us three meetings to come up with a needs assessment instrument that reflected our agreement on format and questions. Each of the different groups represented (student, teacher, administrator, and counselor) had a different opinion, and our task was to resolve their conflicts and negotiate settlements. Our next step involved circulating this preliminary version to several teachers, students, and the principal for reactions —a step that brought to the surface a number of additional concerns. Some teachers, for example, wondered whether the scale would be used by the administration or school board to evaluate teachers' performance and compare one department with another. It seemed that the survey was still regarded as our project despite precautions taken to involve teachers and students in its formulation. Apparently there were still a few unresolved questions among the staff as to our intentions.

We spent the next two weeks revising the survey and resubmitting it to students and teachers. This version met with approval. When we finally administered the survey, we realized that the time taken up in consulting and collaborating with school personnel was more than compensated for by the interest people showed in the scale and their willingness to respond to the questions openly and honestly.

Separate needs assessment surveys were developed for students and teachers. Each survey was anonymous, took no more than fifteen minutes to complete, and was computer scored. The survey revealed several problems we had noted in our informal observations—especially the school's disciplinary procedures and the failure of the college preparatory program to prepare students for their future educational experience.

We had uncovered a multitude of problems related to discipline. The majority of teachers who had cited discipline as a problem wished to assert more control over misbehavior in their classrooms rather than delegate disciplinary action to the assistant principal, Mr. Hill. Many of these same teachers, however, questioned the effectiveness of the techniques they used and were eager to learn better ways of maintaining control in their classrooms.

Although our needs assessment indicated other areas in which we could have begun our consultation strategies, our inclination was to work with teachers on general issues and techniques of behavior management. By describing our focus as behavior management rather than discipline, we hoped to minimize resistance from Mr. Hill—who had already shown signs of being mildly threatened by teachers' responses indicating a desire for more control vis-à-vis discipline. About one week after the data were compiled, we set up a meeting with those who had aided directly in the formulation of the assessment. Moreover, we extended an invitation to Mr. Sands, since it was our impression that any proposals we made would be more likely to succeed with his endorsement.

As we outlined the findings of the needs assessment, we were struck by the generally accepting attitude of our audience. Perhaps the only indication of skepticism or defensiveness came from Mr. Hill, who defended many of the extant disciplinary policies. Mr. Sands made very few comments concerning the content of our presentation; he praised us for the job we had done and asked how we might do something about many of the uncovered issues. We suggested to him that we present our results at the general faculty meeting later that week. Among the various alternatives we discussed, we thought that the formulation of a teacher consultation group in classroom management was necessary and logical. After we had made some progress in this area, we planned to take a closer look at general disciplinary procedures as well as aid in developing the college preparatory curriculum.

Intervention at the Staff Level. Two days later at the general faculty meeting, we presented the results of the needs assessment. We were again somewhat surprised at the lack of negative response about the results. We reiterated our possible role and function as we had done at the first general meeting. We also stated that we were contemplating a behavior management group and passed around a sign-up sheet for those who might be interested. We then discussed procedural details and emphasized that we would accommodate our schedules in any way possible to meet at times convenient for all the school staff. We told the group we would like to meet once a week for six consecutive weeks. Each weekly period would last about forty-five minutes. Following a brief question and answer period, Mr. Sands thanked us and encouraged teachers to participate in our program.

Of the total pool of staff and teachers, twelve teachers and two guidance counselors (about 15 percent of the staff) expressed an interest in the proposed group. All interested participants expressed a strong preference to hold group sessions as close to the end of the school day as possible. Since there were several conflicts regarding the day, we scheduled groups for Tuesday and Thursday afternoons from 3:00 to 3:45. All the teachers expressed satisfaction with the schedule. We also wished to hold these sessions in a comfortable room centrally located in the school. After a brief meeting with Mr. Hill about room scheduling, he arranged for us to use the conference room off the main area of the library.

Considering the many demands placed on the teachers at

Central, we were moderately pleased to have fourteen participants sign up for the group. We did not, however, receive expressions of interest from the teachers who appeared to have the greatest need for such a group. Our total group consisted of two guidance counselors, a special education teacher, six regular classroom teachers, and five teachers from the commercial education or nonacademic areas (two shop teachers, a physical education teacher, and two business education teachers). Among the regular classroom teachers were Ms. Horn and Ms. Updyke, both recognized as outstanding teachers.

It was now mid-October and although we were eager to begin our group, we were somewhat disappointed at our slow rate of progress. We decided to codirect the two teacher groups. We had on several other occasions conducted groups and workshops together and thought we could do a better job jointly than alone. The format of our groups generally followed the thematic outline of Axelrod (1977). The initial sessions were designed to cover basic principles such as different means of increasing and decreasing behavior and other processes affecting behavior (imitation, discrimination, and the like). The aim of these initial sessions was to underscore the basic importance of understanding behavior management and being able to apply these methods in the classroom. We described procedures derived from fundamental behavioral principles and found to be useful in classroom situations. In this phase we covered such topics as reinforcement variables, programming group consequences, contingency contracting, self-management, alternative behavior management agents (peers, influence of student behavior on teachers, and so forth), and classroom arrangements (seating, reinforcement areas, and the like).

After a brief coverage of measurement of behavior and evaluation and accountability, the sessions dealt with common school problems and their solution. Throughout all the sessions, teachers were given weekly homework assignments related to the topics covered in the session. Most of the assignments dealt with the application of these principles to their classroom.

The final group sessions dealt with the design and implementation of intervention in the classroom. In retrospect, we should have reached the final phases of the groups sooner, since several participants were impatient at the start when we spoke of general behavioral issues that seemed irrelevant to their own classroom. It was apparent to us that the group participants wanted quick solutions to their problems. In view of these needs and interests, group participation and enthusiasm were highest during these last sessions.

We were pleased with the outcome of the group and gratified with the enthusiasm and responsiveness we received from the participants. The group members had actively taken part and seemed uninhibited about voicing their concerns on a variety of school policies. We formally assessed the effectiveness of our group through a special twenty-item behavior management questionnaire we gave the teachers before and after the workshop. The items on the questionnaire presented a classroom problem and five ways of handling it. The teacher was required to choose the best disciplinary alternative. The results of this brief evaluation indicated that all but one member showed improvement on the management questionnaire. By the time the group ended in early December, we had come to understand the shortcomings of Central's disciplinary policy through cases presented in our group sessions.

Intervention at the Student Level. Shortly after beginning the teacher group, we began to devote a great deal of time looking at the general issues of disciplinary procedures and policy. We learned through our formal and informal contacts, and the results of the needs assessment, that a significantly increasing number of students were truant. Although the truancy rate was 5 percent last year, this represented an increase of 80 percent over the rate two years ago.

We made an appointment to see Mr. Hill, who had primary responsibility for determining whether a child was truant and any subsequent disciplinary actions. When we met with Mr. Hill regarding this problem, it was near the beginning of November and already there were students who appeared to be habitually truant. Mr. Hill explained that any child who had twenty or more unexcused absences for the school year could not receive academic credit. He blamed these truancies primarily on the student's lack of motivation and lack of parental support for educational accomplishment.

We asked Mr. Hill to explain any other pertinent information that would help us understand why truancy had become such a problem and what measures had been attempted to alleviate it. He informed us that besides withholding credit for the academic year, common disciplinary tactics involved suspension from school and in-house school suspension—a self-contained classroom in which a variety of children were excluded from regular classes for various infractions of the school rules. In addition to restriction from their academic classes, students were also required to eat their lunch in the classroom. Graver and repeated offenses were punished more severely. Mr. Hill said some children were given as much as two weeks of in-house suspension. He felt that since in-house suspension had little effect on truancy, something else "psychological" could be done. He was quite pessimistic about obtaining any positive results, however.

When Mr. Hill asked if we would like to see the in-house suspension classroom, we quickly accepted the offer. Our walk to the classroom took us down a long, poorly lit wing of the school. At the end of the wing, just adjacent to the school cafeteria, probably the most noisy part of the school, was the room. Students walking in and out of the cafeteria peered into the classroom through the small window in the door or knocked on the door itself.

As we entered the classroom, the teacher in charge, Mr. Moore, was reading a paperback novel. He arose quickly, hastily closed the book, and greeted us. The room itself was stark. A number of old desks were scattered about the classroom with students engaged in tasks ranging from homework to sleeping. Mr. Moore assured us that his duty was to provide the instructional assistance each child was missing as a consequence of being suspended. The classroom, however, was far from conducive to learning. It seemed to be more of a place where students idly bided time. After our brief conversation with Mr. Moore, he returned to his desk and made only perfunctory efforts to interact with the children. As we left, Mr. Hill informed us that Mr. Moore had taught science for three years at Central; he had a reputation as a poor teacher but an effective manager of children's behavior.

We said goodbye to Mr. Hill and thanked him for his time in meeting with us early in the morning and for the tour of the in-house suspension room. We told him that he provided us with valuable information. After we had a chance to think over the things we learned today, and discuss some alternatives for dealing with truancy, we would get back to him later in the week.

Back at our office we discussed some of our concerns over the current policy. First, it appeared quite paradoxical to us that someone who failed to attend school was punished by being suspended. Second, it appeared to us that for many of the truant children being away from academic classes was more pleasant than attending. If we wanted to create a more deisrable situation for children at school, it certainly could not be created by placing a child in the in-house suspension program upon reentering school. We decided, however, that nothing could be gained by voicing objections to Mr. Hill. Because we had attempted to involve him actively in our activities, we were on good terms and had managed to reduce his resistance. We did not want to jeopardize these gains by implying there was something wrong in his handling of truancy problems. Instead, we decided to devise an alternative program for dealing with truancy—one that did not compete with the suspension room and could be used in addition to it if school officials steadfastly argued for the continuation of the present suspension program.

To gain support, we asked members of the guidance staff and administration if they would be interested in helping us devise and implement a truancy intervention project aimed at increasing school attendance. Both Ms. Lutz and Ms. Loren, who also were participating in our behavior management group, wished to aid us, but no member of the administration staff voiced any desire to participate. Mr. Sands wrote us a cordial note saying he did not have the time to contribute; he wished us good luck, however, and said that any help we could give him would be appreciated greatly. Mr. Hill said his time was limited, but he agreed to consult with us on both the data collection and intervention phases of the project. We wanted to keep him informed of what we were doing and needed to know what programs had been tried in the past. To limit the scope of the survey of truant characteristics, we decided to screen the names of only ninth and tenth-grade students. Perhaps we could prevent these children from dropping out of school later.

For the next several weeks, we, along with the two guidance counselors, examined the attendance records of all ninth and tenth-grade students. After we found the names of children who were accumulating a substantial number of unexcused absences, we systematically gathered information about them. Of the nineteen students showing high truancy rates, most were male and from single-parent homes; nearly one-fourth of them were receiving some form of special education assistance. Nearly all the children were considered marginal and participated in few, if any, extracurricular activities.

We were well into November when we completed our truancy information search. In fact, it was less than four weeks away from the school's Christmas break. In view of our time constraints, we decided to spend the remaining time before Christmas to design an intervention strategy. As we discussed the characteristics of the truant group, we were impressed by the low level of peer interaction—we felt that it was extremely important to have group experience as a component of intervention. The counselors suggested a nondirective approach involving value clarification, vocational education, and other strategies to help students realize the importance of school attendance. Both consultants, who are primarily behavioral in orientation, suggested contingency contracting as an adjunct treatment. All four of us agreed to implement this multitreatment intervention. In view of the enthusiasm shown by Ms. Lutz and Ms. Loren, we asked them to take joint responsibility with us for conducting the group. After receiving approval from the head guidance counselor, Ms. Gregory, they accepted our invitation and we now worked closely on refining the details of our treatment project.

We scheduled planning sessions twice a week until the vacation break. One of our primary concerns was how to inform the truants about the project. We learned that most of the students attended school at least one or two days or part days per week, so we planned to call these children to the guidance office to explain the project and determine their interest. We also learned that many of the children who were reported truant were at or near the school building before the homeroom period. In fact, many of the truant students could be found at the convenience food store near the corner of Central. We were also concerned over the selection of potential reinforcers for the contingency contract portion of the intervention. We therefore developed a "reinforcement menu" questionnaire that would be given to the students to determine potential reinforcers.

Although administrative staff members assured us that they supported our project, they were unable to give us financial support. We therefore solicited contributions of gift certificates from a variety of York merchants and businesses. Ultimately we found that a number of fast food chains were eager to help us and gave us an ample supply of coupons that could be exchanged for food items. Moreover, a local radio station offered us the extra promotional records they received from record manufacturers. We also acquired a variety of low-cost items from local merchants.

These planning stages were completed just before the beginning of the Christmas vacation. We planned initial interviews with all the students during the first two weeks after vacation. These sessions were designed to explain the counseling group and have the students complete the reinforcement questionnaire.

We had decided to have two groups of five to seven participants each; the groups would meet twice a week for eight consecutive weeks. The contingency contracts were to specify that perfect attendance for the whole week earned a reinforcement. We also agreed to work in pairs of one guidance counselor and one consultant, since both counselors wished to observe our techniques and to be actively supervised by us. We had successfully employed a collaborative team model in some of our other high school consultation work (Kramer and Nagle, 1980; Medway and Elkin, 1975).

During the first two weeks after vacation, we attempted to reach all the truant students. We were able to solicit interest from fourteen of them. We were fortunate that the students reported the greatest interest in food reinforcers, since they were the most plentiful items on the reinforcement questionnaire. We divided the entire group into two groups of seven students (five males, two females).

Almost from the outset of the project, attendance rates increased dramatically. As early as the first week, the majority of children were showing perfect or near perfect attendance. Through our informal contact with teachers, however, we learned that five students were showing up for the group early in the school day and promptly leaving after the session. In response we asked teachers to report class absences to the guidance counselors. Class attendance was then made part of the contingency contract.

The counseling sessions revealed that for most of the students school had become boring and often irrelevant. It became apparent to us that to keep these children in school, a more relevant curriculum that promised success and satisfaction was necessary. It was fortuitous that the guidance counselors were working with us, since they were the people who would be primarily involved in such future educational programming. We also noted a growing concern of the group members for one another; ultimately the students supported each others' attendance at school.

The high rates of school attendance were maintained throughout the project. Ten of the fourteen children showed perfect attendance during the last four weeks of the project, for example, while two others averaged about four days a week. Of all the subjects, we were unable to change the attendance of two females who had active social involvement outside school.

As our project geared down, we made plans for the guidance counselors to maintain the project in a more limited form by phasing out the contingency contracts and then the group sessions. We were confident they would be able to continue these procedures themselves since they appeared to benefit from participation in the teacher consultation groups as well as the truancy project.

Throughout the truancy project, we kept Mr. Sands and

Mr. Hill aware of the gains that students were making in their school attendance. They were astonished to find that twelve of the fourteen participants had either no unexcused absences, or very few, during the final weeks of the project. Impressed with our findings, Mr. Sands asked us to expand the project to the eleventh and twelfth grades. He also asked us to participate in a school committee he was forming to revise and systematize the school's disciplinary policy. We were pleased to receive Mr. Sands' invitation and were able to participate. By this time, Ms. Loren and Ms. Lutz felt able to handle the truancy groups for the eleventh and twelfth graders by themselves, especially since the administration stood behind them. We were also pleased to learn that Mr. Sands had asked a number of students as well as teachers to join his committee—a committee to which he devoted a great deal of time over the next several weeks. Had he seen the importance of involving all segments of the school in policy-making? We believed that he did.

Intervention at the System Level. Although our main focus involved discipline, we also dealt with improvement of the college preparatory curriculum. The teachers and administration had indicated on the needs assessment that graduates had shown poor performance in their postsecondary schooling. This finding was clearly disconcerting to the school staff since they took a great deal of pride in the number of students who went on to college and technical school. We knew that at the university where we were employed, the Counseling and Human Development Center offered a variety of programs for those interested in improving study skills (reading speed and comprehension, test-taking strategies, note-taking skills, time management). The staff at the center agreed to collaborate on a program designed to teach these skills to students at Central High.

We arranged, after administrative approval, a meeting with teachers in the English department in the eleventh and twelfth grades and the center staff. The meeting discussed the nature, content, and time requirements involved in the "study skills package." About half the teachers agreed to participate; children in the other classes were invited to enroll in these classes at the center, which was several miles from Central High. While we did not evaluate the program formally, we later learned that many of the teachers incorporated various aspects of the instructional program into their classroom procedure. We also began to receive requests for more information about the program from teachers in other subject areas, and thus we formulated plans to expand the program. This program is noteworthy in that it illustrates the effective use of community resources in alleviating a school system problem.

This concludes our case presentation. After the year we spent together, Medway was asked to extend the training centers into another school district while Nagle was assigned to similar administrative duties at an on-campus clinic and research facility at the university. Our positions at Central were filled by other faculty in our training program.

It is now several years since we left Central High and we are perhaps in a better position to evaluate the impact of our presence. Certainly we were unable to accomplish all that we wanted that year. Orientation to the school and planning took a great deal of our time. Much of the time we worked with problem adolescents, though our work with the discipline policy committee and the study skills program did reach more students. Several problems had their roots in teachers' low opinion of students, the barren physical environment, and the high rate of marital disruption in the community. And yet we did not have the time or resources to tackle any of these issues. Looking back, however, we now see that many things have changed for the better. The guidance staff has expanded its role and function, there are now systematic procedures based on sound organizational principles to deal with truancy and misbehavior, there is a greater acceptance of consultation practices in the school, there are the beginnings of student and faculty influence on administrative decision making, and there has been expanded collaboration between the high school and the university.

Some Lessons for High School Consultants

We feel that a number of important lessons of interest to consultants can be learned from this case study. In high schools in particular, the existing culture has a great impact on the behavior of staff and students. This is true with regard to the physical characteristics of the school, the organizational structure, and the interpersonal and group dynamics. Although we attempted to assess through informal interviews the general culture at Central as well as the surrounding community of York even before we made our initial contact, our information was very limited. We were unaware, for example, of the we-they attitude that pervaded Central in terms of distinct separation of power between administrators and staff and between staff and students. And yet, on closer examination, it is now easy to see how certain aspects of the school's physical layout and social environment contributed to this distance. Teachers were physically distant from colleagues teaching in different areas; problem students were placed in a remote and barren suspension room close to a noisy cafeteria; the administrative staff was somewhat inaccessible to teachers and students (remember the imposing plastic counter in the main office); both staff and students felt burdened with meaningless custodial details and rules.

The general educational philosophy of Mr. Sands was mirrored in the day-to-day life at Central. Recall that Mr. Sands had originally described himself to us in terms that suggested he was a "laissez-faire" leader. Although we did not give this admission much importance at the time, we can now see how revealing this statement was. Indeed, when it came to meaningful educational administration, Mr. Sands tended to react rather than initiate. His monitoring of our activities was merely cursory. And even though we cleared our actions with him and kept him up to date on our progress, these efforts may not have been necessary, since Sands either saw that we could function independently or, more likely, did not have the inclination to oversee our activities. Mr. Sands also had trouble handling complexity. The orderly environment of the halls and academic classrooms attests to this attitude. If certain policies did not work, they were abandoned or left ambiguous—witness the dress code. Mr. Sands' leadership was also characterized by maintenance of the status quo. Certainly he failed to question the existing disciplinary policy, which was primarily administered by the vice-principal, Mr. Hill. This policy was based on social control of truants rather than the creation of alternative or special services to deal with truancy. Perhaps from Mr. Sands' vantage point, it was not worth the risk of conflict to examine discipline issues. Moreover, it was extremely difficult for him to support any change in policy unless it was clear that the change would be beneficial. It was only after we had demonstrated success in the truancy project that he endorsed change in existing policies. Our experiences suggest that an awareness of leadership styles is essential for the high school consultant. According to Lippitt and White (1943), laissez-faire leaders do not create strong work motivation, group cohesiveness, and self-direction in group members. We saw many examples of such behavior in the teachers and students at Central.

Another important aspect of the culture is often overlooked: the assessment of system problems that appear to have a direct impact on the system's readiness for change. Most school personnel trace the causes of different problems to persons (lazy students, unconcerned parents) or to the school environment (teachers' attitudes, type of instruction, school policy). (See Vernberg and Medway, 1981.) At Central, students and staff (particularly Mr. Hill) were apt to blame external forces that were not under their control. This attitude merely increased the general feeling of powerlessness in the school. Although we consultants were willing to assume responsibility for solving these problems, it was not easy to get a similar commitment from the staff. In our months at Central we were certainly not able to involve all the staff and students in our work; in fact it is quite likely that the teachers who sought us out were the ones who needed consultation least. Many teachers apparently did not consider consultative problem solving as an aspect of their role. For the most part, we worked best with staff who shared our values and were near our age like Ms. Loren and Ms. Lutz. We were pleased with our involvement with students. Many sought us out just to chat during our first weeks at Central. We found it much better to mingle with students in the halls rather than in a psychologist's office, since this helped reduce the distance between us. We tried to deal with the students' feelings of powerlessness by actively involving them in our programs. Their contributions were very important in helping develop the needs assessment survey because of their perspective on their peer adolescent culture.

Another lesson concerns the process of problem identification. When we began at Central we quickly realized that it was meaningless to view the problems of individual teachers and students outside their context. Accordingly, our initial diagnosis examined existing relationships at the community, school, and classroom level (see Alpert, 1977). We chose to make our first intervention at the classroom level. This was done for several reasons. School personnel regarded classroom disruption and truancy as pressing problems. Teachers felt somewhat more control over these concerns than those at higher levels, and it was our intention to get them involved in the problem-solving process. And, finally, we wanted to start with a limited project we were reasonably sure we could carry to success. Many school personnel were not optimistic at our chances for success, even with our limited goals, and were not much help in providing even the small amount of money necessary to purchase food reinforcers for our group. Had we begun with a grandiose project, school support would have been less and the chances of failure greater. Once we were able to demonstrate successful consultation at the classroom level, the way was cleared for greater involvement at the school level (our work on the discipline policy committee) and the community level (our work on the study skills project).

There is a final lesson to be learned from our case: the importance of flexibility. When we began our consultation efforts we did not have a particular plan in mind and, as it turned out, this proved to be the best approach, since we were more open to allowing school personnel to share in diagnosis, intervention, and policy determination. Being familiar with different models of consultation made it easier to choose the right approach for the right occasion; most of our time was spent in consultee-centered case consultation and program-centered administrative consultation (Caplan, 1970). We also made use of more than one type of intervention strategy. Alpert (1977) reviewed three basic intervention strategies for school consultants: empirical-rational, normative-reeducative, and power-coercive. Empirical-rational strategies involve attempts to provide consultees with information. We made ample use of an empirical-rational approach in our group work with teachers. Normative-reeducative strategies involve changes in norms, rules, and attitudes that influence behavior. Throughout our consultation work we used this approach in our attempts to improve communication and shared decision making in the school, coordinate different school subgroups, and bring about changes in maladaptive school policies. These changes were introduced slowly and gradually. For the most part, we did not uncover new issues; rather, we made the administration more aware of the importance of issues like discipline for the staff. This, coupled with the involvement of higher-level personnel like Mr. Hill, helped reduce the need of administration to defend existing policies. We were not in a position to make use of power-coercive strategies involving legal and economic sanctions. Even if we had been in such a position we would not have used power tactics. Such an approach would have increased the distance between us and school personnel and thereby hindered the collaboration that was necessary to reduce the initial mistrust and suspicion directed toward us.

In conclusion, the process of consultation in high schools is far from straightforward. Theory is limited in this area and there are few guidelines for practice. Even consultants who are sensitive to the general influence of environmental, personal, and social-organizational factors on consultation practices must recognize the variation that exists among high schools and in any high school itself—variations that will necessitate departures from the techniques that proved effective for us at Central. We believe, however, that certain principles are basic to the process of successful high school consultation. Among these principles are the importance of collaborating with school personnel, multilevel intervention, and serving as a link between administration, staff, students, and community. In presenting this case study and analysis, we have tried to convey our belief that high schools are fertile ground for mental health consultation.

Promoting Faculty Development in a College

7

Jack I. Bardon

One autumn day, I received a telephone call from the dean of the School of Education at the University of North Carolina at Greensboro inviting me to consider a position in his school. The offer was unexpected and so grand in design that it compelled serious attention. My notes of that telephone conversation read as follows:

Help us plan for the future. What will we need? How can the school and the university get together? How do we get new

Note: A case study should be as accurate as possible while protecting the identity of those whose activities, ideas, and perceptions are discussed. In this chapter, I have tried to be both accurate and ethical. While reporting events as they occurred, I have deliberately distorted the identities of persons. Thus what you will read is true in general but not in its specific details.

ideas into our curricula? We need a developer, intermediary, interpreter, entrepreneur of educational change. The position will not be a regular faculty position but a special one. Be our school psychologist. Do what you think will help us to improve the quality of life in our school.

I did not accept the offer, but I certainly did not refuse it either. We agreed to talk further about his ideas and his school's needs and also about the conditions of employment that would induce me to change positions.

Additional telephone conversations with the dean provided more information. The University of North Carolina at Greensboro (UNC-G) is one of sixteen of the state's public colleges and universities. It is one of only three authorized to offer doctoral degrees and is by far the smallest of these three. Until the early 1960s, UNC-G had been the Woman's College of North Carolina, a highly respected undergraduate liberal arts college for women. Its name was changed and it became a coeducational institution of higher education with no clear mission of its own. The university, then with a population of about 7,500 students of whom about 2,000 were graduate students, serves the needs of those within commuting distance. It is one of eight colleges and universities in the tricity area encompassing Greensboro, Winston-Salem, and High Point, all within about a twenty-mile radius and with an overall population of about 700,000. The area is growing. Opportunity seemed unlimited.

According to the dean, UNC-G retained some of the heritage of its Woman's College days. In addition to a strong liberal arts emphasis at the undergraduate level, the traditional "female" career areas dominated the curriculum. Home economics, child development, physical education, recreation and dance, music, education—these were the major disciplines granting graduate degrees. In this setting, the School of Education was a dominant part of the university.

The dean had only recently come to UNC-G. His education and training had been in school psychology and, moreover, we had known each other for many years. I had served as an external consultant when he directed a doctoral program in school psychology at another university. He was familiar with my thoughts on the potential role of the school psychologist as a systems consultant (Bardon and Bennett, 1974), and my views had to a certain extent influenced his career as well as his writings. In his eyes, his school and university both needed an improved sense of identity. His analysis of the problems of his school had led him to believe that the key to improving the school lay in helping its faculty to reach higher levels of attainment and feel part of a vital institution. The total full-time faculty of the School of Education was not large, about forty-five persons. It included educators who had been with the school when it served as a demonstration school as part of Woman's College—among them the previous dean and faculty members he had recruited during his tenure, some of them nationally prominent educators. New faculty were being added who represented areas and points of view encouraged by the present dean. All tended to regard the school and each other from different perspectives, based on their previous involvement in a changing school. The differences among the faculty members and the lack of identity within the university itself had created a climate of apathy, disinterest in others, and, to some extent, distrust. The school, according to its dean, was not likely to make any major contributions to the university or education unless something occurred to change it.

The dean had a plan in mind but had not worked out the details. The immediate problem he wanted solved was this: We need to improve the quality of faculty and student life in our school. One solution was to employ a psychologist who would be given freedom and time to determine the school's needs and use his or her background and skills to help the school meet them. The mechanism by which the psychologist would operate would be the Office of Educational Development.*

I was invited to visit the university to talk with faculty members and to consider further whether or not I would accept

*Some of the ideas reported here were also presented in an invited address at the annual meeting of the American Psychological Association, San Francisco, August 1977, and described in Bardon (1979).

the challenge. Certain facts became clear. The dean was an optimist. He consistently viewed problems as opportunities for change and believed that most problems could be solved. His assessment of the university and his school, according to my observations after two short visits, was essentially substantiated. Especially impressive was the quality of the many faculty members who had come to UNC-G because it was still developing and showed potential for improvement and, not so incidentally, was in a lovely city with a fine climate.

I accepted the invitation to be considered for the position and agreed to go through the procedures to allow faculty and administrators to determine whether they wanted me to join them. Before going through the recruitment process, however, a number of critical decisions had to be made. First, it was necessary to determine my assignments and to assure that I would have both time and support services needed to carry out my consultant activities. It was decided that I would hold faculty rank; in fact, I would be brought to campus as an endowed full professor with a title that conveyed high status in the university. I would be expected to assume the usual faculty responsibilities of serving on university and school committees and doctoral dissertation committees. I would teach one course of my own choosing per semester. This load was considerably lighter than those ordinarily assigned to faculty members, allowing me time to serve the school as a consultant. I was told I would have secretarial assistance and some funds for whatever uses I thought appropriate to carry out my responsibilities.

The dean and I agreed to develop some basic assumptions about my role and functions before faculty was asked to decide whether or not to support the dean's unusual request for my employment. The assumptions are stated more concisely here than they were in our conversations and correspondence, but the general flavor of our agreement is conveyed.

First: Do not decide exactly what you will do until you have had ample opportunity to understand the school and have been at the university long enough to know what is needed. Begin with a general plan and fill in the specifics later.

Second: Help faculty members to know you before you

begin work. Be honest and forthright about what you are trying to do.

Third: The role that will be acceptable to most people is that of consultant. Even though the term means different things to different people, its connotation is generally positive as compared, for example, with terms such as administrator, clinician, or psychologist. The term implies that the ownership of a problem is with the client. It also implies prestige. In an educational setting, it is relatively easy to promote the idea of a consultant, especially to those who value prestige and professional independence.

Fourth: There is special merit in being part of an organization that allows sufficient freedom of activity. Perceived similarity to others who work in the system is helpful. Similarity does not necessarily interfere with the perception of expertise that is necessary if others are to use your services. In schools, including institutions of higher education, after all, everyone is supposed to be an expert at something.

Fifth: There is more to be gained in the long run by knowing the system from the inside than there is to be gained by the sporadic service typically offered by outside agencies providing mental health consultation to schools (Caplan, 1970), organizational management services to business and industry (Schein, 1969), and curriculum and management consultation to institutions of higher education (Pelon and Bergquist, 1979).

Sixth: Needs assessment and assistance to those in the system and to the system itself are better accomplished by capitalizing on the events of the moment than by functioning in a programmatic way.

Seventh: Given limited time for consultation and a large school population, it is generally more productive to work with the influencer than with those who are influenced. In a school of education, it may be better to work with faculty than with students if a choice must be made.

Eighth: The central purpose of having a school-based school psychology consultant is not to cure the ill, handle emergencies, or help everyone to become happy. Rather, it is to do whatever one can as a consultant psychologist to make the system a better place in which to teach and learn. Therefore, the approach to school-based consultation to be employed should not be a mental health model, as commonly understood, but an educational and systems model that incorporates understanding of human needs and system needs and is based as much on social-psychological principles as on personality dynamics. Its central focus is on the professional concerns of those who work in a system; its ultimate goal is to improve the way the system functions.

Ninth: Considering the overall goal of helping the school to improve the way it functions, it is better to regard an internal consultant as a facilitative agent than as a change agent. Although both terms are variously interpreted, the distinction here is between a consultant who works toward the improvement of an institution in a developmental manner as opposed to one who works to introduce major changes in practice and attitude through specific programs. The facilitative approach appears to make the most sense in a university—after all, universities are, by design, made up of people who above all prize autonomy and academic freedom. The purposes of a university are well established; they invariably include research, teaching, and service. Faculty members are encouraged—required—to be independent and creative in the ways they carry out the purposes of a university. Major changes in programs and process are most likely to emanate from legislative, administrative, and legal requirements. Individuals and units in a university can, however, improve their ability to do what they are supposed to do. The concept of a facilitative consultant involves working to improve the academic lives of faculty members individually and collectively while helping the university to function efficiently.

Entry into the System

As part of my official visit to the university to be evaluated by faculty members and administrators and to determine if I wanted to come to UNC-G, I was asked to present a colloquium. I used the occasion to describe in some detail who I was and what might be expected of me if I came to the university. I especially wanted people to know how I thought, how I behaved, and what I would try to do if they decided to have me join them. I was already aware of deep philosophical differences among faculty members in the school and wanted to be sure my participation would not be based on false premises. Some excerpts from my talk will illustrate my approach:

> So far I have said nothing about my theoretical bent or my interest in certain aspects of psychology and education. It is important that these omissions be understood. When you practice as a school psychologist and try to train and educate school psychologists, it soon becomes clear that the problems of schools and people in schools are so massive, so complex, so immediate, so ephemeral, that no single point of view or set of techniques or theoretical persuasion is sufficient to account for all the problems. In attempting to do something that might be helpful to teachers, administrators, pupils, and parents, many of us in school psychology become practicing eclectics, supreme realists, and pragmatic practitioners, with all the attendant dangers.
>
> When I tell you, then, that I am philosophically a humanist, methodologically a scientist, technologically both a behaviorist and an interactionist, and that I am pragmatic in all other respects, you will understand, I hope, that I am not simply confused! My view of most professional problems involves, I trust, deep concern for the rights and values of the persons presenting the problems—including a desire to let them solve their own problems in their own way with my assistance. I hold an abiding respect for data . . . for the questions "How do you know? What evidence are you using to make your decisions? Are you discriminating fact from opinion?" I recognize the power of reinforcement in virtually every aspect of our lives and our need to understand how it works because we respond to reinforcement whether we try to control it or not. I believe it is unwise to think that professional judgments make sense without consideration of the setting. Therefore, I am less likely to think of people as having abiding traits than to think of them as capable of behaving in somewhat different ways in different situations.

Later I tried to describe how I wanted to work if I were employed:

The practitioner role I have envisioned can best be described as applied scientific. You try to define a problem—to determine how it can be solved. You do something or mobilize others to do something about it. You try to assess the results and modify procedures accordingly. You stop when there is no longer any incremental value to your efforts. The role certainly is not that of a clinician in the ordinary sense. The area of concern is whatever *others* are concerned about. In practice, you might be an organizer, entrepreneur, confidant, planner, editor, arbitrator, information disseminator, or data interpreter. The role might best be characterized as open, dependent in large part on what others want done, and system-serving rather than self-serving. It is, above all, highly applied and practical.

It is this kind of role I would put into practice at this university. Doing so is, for me, a logical extension of what I have been doing for a long time. I am not aware, however, of a university employing anyone to practice, or teach, or study what I see as a high level of school psychology practice. Nor am I aware that educators have availed themselves of the use of such practitioners or tried to learn the skills involved in helping others to solve their problems and the skills involved in using others as consultants. In education we have not yet become accustomed to using others to help us solve our professional problems. Nor is the process by which it can be done well understood. Educational consultation ought to be tried and developed somewhere, and I would like to do it at your university.

At the time, I really did believe we were being original. Subsequently, of course, we learned of similar efforts at other universities. (See Parker and Lawson, 1978, and Sandoval and Love, 1977.)

The colloquium was poorly attended. Apart from the members of the search committee appointed by the dean, only nine other School of Education faculty members attended, along with some faculty members from other units of the university who came for unknown reasons. The small attendance was disappointing. It thwarted my first attempt to introduce myself to faculty and also suggested that the assignment I was about to undertake would indeed be difficult. The indifference mentioned by the dean had revealed itself in my very first attempt to interact with members of the faculty.

Nevertheless, I was offered the position and I accepted. My interviews with the university chancellor and the vice-chancellor for academic affairs had gone well enough. Neither seemed to be especially concerned with the details of my assignment. Rather, it was my impression that they had faith in the dean's decisions about the School of Education's future direction and were trying to give him as much support as possible. At least they had allowed my appointment to be made. I was impressed with their willingness to give the dean authority to carry out his responsibilities; their stance seemed to indicate that the university did allow freedom of action and encouraged innovative planning.

Because of previous commitments, I was unable to start work immediately on a full-time basis and therefore arranged to begin as a part-time consultant. For a full fifteen-week semester, prior to my joining the faculty, I commuted between New Jersey and Greensboro one day a week. The purposes of my weekly visits were to get to know the faculty and school and to prepare for faculty consideration a proposal for an office of educational development.

I used my time to meet with almost all members of the faculty, attend faculty meetings, and discuss my future role with the dean. My conversations with faculty members were informal. I learned about their work and their views of the school and told them about my plans. For the most part, their reaction to me was cordial but guarded. It was evident that the dean's plans for the school and for my role had not been developed in close cooperation with faculty members. Most faculty members, while not hostile to the plan, did not think it pertained to them. The general impression I gained during the semester was that of a highly diversified faculty, some excellent and committed teachers, some nationally recognized experts, and some inadequate educators no longer, if ever, functioning well as teachers or scholars. Many faculty members were isolated from one another and did not understand the work of their colleagues. A proportion tended to be self-protective and suspicious of the motivation of others in the university. The dean had been right: The school did lack a coherent identity, and the quality of academic life was wanting in certain respects. A number of faculty members spoke of the need for "a sense of community" and complained of heavy teaching loads and lack of intellectual stimulation. Yet, in general, most liked the university and were content with their positions and their professional lives.

At the conclusion of my part-time introduction to UNC-G, I attended a faculty assembly of the School of Education to present my proposal for an Office of Educational Development. My proposal was so clearly based on the foresight and planning of the dean, however, that I was somewhat embarrassed to present it as I did. Nevertheless, the dean wanted the plan to appear to be other than administrative fiat and supported its presentation.

I had worked hard on the proposal—a five-page document presenting a review of the dean's model for the office, a rationale for its creation, evidence that similar planning had been done at other institutions of higher education, my tentative impressions of the school, the broad scope of the plan, and how it would be implemented. Emphasis was placed on one special aspect of the office I thought would be easily understood by faculty members. This was the most innovative aspect of the plan: the faculty study group, a form of internal sabbatical.

In preparing the report for the faculty, I had formulated some additional assumptions about the school and the Office of Educational Development and discussed them with the dean.

First: An office appended to an existing institution will remain an appendage unless it affects the activities of that institution in important ways. In many institutions of higher education, offices of educational development present lectures on how to teach, provide resource materials for faculty members on a variety of subjects, develop methods to evaluate the effectiveness of teaching, and assist with grant preparation (Group for Human Development in Higher Education, 1974). While all these activities are useful, they are not critical. Such offices do provide information and techniques for those who want them, but they are not intimately related to the institution's daily academic life.

Second: Whether an institution such as a school of education can improve itself cannot be determined by one factor, no matter how successful it is. Support by the state, the priority given the school by the university, the school's leadership, the effectiveness of its organizational structure, the willingness of faculty to help—all are influential.

Third: If members of an organization are given direct support with their critical day-to-day problems, they can usually solve their professional problems. A colleague able to assist in a variety of ways with problems not easily solved by the administration can offer the faculty more assistance than an appended office that is primarily a resource center for materials about teaching and learning.

Fourth: If a small group of faculty members can get to know one another under conditions of mutual support, they will find more in common than they originally thought possible. And if such a group can stay together long enough—a year, for example—with focus on problems of interest to all, they will be able to assimilate new ideas and tolerate others' views to the benefit of all.

Fifth: Given time to arrive at ideas under conditions that promote close contact with others about intellectual and professional concerns, the chances of transferring learning to the work setting is increased. Many small-group experiences intended to have major impact on the participants are held under ideal conditions far from the places people ordinarily work, often with people one will never see again. Can what happens in such groups really influence what happens in the old setting? The assumption is that participation in the faculty study group—as part of the work load for the year, taking place in the same location, with normal contacts and school activities occurring at the same time—will increase the chances that whatever changes occur will continue in the future. Over a period of time, the combined number of faculty members who had participated in the group would be large enough to influence the psychological climate of the institution.

To show how the faculty was informed about the Office of Educational Development, sections of the proposal are presented here:

In my experience, colleges and universities, like public schools, are often lonely places in which to work. . . . For the most part, faculty members tend to go their own ways, doing what has to be done or what pleases them, profiting little from the talents and interests of their colleagues or from the opportunities present to enrich their own scholarship or increase their enthusiasm for teaching through constructive responsiveness of others on the faculty. The atmosphere needed for mutual trust and cooperative effort often is not present. The incentives needed to promote involvement outside one's own immediate sphere of activity are often not available. . . . The proposal for an Office of Educational Development in the School of Education should be put into perspective as one modest attempt . . . to help the school become better than it already is through provision of ways to improve instruction, research, scholarship, and interchange among faculty members.

Objectives of the Office of Educational Development:

1. The office . . . will provide a means each year for a small number of faculty members to work together across disciplines on an applied problem of interest to all involved, that problem to be determined by the group. . . . The immediate goals of this yearlong activity will be:
   a. To work toward the solution of an educational problem that needs clarification or resolution.
   b. To disseminate the results of the effort through joint publication.
   c. To enhance the education of the participants through exposure to the ideas and reactions of colleagues from different disciplines within education in an atmosphere that encourages open discussion, mutual respect, and team effort.
2. The Office of Educational Development will provide assistance in whatever ways its resources permit to any faculty members who are working alone or together on problems of educational merit. . . . The office will also offer consultation or will become involved in other ways to help faculty members find solutions to educational or professional problems. The immediate goals of consultation will be:
   a. To assist faculty to solve immediate educationally relevant problems that are not easily resolved through the

current channels of support and assistance in the university.

b. To advance faculty efforts toward professional and scholarly growth by providing or making available constructive feedback not ordinarily available through other means.

3. The long-range goals of the Office of Educational Development will be:
   a. To increase colleagueship among faculty members in the School of Education.
   b. To foster faculty and student involvement in the multiple efforts of the school.
   c. To enhance the vitality and quality of teaching and scholarship in the school.
   d. To add to the visibility of the school within the university, the state, and the nation.
   e. To attract faculty and students who will contribute to the vigor and excitement of the school as a place to work and to study.

It also seemed sensible in the proposal to say what I would not do:

The office will not serve as the school's research and grant clearinghouse to store and provide information on the availability of grants or on research contract procedures for faculty and students.

The office will not be the research technology center for the school to provide students and faculty with research design, statistical, and computer assistance.

The office will not serve as the center for the organization and implementation of conferences, workshops, training sessions, or continuous education programs.

These activities will be administered in other ways by the divisions, the school, or the university.

The office will not knowingly duplicate any existing activity in the school nor will it interfere with any function, procedure, or activity of its divisions, and it will cease immediately to engage in any enterprise which impinges on those of others not involved in the work of the office.

The office will not presume to be the repository of all intellectual concern in the school outside of coursework. It will serve as only one additional means to encourage an intellectual climate and will assume that comparable efforts are ongoing.

The office will not seek to involve itself in the teaching or research activity of any member of the faculty who does not choose to become involved in its work.

To implement the plan, the following procedures were proposed:

Each division of the school (three divisions) will request its faculty to become volunteers for membership in the office's Faculty Study Group. From these volunteers, each division will recommend to the dean no more than four persons to serve for the next academic year. From this group, a total of from four to six faculty members will be selected to represent a range of academic disciplines and competencies.

Faculty members will be given a reduced load for both fall and spring semesters, with responsibility for teaching only one course per semester (normal teaching load is three courses per academic semester) or comparable released time in advisement, committee work, and other school and university responsibilities.

Funds will be provided to the divisions to cover the costs of employment of adjunct faculty to teach the courses ordinarily taught by those selected for inclusion in the Faculty Study Group.

Faculty members selected will be expected to devote the equivalent of two and one half days per week to the Faculty Study Group and to their own research or academic study. The remainder of their time will be devoted to teaching, committee work, research supervision, administration, or other university, school and professional activities.

It was further pointed out in the document that the plans were deliberately vague. It was understood that the goals of the office would change with time. The proposal called for approval of the plan by the faculty assembly for a period of three years; that its renewal would be contingent upon faculty vote; that the office would be monitored by the school's executive committee each year; and that the office would provide a yearly progress report to the faculty.

The proposal was presented. There was no discussion. Approval was given by a unanimous but perfunctory vote of the faculty members who attended the meeting. In effect, the faculty assembly concurred in the decision but with no indication of strong support. Concurrence is not the same as support, of course. Controversial issues that deeply affect members of a group receive concerted effort and attention. They are discussed and voted on with some degree of passion. Concurrence implies passive consent—that members of the group do not hold sufficiently strong opinions to vote something down and therefore vote for it in the belief that, if it happens, it will not affect them much anyway. Concurrence often allows new programs to come into existence but does not always provide the support needed to make them work.

To this point I was satisfied that I had conscientiously prepared for my work as resident consultant. I had negotiated a contract with the dean that both of us could accept. I had met most of the people with whom I might eventually work, had explained my role, and had at least tried to establish a working relationship with each of them. I had presented a detailed plan to faculty members for their approval. I had developed a consultation role that appeared well suited to the needs of the school. Nevertheless, my initial concerns remained. Was it possible to break through a well-established system of functioning that, even though it resulted in complaints, was steady, comfortable, and predictable? Were the dean's plans for the future of the school unrealistic? Had I accepted too easily the conviction that my activities could introduce changes in the school?

Despite these concerns, I was frankly so enamoured of the role and its possibilities that I was willing to give it a try. In retrospect, it now seems that I was somewhat less objective than I should have been in this phase of consultant activity. The unique opportunity to extend my own career goals, the fancy title that went with the role, the opportunity for a move to an attractive city and a university that was still growing—these were seductive factors that influenced my decision to accept the assignment. Had I been less personally involved, I might have raised questions and insisted on conditions that could have helped avoid some of the mistakes and problems that lay ahead.

Intervention: The First Two Years

The formal life of the Office of Educational Development lasted two years. Although some of its activities continue to exist, I recommended that it be terminated at the end of its first two years of operation. The reasons had less to do with the project and its goals than with the realities of institutional life. In fact, the entire project might be considered as a successful failure: successful in that it did what it set out to do, a failure in that it could not afford to continue. It was in fact too rich for its institutional setting—that is, the institution could not support it logistically or financially without diverting limited sources of support from other activities. Even though the project did not survive, its purposes and the role established by the consultant have continued to serve the institution, but in unexpected ways.

The Faculty Study Group: Year One. Just before the beginning of the fall semester, the dean asked faculty in each of the three divisions of the school to volunteer for the project for the next academic year. In two divisions four faculty members asked to be considered, and the dean selected two persons to participate who were different in educational background and academic specialization. In the third division there were no volunteers; instead, the chairperson of the division designated one faculty member to serve. Although the original plan had been to include four faculty members in addition to the project director, budgetary considerations made it necessary to keep the group small. Thus we began the project with three instead of four faculty members and with one member who was there by command rather than as a volunteer.

The group consisted of me and three assistant professors, two women and a man. One member held tenure as an assistant professor. The other two were in the unenviable position of preparing credentials for review by senior faculty to determine whether they would be permitted to stay and be promoted to the rank of associate professor. One was an educational technology specialist, one an English educator, and the third an educational philosopher.

We held our first meeting just prior to the beginning of the academic year. It was hardly an unqualified success. Although the three participants had been employed in the same school for four years, none of them knew the others well. The meeting was uncomfortable. The tone was one of mild suspicion, psychological distance, wariness, and, at the same time, curiosity. I learned later that all three faculty members were considered by various other faculty members to be mavericks who had established reputations for fierce independence or isolation. Although I cannot be certain, it may well be that all volunteers viewed the faculty study group as an opportunity for self-expression and a change from routine.

Although two of the members had volunteered, the session began with questions. "Why were we selected instead of others who asked to be included? What will it mean to us to be involved? Are we being told something negative about our status here? How are we perceived by the dean?" The only answer I could give was "I don't know." But I did learn a lot from these meetings:

Lesson number 1: Do not have the group coordinator participate in the selection of participants. To do so involves the coordinator (consultant) in authority problems and leadership activities that are inimical to the later development of good group relationships.

A more practical concern had to do with assurances that involvement in the project for at least two days a week would actually be accompanied by released time from other obligations. Although the group members had been told they would teach only one course per semester and be relieved from new advising and committee assignments, we needed to make sure that these promises would be kept.

We next met after the semester began. Some of our time was spent in settling initial organizational planning. When would we meet? For how long at a time? What would we do about secretarial services? How could we safeguard our free time from telephone calls, student visits without appointments, committee assignments? We arranged a tentative schedule and tried to answer these and other operational questions. I assumed responsibility for handling the organization of the project group.

Lesson number 2: Make sure that details of procedure are considered early and a plan for handling problems is developed and agreed to by all.

I then explained a number of basic rules that would govern the group's activities. My experience in academia had led me to believe it would be a mistake to have a nonstructured group organization. I hoped that my rules would be viewed as so reasonable they would not be regarded as the exercise of unwarranted authority. I made it clear that the rules were simply guidelines. I was trying to help the group members learn, and practice, the basic tenets of good consultation:

- Listen to the person who is talking.
- When someone is seeking assistance from the group, concentrate on the problem, not on your reaction to it. Try to be *helpful.*
- If you do not understand what someone is saying, ask for clarification.
- If you want to comment on the remarks of another, consider first how to say it without evoking retaliation or defense.

These rules were intended to counteract the verbal behavior that typifies much of academic interchange. They were tacitly accepted, with little comment, but it took a long time before they were accepted as worth the effort.

Lesson number 3: Do not expect harmony just because some guidelines are posed. It takes time and practice—and, most of all, willingness over a period of time to keep working at them.

We set as our first major task the discovery of a common theme that would give us a basis for working together throughout the year. To determine what themes might be possible, each of us talked about what we were teaching, what we considered our areas of specialization, and the problems we encountered in our teaching and scholarly activities. This open format for discussion proved useful. By beginning with attempts to help others understand our work and buttressed by a set of guidelines, we were able to listen attentively. The result was an early experience of learning from one another, different enough from ordinary interchange among faculty to be reinforcing. We also asked each other to clarify terms and explain concepts. It is one thing to present the basic terminology and concepts of a field to students in a class who are there for credit. It is quite another to do the same thing at the request of colleagues who want to know what you are saying. Without the anxiety created by academic competition and with no great concern for evaluation from others, the members of the group began to enjoy each other's comments. The closeness of a small group, the recognition of sharing with others, the experience of being a student again but this time from the perspective of competence—these were new and stimulating experiences. The members of the group began to appreciate the novelty of the situation.

At the end of two productive weeks, mindful of our decision to find a common theme, I pressed to find where our conversations might lead. I tried to summarize them and to identify areas of commonality. It was a mistake. This attempt to structure our discussions resulted in a kind of self-consciousness that interfered with the experience. Group members were cooperative and listened as I summarized my views about what common themes may have emerged. The results, in hindsight, were predictable. As I attempted to restate what others had said, they noted only the discrepancies in meaning. Even when I was reasonably accurate in my summaries, disappointment replaced enthusiasm and resistance displaced cooperation. It all happened quickly. We were dismayed that we were once again facing each other with distrust. The feeling of mutuality had been fragile and now was gone. At this point we decided to end our session and try to start over again next time.

Lesson number 4: Do not seek closure too soon. If things are going well, let them go on until the next step emerges in a natural way. In a group such as this one, there is a flow of activity. Too much structure stifles initiative and creativity. Too little structure, however, is equally damaging in that the group may lose any sense of purpose. The consultant's task is to keep what is good going and to know when structure should be introduced. One way to do this, of course, is to ask the group rather tell it.

Our next meeting was important. I decided to express my concerns and apologized for my lack of sensitivity to the process in which we had all been engaged. Beginning again on a note of honesty and concern, with mutual recognition that we had all found our conversation pleasant and intellectually stimulating, the group returned to its earlier state of supportive dialogue. It was then that the group members decided to look for the common themes in our conversations.

Lesson number 5: The best way to coordinate a faculty group is to practice what you preach. Maybe it is the best way to do anything.

By now we had met five times for a total of about twenty hours. We did not reach agreement at this meeting or even the next. Rather, agreement to try to agree led us into a way of talking that characterized the rest of our work together. We would begin in one direction and end in another. Each of us expressed a major concern. The rest of us listened and tried to help the speaker clarify ideas. One idea led to another in a sequential way—orderly but not necessarily logical. My role was that of a participant but also a coordinator of activities with special responsibility to remind the group of our purposes and guidelines for conducting the meetings.

When we finally agreed on a topic three meetings later, we realized that we were all interested in teacher education but from different perspectives. We therefore developed a general topic and individually pursued areas of special interest with the understanding that the others would help us refine our special topics—not as experts but as colleagues who had much to learn from the efforts and ideas of others.

As we continued to meet, we developed new rules. We decided not to meet as a group unless all four could be present. We were determined not to establish subgroups. Despite our best intentions, our schedules continued to fill with traditional family tasks and events.

Lesson number 6: There is no way to keep the ordinary activities of academic life from impinging if you remain on campus. Although the amount of activity can be contained, committee work, student advisees, professional activities, the lure of consultantships, and requests to give speeches continue. The idea of an internal sabbatical is not as easy to manage as it may have seemed. But, despite all these distractions, the experience can still be worthwhile.

We tried various ways of organizing our two and one half days of development work. Our pattern was to organize one day with a morning meeting of about three hours, lunch separately, and a short afternoon meeting. The remainder of the time was given to study, research, and whatever pursuits seemed appropriate. I cannot recommend an ideal way to organize groups of this kind. Each group will find its own way.

During the academic year, we met for a total of 135 hours. Each participant probably spent a comparable amount of time reading, writing, and thinking. I spent considerably less time in related activities outside the group, as my role was a continuous one and my writing and research activities were not directly related to the project. What did we talk about? Here is a list of some of the topics we discussed:

- Teaching in the ghetto
- Sex education in the schools
- The effects of poverty—how the poor view the world around them
- Moral education in the schools
- How we can help teachers be better teachers

- The significance of Piaget's work in education
- How we teach and how students respond—differences in professional style and their origin
- How consultants work in and out of education
- Mental illness—how we decide who is mentally ill
- Philosophy and science—terminology, similarities, differences
- Evaluation of teachers and professors
- Admissions policies to colleges and universities and their implications
- How to study—problems that keep us from reading and writing
- Special education and the law
- Democracy and control—centralized and local control of schools
- Right-to-work laws—teacher unions and professional organizations
- Philosophy of finality—the meaning of death, suicide, reasons for living
- The value of questions and answers in teaching
- The purpose of higher education—its time arrangement, grading, policies
- How change does or does not take place
- Educational injustice—what to do when school personnel harm children (what constitutes harm?)
- What professors of education can offer school systems
- Differences in undergraduate and graduate teaching
- Technology in education—its place and purposes
- Integration, busing, and equality in education
- Power and prestige in higher education—their effect on teaching and scholarship

This list does not mean that we organized meetings to talk about these topics or came to firm conclusions. We did neither. We talked about these topics in and out, back and forth, over and over again. We read books in common; we read books or articles in others' fields. We exchanged book notices, reviews, and articles. We wrote notes to each other during the week about our discussions. At one point we decided to write personal essays on teaching and learning to clarify what we were saying. We exchanged these essays, commented on them, exchanged comments, and rewrote. A lot of written material passed among us that year.

One member of the group invited us to visit his classes, and two of us were able to accept his invitation. We gave him our views of what was happening in class and discussed our impressions in light of his special area of interest in our group.

Through contacts made by one member of the group, with the help of consultant funds made available to us by the dean, we brought to campus a group of educators and parents from an inner-city school in another state who had developed an innovative community-based elementary school. We invited faculty and graduate students to meet with them.

Putting these events on paper cannot do justice to the process or content of our year's activities. When we met in the halls during the week, there was an assumption of mutuality that was gratifying. We talked about our work with other faculty members and graduate students. The group members teased each other about the differences in their activities this year as compared with previous years, but they were clearly proud of the differences. Three group members wrote more than they had in the previous four years combined.

While much of what appeared to happen tends to happen in any intense, intimate, long-standing group, it is important to point out that the faculty study group was not engaged in group therapy as usually understood. Our focus was consistently on intellectual concerns. We talked about ourselves only to clarify the topic under discussion. We did not share personal experiences for the sake of doing so. We preserved our independence and our right to privacy. We were people who would in all probability work together for a long time to come, and we reserved the right to keep personal distance while encouraging professional closeness.

Lesson number 7: A faculty group must not be allowed to become group therapy. Its goals and the nature of professional life in an institution of higher education dictate a more limited purpose. If faculty development becomes group therapy, it loses its special meaning.

At the end of our year together, we disbanded as planned. We had learned a lot about ourselves as academicians, about other disciplines in education, and about how to live and thrive in our university. We believed we could now interact with other colleagues in ways that would be mutually enhancing and that our own careers would become more productive.

The Faculty Study Group: Year Two. In the spring of the first year of operation, a request was made for volunteers to participate during the next academic year. Eight faculty members at all ranks volunteered, approximately 18 percent of the school's full-time faculty, presumably because they had heard good things about the group—above all, that it had been useful. The dean selected four persons to represent diversity of disciplines in the school: three assistant professors and an associate professor, three men and a woman. The areas represented were curriculum theory, mathematics education, reading, and educational psychology.

The same format was used at the beginning of the semester as during the first year, but it soon became clear that the dynamics of this group were quite different. Based on what they had heard about the first year's activities, group members had specific ideas of how they wanted to use their time. Each of them wanted to work on specific projects requiring time for extensive research and reading. Therefore, meetings together were limited first to four hours a week and then to two hours a week. While less time was spent together, the major purpose of sharing ideas among disciplines was carried on, and the benefits reported by those who participated were similar to the benefits reported by the pioneers of the first year. We never reached the level of intellectual stimulation attained in the first year, but our efforts seemed to result in understanding of other disciplines, mutual respect, improved consulting skills that could be used with other faculty members, and professional productivity.

Consulting with Faculty

My experiences as an internal consultant were similar to those I had experienced in the public schools. Educators do not easily turn to a colleague for consultation. Acquaintances, however, do turn to each other regularly for assistance and support. Informal consultation begins when someone with whom you work asks for assistance. If you are helpful, that person suggests to someone else that you might help them. With each success, more educators turn to you with requests for assistance with increasingly complex problems. At some point it becomes established that you do have a special role to play and it is legitimate to use you in that role.

Even though I had announced my role as consultant to faculty, faculty members did not line up at my door. Rather, I assumed my regular responsibilities, talked with faculty members in the mailroom, met some for lunch and at business meetings, and engaged in the normal professional and social interchange that takes place in a university. There was one difference, however. If a question arose, I always stayed with it and always took it seriously. I offered to be helpful. If encouraged further, I tried to be helpful. I did not use the term *consultant* in my general conversations with faculty members; rather, I intended to be helpful and seized on my opportunity to do so.

This approach seemed to work well. During the first year I "consulted" with fifteen School of Education faculty members in addition to my work with the three members of the faculty study group. In the second year, I "consulted" with nineteen members of the school's faculty in addition to the four members of the faculty study group. Each year I met with 30 to 40 percent of the faculty members in one way or another in a consultant capacity. I put "consultant" in quotation marks to indicate that what I did in some instances may stretch one's view of school-based consultation. Some who received assistance from me would not have viewed my activities as consultation; others definitely understood the nature of our relationship and accepted it.

My experience suggests that consultation in higher education would be especially difficult for anyone whose credentials in the traditional areas of academia are wanting. A record of scholarly productivity, professional activities, and good teaching are valuable assets. It was useful to be viewed as an expert in general areas of higher education and to have established credibility in a special area. My staunchest supporters were the members of the faculty study group who told their acquaintances I could be trusted and was efficient, sensible, and knowledgeable.

Over the two years, faculty problems brought to me seemed to fall in the following categories:

- Reviewing manuscripts for submission to journals
- Planning career development or career change
- Planning possible research projects or articles
- Improving communication with other faculty members
- Requests for classroom observation as a way of improving teaching
- Planning adjustments in work load
- Planning for improvement of teaching
- Planning new courses
- Assistance in planning for new committee assignments
- Assistance with grant preparation and application
- Preparation of materials for promotion, retention, tenure
- Exit counseling (when a faculty member's contract was not renewed or a change in location was being considered)

Most of these activities involved planning. Sessions varied from one to several in most instances. Follow-up was informal and easy to do, as we saw each other often in the halls and at meetings. In some instances, editorial work and direct instruction in methods and approaches were required. Many of the problems brought to me were of great professional consequence to those involved and required continuous contact over a period of months. One senior faculty member, highly respected by her colleagues, had become almost wholly unproductive, was no longer interested in her long-standing area of scholarly inquiry, and was despondent about her future. In her eyes she was expected to be good at what she did, and it was hard for her to let others know of her boredom with teaching and research activities. This faculty member had volunteered to be in the first-year faculty study group but had not been admitted. Through our contact, she decided to talk with the dean about her concerns and received his strong support for change. We explored different areas related to her work and engaged in wide-ranging discussions of topics in which she already had some knowledge and interest. I recommended readings to her; I shared my writing with her. By the end of the spring semester, she had developed an outline for a revised course in a related subject and had enrolled in a summer program to study a specialty about which she expressed considerable enthusiasm.

Another member of the faculty who had recently completed his doctoral degree was unable to get himself to begin the research and writing that would be necessary if he were to be retained. He had found it difficult to complete his dissertation and remembered his orals with horror. Eventually we were able to overcome his resistance to reviewing his dissertation. I helped him to outline an article based on his dissertation and then to organize and edit his first draft. The article was accepted for publication.

Another unexpected outcome of the faculty study group was that a few faculty members asked me to provide an objective view of their teaching. Since two of us had already visited the class of one member of the group who not only survived but had profited from the observations, first one and then another faculty member asked me to visit their classes. Observations were made and descriptive reports prepared, followed by consultation meetings in which we discussed my observations and their implications for the improvement of instruction.

I almost hesitate to mention committee work in this case study, but it did occur. Perhaps it is worth thinking about as an unusual form of consultation especially appropriate to internal consultation in institutions of higher education. As a member of the faculty, I was both assigned and elected to a variety of committees in the school and university. In my experience, participation on committees is often considered a chore, a way to protect one's territory, or a duty to be performed as best one can.

Futility and cynicism are common reactions to committee work in universities.

In some of the committees in which I participated, my role in the university was discussed as part of normal conversation. One committee member jokingly suggested that the committee itself could use a consultant. I took the remark seriously, though, and asked how the group would feel if I took a consultant role as part of my committee activity. There was no overt objection, so I participated in the committee's work but assumed responsibility for reviewing the ground we had covered, reminding the group of the committee's purposes, and commented on process when conflict arose among committee members. My interjections were viewed as helpful, and I continued the role throughout the year.

After this experience it occurred to me that committees are, after all, assemblies of faculty members from varied disciplines, much like the faculty study group. They carry out the work of the schools and university, and each has the potential to move the university toward improved practices and policies —toward gradual change. I have written about consultation to committees elsewhere (Bardon, 1979), but I want to point out here that committees have been much maligned. They are potent forces for good or for harm in an institution. They are complex groups and should be taken seriously. Therapy and training groups do not have monopolies on interesting problems or group dynamics. From a consultation viewpoint, it is fascinating to follow the flow of interchange, detect the hidden agendas, and observe the influence of leader style on committee activity. It is possible to help members accomplish the purposes for which the committee was established or to help them understand that their purposes cannot be carried out unless changes are made in responsibility. Committee members can learn to accept each others' view and respect the differences. Participants can come away from meetings feeling they have not wasted their time. Actions can be taken that improve the school. Every committee brings together people who often suspect that those unlike them are muddleheaded, wrong, or beneath consideration. Every committee meeting is an opportunity to clarify erroneous impressions and enhance interchange among faculty members.

One problem that remains unresolved is my unwillingness to impose the role of consultant on a committee. In the one committee where my role as consultant emerged naturally, it was possible for me to clarify my position and gain special status in the group. I asked myself what might happen if I took my participation as a committee member or chairperson seriously and sought to clarify committee purposes and induce committee members to work together harmoniously. Could I do this without imposing on others or interfering, unasked, with the prerogatives of the committee chair? I decided that it was not underhanded or unethical to help committees accomplish their goals, enhance group cohesiveness, and diminish unproductive group conflict. Although I was using consultant skills, I was not *being* a consultant in a formal sense. There is nothing wrong with being a good committee member in a special way—after all, every member brings to the committee special skills and experience. Therefore I could deliberately be consultative without being a consultant, just as one can be therapeutic without having the formal designation of therapist. I have continued to function on committees in this way and am considered a constructive and cooperative committee member and chairperson. Nevertheless, I am still concerned about the appropriateness of my stance.

The Project in Retrospect

During the first year of its operation, it became clear that the Office of Educational Development, especially the faculty study group, was expensive. The dean was unable to provide all the support funds (travel, consultant visits, research assistants) he had promised. Release of one faculty member from two courses per semester required covering four courses a year per faculty member with adjunct faculty or requesting other faculty to take teaching overloads. I wrote a grant proposal for foundation support during the first year, only to learn that no granting foundation would support efforts for faculty development in only one unit of a university. The one foundation that expressed interest wanted a total university commitment to the plan.

In the second year of operation, I proposed a university-wide plan—extending the idea of the faculty study group across academic units and establishing consultant services for the whole university. This plan, while strongly supported by some of the deans, was not supported by central administration. In its view, faculty development and consultant services were best done by department chairpersons in their official capacity as supervisors and administrators.

Within the School of Education, a number of faculty members became increasingly vocal in their condemnation of the faculty study groups. Some were ideologically opposed to empirical research, behavioral psychology, and the importance of psychology in education; they viewed my leadership in the project as administrative support for a point of view they did not want to encourage. Members of the study group reported that remarks had been made that they were in the "special education class." Justifiable complaints were made about excessive teaching loads created by released time for study group participants and lack of school funds available for other projects because of the cost of the office. It was clear that the project was promoting counterforces that could destroy the very purpose of the office.

Just before the end of the second year of the project, I submitted my second-year evaluation report to the dean and faculty. I recommended that the Office of Educational Development be discontinued in its present form; without outside funding or additional support from the university, its merits (and there were many) were outweighed by the problems caused primarily by lack of adequate financing. I agreed to continue to serve the school in a consultant role without the office. The dean, with reluctance, accepted my decision and admitted that he too had become increasingly concerned about the office's cost and the few faculty members who were unhappy with its activities.

Since the office terminated, I have continued to serve unofficially as a consultant to faculty members. My sphere of influence in the school, however, has narrowed to only a portion of the faculty, as the rifts in the faculty that influenced my decision to disband the office have created major schisms and tensions among faculty members. However, through the same process that worked earlier in encouraging faculty members to seek me out, I am now serving informally as a consultant to faculty members in other units of the university. The major sources for consultees have been my activities on university and school committees and referrals from those with whom I have worked. I have continued to use, with considerable success, consultation skills and process in many aspects of my work in the university. I am currently serving as chairperson of the university's planning council, charged by the chancellor with developing a revised mission for the university into the twenty-first century. The assignment involves the coordination of the work of a council and eight task groups, a total of 135 faculty members, trustees, alumni, and undergraduate and graduate students. The role is best described as consultative–collaborative, assisting with decision making, supportive, clarifying, synthesizing, conflict resolving, all toward a common goal. I have developed a graduate course called Consultation in Education: Theory and Process and would like to be regarded as a professional consultant who views his role in the university as helping others to resolve their professional and academic problems.

Of the seven people who participated in the faculty study group, three were promoted from assistant to associate professor with tenure. One was not offered a contract and has left higher education. One chose not to seek promotion and has left the university as a result of decisions made while in the study group. Five of the seven have published articles in some way influenced by participation in the group. Relationships among those still at UNC-G are cordial but not close, influenced more by subsequent problems and discord in the school than by past associations.

In retrospect, two questions occur to me. Would it have been better to undertake the project—to try to achieve the dean's goals for the Office of Educational Development—by using an outside rather than inside consultant? And if I were to begin over, what might I do differently?

An outside consultant, if carefully selected, could certainly have organized and conducted a faculty study group not unlike the kind reported in this chapter. This person could also have offered consultation on professional problems to individual faculty members. Use of an outside consultant might, in fact, have been a less expensive way to offer leadership to the study group. The outside consultant would have had to be available on a regular basis over an extended period of time, however. Moreover, some of the major benefits noted by members of the study group might not have occurred with an outside consultant. Intimate knowledge of the daily activities of the school and university were valuable assets to me as group leader/consultant. The group members were not always concerned with subject matter; they were concerned with their life in the institution. I cannot easily conceive how an outside consultant could have known enough about the subtle aspects of life in *this* school and *this* university to deal with the issues and problems that arose in the group meetings. Group interaction took place in the mailroom, in the lounge, in faculty meetings, and in informal conversations throughout the year. As part of these interactions, I believe I was more helpful and influential than an outside consultant, available only periodically, would have been. Consultation to individual faculty members was facilitated by easy availability. I believe that many faculty members would not have sought assstance if they had had to make an appointment. And, of course, consultation to committees would not have occurred at all if an outside consultant had been used.

Perhaps many of the purposes of the faculty study group might have been achieved in shorter, more intensive workshops or meetings or faculty retreats. Perhaps. But my own experience has been that the carryover from isolated short meetings to daily life is inevitably tenuous. I continue to believe that the best way to influence an institution is by living in it day after day. Despite the problems involved in being an inside consultant, I still contend that more can be accomplished to facilitate faculty development and institutional improvement from the inside than the outside. The only exceptions that make sense to me are the outside consultants who enter the institution with either expert or coercive authority to recommend changes—using their power, that is, to persuade people to do things they might not otherwise do. For example, coercive authority might best be used when a person consults on a preliminary site visit in preparation for an accreditation visit. Expert authority might best be used when faculty members know what they want to do about a specific activity and seek assistance in getting it done well.

What might I do differently? I would pay attention to the mini-lessons in this chapter. I would report to the entire faculty more often, involving members of the faculty study group in reporting. I would discuss problems in offering consultation services with the faculty on an ongoing basis so that rumors and false assumptions about the consultant's work do not develop. I would reorganize the entire project to include less faculty time in order to cut costs. I would preview the work of the faculty study group in open sessions as a way of recruiting faculty members and helping them understand what the group can and cannot offer them. I would be more open about my role as a consultant to committees and extend my services to committees on which I did not myself serve. I would work harder to keep the university's administrators informed of my activities. I would try to help them understand the difference between consultation from a department chair—who must make hard decisions about faculty members and sit in judgment on them—and a consultant whose purpose is to help faculty do what they want to do in their way, regardless of merit pay requirements, tenure decisions, administrative ratings, and all the other activities that prevent chairpersons from being collaborative and neutral consultants.

I must say, however, that if I had done all these things, I am still convinced that the project would have been discontinued. It would have been discontinued because the university's budget became increasingly strained; outside funds for faculty development activities were no longer available; administrative changes in the university took place; and dissident faculty members would have continued to thwart any activity they opposed, especially if it seemed likely to succeed.

Lesson number 8: Things work out but not always the way they are planned. Yet planning is necessary in order to get started. If you do not have a thoughtful and carefully constructed plan to put into effect, you cannot do much. If you persist with the plan even after evidence suggests it will not work, however, you will fail to grow. Institutions are at the mercy of so many complex factors, it is axiomatic that change will take place but not always in a predictable way. Anyone who wants to serve as an inside consultant in institutions of higher education had better be prepared for change, disappointment, and success in unexpected ways.

Setting Up and Disseminating Training Programs for Social Problem Solving 8

Ellis L. Gesten
Roger P. Weissberg

The list of challenges facing our public school system in the 1980s is by any account staggering. Directly or indirectly a majority of these problems are a reflection of stresses facing the community at large. As society changes, schools are forced to accommodate whether or not the resources to do so are avail-

We regret not being able to recognize individually the many teachers, university students, school administrators, and children who over the years have made important contributions to the social problem-solving (SPS) program. Among those whose imprimatur appears most unmistakably on final SPS products are core groupers Roberto Flores de Apodaca, Mark Rains, Bruce Rapkin, Ed Davidson, and Nancy Liebenstein. We are deeply indebted also to two extremely capable former undergraduates, Kathy Doherty-Schmid and Julie Polifka; to Helen Oosterveen-Amish, our

able. These days they usually are not. Many of the current crises facing teachers and administrators can be traced to shifts in cultural patterns, economics, and demographic trends over which there is virtually no local control.

The increased incidence of marital disruption is a prime example of one such cultural change that has severely affected the school system. In 1976 there were five divorces for every ten marriages, and the gap has narrowed still further since then (Bloom, Asher, and White, 1978). It has been estimated that nearly half of all children born in 1980 will spend at least some of their formative years in a single-parent family. Not only were there far fewer children of divorce in the 1950s and earlier, but the topic was discussed less openly in the schools. By contrast, in many schools today the majority of children have experienced a breakup of their family, some more than once, and what used to be a rarity has become the norm. Divorce is a frequent topic of discussion among classroom teachers seeking ways to assist their students, as well as among children themselves. One perhaps extreme example of the relevance of divorce is given by a fourth-grade class in a Connecticut school that conducted a year-long project on the subject. Interviews with judges, talks with mental health professionals, and extensive class discussion of their own personal experiences led to the publication of a book by, for, and about children of divorce that promises to be a big seller.

A significant proportion of the increased demand for mental health services in the schools stems from stress created by divorce and other life events. Teachers have in general become more sensitive to the acting-out and at times depressive symptoms associated with divorce that interfere with children's ability to learn. Rarely, however, does a school mental health referral solve these problems. There are simply too many youngsters with vast unmet psychosocial needs for attention, support, and guidance than support staff can handle. This stress on the

---

master master teacher; to David Rose, videotape artist; to Sharon De Vita, supertypist and friend; and, finally, to Emory Cowen, Primary Mental Health Project director and mentor in the finest sense of the word.

system has been further fueled by the passage of Public Law 94-142, which requires schools to provide a free, appropriate education in a minimally restrictive environment for all children with special needs.

A second challenge facing our schools, with implications for the increased service load, is tied to the present state of our national economy. Spiraling inflation, high interest rates, increased taxes, food and energy costs—all have left fewer dollars available for education. Federal and state funding cutbacks are matched by the reluctance of many local communities to raise local property taxes needed for their schools. As more and more school referendums fail, schools have been forced to operate on an austerity plan cutting out such "extras" as sports programs and library acquisitions. While some districts have found creative ways to generate income, others have gone bankrupt and been taken over by the courts. In all but the wealthiest of areas, schools are being asked to do more for less money. Accountability and cost effectiveness, concepts previously reserved for the business community, are now tossed about quite commonly in district administrative offices. Once again it is ultimately the front-line workers, teachers, who feel the pressure.

A third crisis affecting districts to varying degrees has been created by the demographic shift to smaller families as the population bulge known as the baby boom completes its education. This trend is reinforced by the increased acceptance and availability of birth control and abortion and the high cost of raising a large family these days. With fewer children in each successive entering class, younger teachers are being laid off, often despite as much as ten years of tenure credit, and schools are being closed. This phenomenon is particularly prevalent in the Northeast and Midwest. One suburban district in which we worked has seen the average age of its teachers steadily climb to the point where there are few staff members less than thirty years old. These school closings have serious consequences—great anxiety among teachers whose jobs are threatened, protracted conflict between parent groups and school officials over the loss of neighborhood schools, the absence of young, energetic teachers fresh out of school along with the new ideas and willingness to take risks they bring, and frequent overcrowding in the schools that remain open and receive the overload.

This list of concerns is by no means exhaustive, omitting as it does such key issues as strains caused by busing to achieve racial balance and the psychosocial abuse and physical violence to which increasing numbers of teachers are exposed. Nonetheless the point is clear. There is a confluence of pressures threatening the ability of our public schools to perform their traditional mission, which moreover has created a series of new roles for which schools and teachers are ill prepared to cope. As parents from intact families pursue dual careers, and single parents struggle to remain solvent, children receive less parenting than previous generations. School staff are forced by default to take on more responsibility for the socialization of their charges. As these pressures increase, teachers as a group have become more dissatisfied and suspicious. "What next?" is a question frequently heard in the teachers lounge. A new term, *teacher burnout,* has even been coined to describe the syndrome of frustration that has led many to seek new careers outside of education.

Active concern and involvement with these issues permeated the school climate of the district in which our skills training project was based. In many ways, the existence of these challenges created the opportunity to develop the program, helped to define the intervention structure and process, and set limits as well on how much we could hope to accomplish. Teachers were frustrated by the impossibility of simultaneously teaching the three Rs, maintaining classroom discipline, and meeting the enormous psychosocial needs of their children as well. At the same time, to ask for help was seen as tantamount to admitting inadequacy, difficult at any time, but especially so during periods of mandatory cutbacks. Administrators for their part were aware of the tension and the need to respond to teachers' concerns. In casting about for solutions a specialist was brought in to implement small-group components of Glasser's Schools Without Failure program in elementary classrooms. The project collapsed after the withdrawal of the consultant, however, and did not produce an objective record of accomplishment. Of greatest importance for our own work was the anxiety expressed by some parents that teachers were getting away from academics and instead doing "sensitivity training." Spring of 1976 found the district not only suspicious of any program that smacked of "affective education" but with extremely limited program development and in-service training funds.

Having identified the broad context, in the following pages we describe a training program developed to improve the teacher's ability to cope in the classroom and to enhance children's adjustment. The Social Problem Solving (SPS) training program was designed to teach children a cognitive-behavioral approach to the resolution of daily interpersonal conflicts. The curriculum package made extensive use of modeling and role playing to teach the component skills and promote transfer of learning beyond the classroom. This primary prevention project has progressed from a pilot phase during the 1976-77 school year through successive modifications, local expansion, and attempts at large-scale dissemination. Though extensive evaluations have been conducted (Gesten and others, 1982; Weissberg and others, 1981; Weissberg and others, 1981), results of these studies will be mentioned only briefly here. The focus will instead be on problems and processes associated with entry, program development, local expansion and program continuity, and dissemination. Our struggles, failures, and partial successes likely have the most meaning for the consultant seeking to develop a long-term relationship with a host school or district. In our experience this sort of consultative role seems to offer the best prospects for significant system change.

Entering the System

We began neither as outsiders nor insiders to the school district, occupying instead an intermediate position that provided both ambiguity and flexibility in our negotiations. Gesten had worked for three years as both coordinator of research and clinical consultant for the Primary Mental Health Project (PMHP), a preventive mental health program conducted jointly by several local school districts and the University of Rochester. In this capacity he had consulted frequently with both teachers and school administrators and established close associations with many. This history of positive relationships via PMHP helped greatly in securing permission to develop the present project. Weissberg was at the time a graduate student in clinical psychology at the University and a PMHP trainee. The project's twin goals are early detection and intervention with children experiencing school adjustment difficulties. Its 23-year history has been extensively documented elsewhere (Cowen and others, 1975) and will not be recounted here.

Several aspects of the Primary Project are, however, extremely relevant to the development of our training model. Its basic structure involves the use of school-based paraprofessionals working under the supervision of a school psychologist and social worker. These individuals meet one-on-one or in small weekly groups with primary graders identified as at risk through systematic screening. While extremely supportive of the program, many teachers were openly jealous of the initial training and professional consultation provided project aides. In spite of their own pivotal role in many PMHP school conferences, teachers, unlike the aides, lacked a forum designed expressly for them. They wanted help dealing with the child's emotions and behavior when he or she was not with the aide—that is, most of the school day.

Apart from the special attention given paraprofessionals, a second characteristic of the program created stress: the requirement that children be removed from the classroom for treatment. This mode of service delivery provided, as a byproduct, welcome short-term relief for some teachers, but it created scheduling nightmares for others whose youngsters were already enrolled in a variety of special programs. How could they be expected to achieve already difficult academic goals when children were available only one or two hours per day for instruction?

A final, at times irksome, issue—for both our central planning group and school district administrators alike—related to referral rates. If this was indeed a preventive program, and children were improving as our data suggested, why were referral rates still on the upswing? While much of the trend seemed to be a function of increased numbers of troubled children and the greater diagnostic sensitivity of referring teachers, the question was still legitimate. We determined that something more truly preventive should be done even earlier in children's history to reduce the need for later intervention.

With these observations, we decided upon several a priori decisions in the form of procedures and objectives. First, a skills building or educational approach, rather than a traditional mental health approach, would be used to inoculate youngsters against stress from life and conflict. Second, teachers, rather than outsiders, would be trained as the primary agents of change. This would eliminate the need to pull children from class, maximize teacher involvement, and improve the prospects of the program's continuity beyond year's end. The enhancement of competence in the host community rather than perpetuation of the consultant's role is for us and others (Iscoe, 1974; Kelly, 1971) a hallmark of both sound community psychology and consultation practice. Finally, it was agreed that the content of the program would center on social problem solving. Our reading of the literature indicated that this area held much promise for the promotion of children's adjustment (Spivack and Shure, 1974) and could easily be expanded to include a classroom management component for teachers.

Once we had diagnosed the problem and set preliminary goals, one crucial step remained before schools could be approached—the development of an intervention team. Key project staff were drawn primarily from the clinical psychology graduate program at the University of Rochester. Students from the university were regularly involved in training and service projects at the Center for Community Study, an outpost of the psychology department directed by Emory Cowen that served as headquarters for PMHP and other community programs. The precedent for placing graduate students in applied settings as part of their community training was well established. Indeed, the long history of productive collaboration between the university and several local school districts had created fertile soil for the growth of new ideas and projects.

Weissberg, the first graduate student to express interest in the project, remained a member of what became known in-house as the "SPS core group" even as other students came and left over the years. During the pilot year, the group headed by Gesten included Weissberg and two other graduate students. Since each person had many other responsibilities in addition to the development of the project, a system of regular twice-weekly meetings was established. This system broke down, however, as we quickly determined that the project was day by day becoming larger than we could imagine. Moreover, the purpose for which the group had initially been formed—division of labor—was modified long before the first lesson was ever taught. The paramount importance of the group as a social support system, the key buffering and energizing purpose it served, would be hard to overestimate. Accordingly, we have come to view the establishment of a healthy work setting for oneself as an important, if much overlooked, phase of the consultation process.

A critical decision confronting our working group related to the selection of an appropriate point of entry to the system. From whom should we be seeking official permission? And, beyond this, whose active support and cooperation would be required for the project to succeed? We were in agreement that the preferred strategy would have been to secure formal sanction from the highest administrative level, working our way down to the many principals and teachers with whom we had PMHP contacts. Having secured this degree of commitment, we would be able to proceed with maximum freedom and could reassure school staff that their involvement would have administrative backing. This agreement notwithstanding, plans for a meeting with the superintendent were abandoned for what seemed like good reasons in favor of a somewhat more risky strategy.

The reasons for the change were highly pragmatic. Long a supporter of mental health services in general, and the Primary Mental Health Project in particular, the superintendent had made several recent comments concerning the Back to Basics movement that was gaining momentum in the community. It was feared that this shift in position might jeopardize support for a new mental health oriented project. A second worry was that an effort might be made to house the project under instructional services rather than mental health. Given the bias shared there against any affectively oriented program, this arrangement did not seem desirable.

Initial contact with the district was made instead at the grass-roots level of individual principals and teachers. As a program consultant to Hawthorne, PMHP's laboratory demonstration school in that district, Gesten knew the principal to be a risk taker and advocate of innovative programming. The task was to obtain the principal's support along with an agreement not to mandate teacher involvement. Permission was readily given, along with helpful validation of the negotiating strategy devised by our group. The superintendent was in fact under pressure from several quarters and this was not the time to present him with new initiatives, even if they were at no cost to the district. Perhaps most importantly our colleague felt confident he had authority to approve the project at his level.

Of perhaps greatest value was the assistance provided by this principal in identifying the two other schools needed to complete the intervention/evaluation design. District staff understood that each of our demonstration projects included a strong evaluation component. The type, but not the fact, of evaluation was open to discussion and compromise. The principal, call him Mr. Millman, confirmed what we already suspected—that the school was simply too small a community to provide all the teachers we needed. It would be impossible to keep experimental and control teachers from knowing about each other's activities and perhaps sharing information about new skills being learned. With the principal's help we selected two other demographically comparable schools whose teachers would receive either an abridged version of the program to establish the effort required for skill acquisition or no treatment (a standard control group). Mr. Millman's personal contact with the control school's principal, an extremely conservative person who generally did not support new programs, was influential in obtaining entry there. The third principal was new in the district and a strong advocate of mental health.

Approval of the principal was seen as a necessary, but not

sufficient, step toward recruitment of teacher trainers. Since this was an experimental project and we would be making many demands on participants, we wanted to be sure that teachers were true volunteers. Given the lack of control over school policy and low status that teachers generally experience, every effort would be made to develop a spirit of collaboration.

The procedure for soliciting teacher interest was somewhat different in each setting, dependent largely on our history with various school staffs and the principal's leadership style. At Hawthorne, where previous collaboration had established a high level of trust, the principal was willing to absent himself—thus removing a key element of pressure teachers might otherwise feel. Since our program plan called for three third-grade teachers per school but there were only four or five in each, we had very few degrees of freedom. Based on a bad experience the previous year in which the presence of one vocal skeptic quickly polarized a small group and ultimately quashed plans for another project, we decided to contact teachers individually. Although this approach took far longer, it provided a better format for dealing with reluctance to take on a major obligation, many details of which were not yet known. After discussing with teachers the classroom behavior problems they faced every day, we explained that the social problem-solving program we proposed could be viewed preventively as a kind of survival kit children could use to solve interpersonal problems effectively and independently. We expected in addition that the program would aid classroom management by providing the teacher a clear framework for discussing and resolving conflict—whether with an individual child, a small group, or an entire classroom. Teachers were at the same time invited to participate in curriculum development to whatever extent their interest and time permitted. Much to our excitement and relief, three of the four teachers agreed to participate, two eagerly and one with some anxiety about the amount of work involved.

The initial teacher meeting at Parker School—the proposed site of our shortened training—was a near disaster. The principal insisted on a group format and his presence at the meeting. Though his intentions were positive and supportive, we were concerned that his lack of knowledge about the project, combined with the pressure to volunteer that his presence implied, would turn teachers away. This is exactly what happened. Instead of viewing the program as an opportunity for prevention, they wanted to know why *their* school had been selected. The implication was that some sort of sinister criterion had been used. Did we think their classes were more poorly managed than others in the district?

Just as the situation seemed bleak, the principal was called to the office and we were left alone with the teachers. After some initial discomfort the ensuing discussion revealed that their objections had less to do with the merits of our proposed program than with their resentment of all the changes the principal was attempting to institute at once. Whereas the previous principal spent most of his time in the office and viewed his role as a crisis manager, Mr. McDonald frequently visited classrooms unannounced and saw himself as a program planner. Teachers were unprepared for the dramatic change. Convinced that we understood their position, and that they could indeed choose not to become involved, much to our surprise all three volunteered to join the project. For us this incident demonstrated the feelings of powerlessness and unmet needs for support that teachers share. In addition to teaching specific skills, our project would likely have to provide assistance for teachers in these areas as well.

A further serendipitous benefit derived from a debriefing with the principal at which he expressed both surprise at the teachers' decision and interest in examining what had occurred. He shared his frustration in getting staff to go along with his ideas and, essentially, solicited our observations and assistance. In the end what had appeared initially to be a serious crisis helped us to solidify our relationship with the teachers and principal.

It was in the third and final school that we anticipated the greatest problems securing cooperation. We would not be offering any services there and believed from prior experience (Cowen and Gesten, 1980) that teachers and principal alike might resent being a comparison group. In the interest of sound evaluation practice we were nervous about even mentioning that a comparative study was under way. After much debate in our group, it was decided that our relationship with the schools was of paramount importance. If we were to maintain open communication, the basic nature of the design would have to be shared. For teachers to have learned about the evaluation secondhand, a near certainty in such a small district, would have been far too damaging at a time when teachers felt so insecure about their jobs and trust was such a key issue. This direct approach, combined with an expressed willingness to train control teachers after the evaluation, enhanced our rapport with teachers, but it created some problems for the evaluation that will be mentioned later. One of the third-grade teachers whom we knew personally agreed to introduce us to two other teachers, and all three were willing to serve as controls. In retrospect, the fact that the anticipated reluctance to participate never materialized was likely due as much to our friendship with the one teacher as anything else.

The final element of our recruitment effort relates to teacher motivation and reinforcement; it has been saved for last because of its key but often overlooked role in the consultation process. Even a casual inspection of the program demands being placed on teachers revealed that we were asking a great deal from them. Participants were required to commit themselves to attending weekly training sessions, teach a new curriculum, and cooperate with an evaluation. Their role in the latter would require the completion of rating scales as well as the disruption of their class for a week both before and after the program when individual, small-group, and class measures were to be administered. Although we assumed the program would have tangible benefits to teachers in the form of improved class management and better-adjusted children, we could not be certain—and in any case the payoff would not come until near the end of the school year. Recognizing this inequity and the related fact that the reinforcement system of university-based consultants and teachers are quite different, an arrangement was made with the university to recognize teachers' special efforts. Participants in both training conditions were given the option of receiving tuition-free graduate credit in return for the heavy commitment we required. Although teachers were generally not informed of this option until they had agreed to participate, the use of course credit helped both teachers and ourselves feel better about the program's demands. Teachers reported working harder for this "course" than any other, and they were able to apply credits earned toward merit increases.

Developing the Program

Teacher Involvement. Ostensibly ready to roll up our sleeves and begin developing detailed lesson plans, we found ourselves confronted by issues of teacher involvement and program ownership. Although we had identified a bona fide gap in school services and targeted a problem to which teachers in particular could easily relate, the proposed solution was thus far entirely our own creation. For the program to succeed it seemed desirable that teachers become actively invested in the program from the start. This was important for a number of reasons. For one, while members of our planning group had worked previously to develop intervention programs and had treated children in clinical settings, we had limited classroom experience with young children. For a short period Gesten had taught emotionally disturbed children aged seven to nine. Sharing that piece of history had helped to establish credibility with teachers, but it was of little value when it came to answering key questions. How long should lessons be? What is the vocabulary level of third graders? How many new concepts can be introduced in a single class period? At what point does the repetition required for effective learning become simply boring? To answer these and other questions, the teachers' involvement was essential.

A second reason for wanting teachers to develop a personal stake in the project related to continuity. Without prejudging the outcome of our evaluation, we hoped it might be the first in a series of efforts to promote social skills in the classroom. To accomplish this would require a cadre of teachers with both the necessary skills and motivation to continue the program.

Our efforts to involve teachers in the development of the curriculum were only partially successful. To begin with, we informed teachers that program content would be largely built around children's classroom and playground problems with peers and adults rather than conflicts in the home. The latter were too emotionally charged for some teachers to deal with initially, and by structuring the program around classroom issues teachers' needs were given top priority. Each participant was asked to rank children's interpersonal problems that occur with some frequency in the classroom and are difficult to handle. The group had little trouble coming up with ten or twenty problem situations each. Their lists ultimately formed the basis of several class lessons as well as a series of modeling videotapes. Teachers could see both in words and on film the results of their contribution.

Problems developed, however, when we attempted to have teachers join in the writing of specific lessons. We had by then already collected information from several similar programs directed to a different age group or type of child than our own target group. Spivack and Shure's (1974) work at Hahnemann was limited to inner-city preschoolers and kindergartners. Analysis of the Hahnemann project among others (Allen and others, 1976; Elardo and Caldwell, 1979; McClure, Chinsky, and Larcen, 1978) suggested that a new approach was needed—an approach combining the strengths of prior interventions with a highly structured, behaviorally oriented curriculum. Teachers politely, but firmly, declined the opportunity to join our writing team by citing team pressure and the fact that we were the experts, not they. A compromise was struck that seemed to satisfy nearly everyone. We would write a rough draft of each lesson and the teachers would then modify it. Additionally, teachers helped us to develop a consistent framework for each lesson, including sections for objectives, materials, procedure, special instructions, and enrichment ideas. After each lesson the teacher was to complete an evaluation sheet rating such things as clarity of instructions and children's understanding of the concepts taught, as well as recommendations for change. This evaluation formed the basis for a postprogram curriculum revision.

The Curriculum. Although our primary focus is on consultation process, to understand the project as a whole requires some knowledge of the concepts being taught. During the pilot year the full-package program was divided into seventeen biweekly lessons taught from February to mid-April 1977. Each session consisted of two to four distinct activities and required thirty-five to fifty minutes. The four-unit curriculum was built around the teaching of six problem-solving steps:

- Prerequisite skill: Look for signs of upset feelings.

1. Problem definition: Know exactly what the problem is.
2. Goal statement: Decide on your goal.
3. Restraint: Stop and think before you act.
4. Generation of alternatives: Think of as many solutions as you can.
5. Consideration of consequences: Think of the different things that might happen.
6. Implementation: When you think you have a good solution, try it.

- Recycle: If your first solution fails, try again.

Unit 1 consisted of five lessons and was divided: Part 1 was Introduction to Feelings; part 2 was Problem Sensing and Identification. Children were first taught how to recognize and label feelings in themselves and others. Games, role-plays, and cartoons illustrated that feelings—even strong feelings—are a normal part of life in school and elsewhere. The problem-sensing section developed an orientation to interpersonal rather than personal or impersonal problems. For purposes of the program it was explained that "a problem is something that happens between people which gives someone an unhappy or upset feeling." The first three problem-solving steps were introduced during this unit.

Units 2 and 3 each included four lessons and focused on the two problem-solving skills considered crucial for the age group: generation of alternative solutions and consideration of consequences. Solution generation (SPS step 4) is simply brainstorming in which both teachers and students are instructed to defer judgment about the quality of a response. The rationale for this component is that the more solutions, the greater the likelihood an effective option will be found. Teaching children how to anticipate and then evaluate the consequences of potential solutions was the most difficult part of the program. They were taught to "think ahead to what might happen next" (after each solution) and decide if it was something they would want to happen. The last two problem-solving steps were taught in this unit. The final segment of the curriculum consisted of a four-lesson review unit in which the entire problem-solving sequence was integrated and practiced. All the concepts were applied to real-life school, neighborhood, and family problems via role playing. In this fashion an attempt was made to promote generalization of skills and behavior taught during formal lessons.

Emphasis was placed on class discussion, modeling, extensive role playing, and behavioral rehearsal. At least one lesson from each unit involved videotapes in which new concepts were introduced and children were shown using the problem-solving steps. Each narrated videotape vignette consisted of the real-life problems supplied by teachers; these situations were acted out and often written with the help of a cooperative third-grade class from a nonparticipating school. Specific situations dealt with problems of equity, bullying, stealing, copying, teasing, joining a group, and destruction of property. Tapes were accompanied by a discussion guide outlining points to be highlighted during class discussion at planned stopping points.

The production of training videotapes is an example of a task that would not have been accomplished without an effective support group. Two group members charged with this task seriously underestimated the time required, as well as the technical complexities of writing, typing, and editing five training tapes lasting fifteen or twenty minutes each. Fortunately, we were assisted by a friend who generously volunteered his videotape expertise and were able to secure a limited budget to rent time at a local television station's production studio. The entire project team pulled together working around the clock on several occasions to meet final deadlines. Our failure to assess realistically the resources required in advance had nearly scuttled this component of the project. At the same time, however, this crisis more than any other strengthened the personal relationships among SPS group members.

Whereas the videotape series constituted only one component of the full-package curriculum, the abridged program consisted exclusively of these training tapes. Each was developed to be a self-contained teaching package demonstrating one or more social problem-solving steps. Teachers using the tapes alone began each lesson with a brief review of previous material; they ended with a discussion of that day's training tape. This shortened training was included to determine whether modeling alone would be sufficient to produce significant skill acquisition and adjustment gain. Given the increased time and effort required to teach the complete program package, the availability of a cost-effective alternative would have important implications for widespread dissemination.

Teacher Training. Two days before teacher training was to begin we received an upsetting call from one of our teachers in Hawthorne School. She had talked the project over with her husband and both agreed that this was not the time to take on new responsibilities. With regret and guilt about the difficult position in which we were being placed, she was nonetheless withdrawing from the project. After coping with our disappointment and anger, we realized there had been early signs we had chosen to downplay or ignore. In order to recruit enough teachers to satisfy the requirements of our design, we had minimized concerns about the amount of project time required—concerns that this teacher had expressed from the very start. Having gone to great lengths to shelter teachers from the principal's pressure to volunteer, we had in fact applied pressure of a different sort ourselves. While the timing of the object lesson was unfortunate, it would no doubt have been far worse had the teacher informed us after the program began.

This crisis provided our group an excellent opportunity to utilize the same problem-solving steps we were about to teach children. After we got over the feeling that the sky had fallen, we created a remarkably long list of alternative solutions. These ranged from asking the teacher if we ourselves could teach the lessons in her class to delaying the project's start and identifying another target school. Consideration of the consequences associated with each solution led to the choice of a strategy that had both positive and negative elements. Our decision was to invite a highly regarded second-grade teacher from the same school to join the two remaining third-grade teachers. We felt that the curriculum, with only slight modifications, was applicable to that age group; and the teacher concurred. She had been an important inside contact during the planning stages and would therefore require little additional preparation. In the more personal sense, she was well liked by her colleagues and had remarkable enthusiasm. Her presence would allow us to test the potential applicability of our model to younger children. On the negative side, our evaluation design was compromised and we were confronted once again by the constraints of reality and the hazards of field research.

Based on an analysis of implementation problems associated with most school curriculum innovations, considerable emphasis was placed on teacher training. The importance of providing appropriate orientation, ongoing training, and feedback was dramatically illustrated several years previously during an attempt to implement a new reading program locally. While in agreement that a revision in the district's approach was long overdue, and generally supportive of the program in question, teachers disliked the manner of its introduction and lack of subsequent follow-up during the year. After a brief introduction to the program during a large group meeting, teachers were expected to begin implementation the following week on their own. By the time corrective measures were taken by district administrators, the reading program was in shambles.

To help ensure that teachers would be comfortable conducting our program, and that concepts would be taught consistently in all classrooms, training was ongoing throughout the nine-week program. Weekly sessions were held separately for teachers in each experimental school led by at least two members of our core group. Also present at sessions for the full-package training group were undergraduate aides, two per classroom, assigned to assist teachers, particularly with small-group role-playing activities. These specially selected university students were enrolled in a seminar/practicum taught by our group entitled "Community Psychology in the Schools." Their enthusiastic involvement with the project helped provide a much more intensive training experience for children than would otherwise have been possible.

Training sessions followed a format developed with the participants and were held at school to minimize any inconvenience for them. Teachers received one unit's worth of lessons at a time and were instructed to review the material before each training session. The initial portion of the meeting was spent evaluating the previous lessons and discussing implications for the current week's work. Next came a presentation of new material by one of us, followed by role playing of each lesson. Teachers were generally unwilling to participate actively in this last segment, particularly during the first few weeks. Reluctantly, we agreed to their request that we model the teaching of each lesson. It soon became clear that teachers were made uncomfortable not by our presence but by the prospect of performing in front of their peers.

Their attitude should not have been surprising, considering the isolated context in which they work. Teachers virtually never observe their colleagues teach, and they are unaccustomed to giving and receiving feedback. Understandably, it was not until people grew to know and trust each other, and we had established ourselves as teaching amateurs, that teachers themselves began to lead the lessons and solicit response. Several people have commented over the years that the opportunity to observe other teachers during both training and live lessons was for them a highlight of the program.

The final segment of each session was spent in smaller groups dividing up responsibilities for the following week. Teachers met with their classroom aides to decide who would teach each portion of the lessons and how to conduct activities requiring both.

A second consultation, exclusively for teachers, was held before school each week. These sessions lasted twenty to thirty minutes and generally served more of a troubleshooting and support function than instructional purpose. Although they had to come to school early, teachers seemed to appreciate the chance to talk about the program and other unrelated issues in a more relaxed manner (usually over donuts we brought and coffee they provided). Our other longer session was too jam-packed and hectic to allow much informal exchange. During morning meetings we were able to discuss the performance of our undergraduates openly and thus collect information useful for supervision.

Evaluation. The response from program participants during the first year was positive and supportive. Teachers reported that children learned the social problem-solving concepts and with encouragement were able to apply them in the classroom. They themselves had been taught to use the problem-solving approach to handle spontaneous individual and class problems. This technique had reportedly reduced time spent on classroom management and helped them feel more comfortable assisting children with school and home problems.

Both children and parents shared incident after incident in which these concepts had been applied at home with parents and siblings. One extremely shy third-grader described how she had used problem solving to join a group of friends at the local bowling alley instead of holding back and looking sad—her typical solution—in hopes someone would respond. Nervous about parental reaction to the program, we were relieved to get many positive reports from home. Our second-grade teacher received so many program inquiries that we arranged a special videotape showing of one class lesson for parents. The excitement and support expressed at that meeting led us to consider involving parents more actively in possible future programs.

Having sat in on many lessons, we shared some, but not all, of the positive impressions of others. Children did seem to understand the concepts and know how to apply them, especially in the full-package program. We felt, and others confirmed, that youngsters exposed only to videotapes were much less involved in the program and required considerably more prompting to implement the process. It appeared, moreover, that teachers varied a fair amount in the extent to which they incorporated the approach into their daily teaching and classroom management style. We were not sure what effect, if any, this would have on overall results. Also difficult to assess were the anecdotal reports from principals, teachers, and undergraduates that children appeared better adjusted at year's end. We ourselves lacked the day-to-day, longitudinal perspective to make those judgments, especially in the absence of comparative data from untrained children.

The formal empirical evaluation, conducted with the aid of a second undergraduate group, consisted of preassessment and postassessment and a one-year follow-up. While generally positive, the results were also contradictory in places and defy simple summarizing (Gesten and others, 1979; Gesten and others, 1982).

The most clear-cut results were obtained for skill acquisition. Children trained with the full-package program were superior to both comparison groups on cognitive and behavioral measures of problem-solving skills immediately after the program. The cognitive measure assessed each child's ability to solve hypothetical peer problems portrayed verbally and pictorially. Using a simulated problem administered outside the classroom context, the behavioral measure provided an index of generalization, indicating that children could use the concepts spontaneously even when not under the teacher's watchful eye. At the one-year follow-up, the full-package group maintained its advantage on one of two skills (consequential thinking) from the cognitive measure.

Adjustment findings were far more difficult to interpret and reflected both bad and good news. On the negative side, the immediate postprogram teacher-rated adjustment data failed to corroborate positive, impressionistic observations; moreover, they favored untrained controls on several measures. Sensitive to the potential bias of teacher rating scales, we had encouraged experimental teachers not to let positive feelings toward us or the program interfere with their ratings. In the absence of a class program, control teachers were on the other hand rating their own effectiveness over the year. This likely contributed to their extremely high end-of-year ratings. Combined these two rating sets may have contributed to our initial disconcerting adjustment results.

The good news did not appear until follow-up. With a full year to integrate and utilize newly acquired social problem-solving skills, and in turn receive positive feedback from their environment, the full-package and videotape-only groups were rated more positively than controls on seven of ten teacher-rated problem behavior and competence variables. These results were much less influenced by possible response bias for several reasons. First, ratings were made by a new group of teachers with little knowledge of the prior program. Second, program participants had been scattered across sixteen third and fourth-grade classrooms—including children not previously tested as experimentals or controls as well as those new to the school entirely. Teachers were unaware of the prior program status of their students. Finally, the fact that positive teacher ratings were largely mirrored by peer sociometric results favoring trained youngsters was seen as particularly encouraging.

Extending the Program

Buoyed by our skill acquisition results, and both confused and upset by preliminary postprogram adjustment findings, we began work the following September to regroup our forces, modify the curriculum, and try again. Our new core group was assisted in those efforts by a grant from the state of New York that allowed us to think about expansion and recruit more help.

During both the second and successive program years we were confronted by some of the same consultation issues already discussed, as well as a series of new challenges. Though we were somewhat better prepared the second time around, there were nonetheless plenty of opportunities for new learning. The purpose of this section is to describe two consultation/program development issues extracted from the matrix of concerns faced during the second and third program years. The first issue revolves around resistance from a parent group as the program included parents and expanded into an inner-city school for the first time. The second issue, while always present, came into sharpest focus during the third program year when eighteen teachers (three times the first-year group) were trained; this issue revolves around the question of program continuity.

Expansion to the Inner City. Although the pilot program was housed in a suburban setting, it had been our intention from the start to branch into an inner-city school as soon as that proved practicable. Spillover of behavior problems from the home into the classroom was more pronounced in the city than any of the surrounding suburban districts. In spite of this obvious need, we chose to begin our work in a setting whose problems were less severe but which offered greater support and prospects for initial success. Having taken a year to develop the basic program, identify a target city school, and secure funding, we spent late September and early October negotiating entry and establishing a contract with the school.

Whereas the previous year saw the SPS program established on the coattails of the Primary Mental Health Project's success, we did not have that advantage in the city. The problem was made more complex by the fact that negotiations to begin both a PMHP and SPS program were occurring simultaneously. The student population of this school was nearly 100 percent minority and included a high proportion of single-parent families receiving public assistance. The needs for service were thus enormous, and it was on this basis that district administrators recommended the school to us.

Preliminary discussions went extremely well with the principal and a highly competent third-grade teacher he had suggested as a possible social problem-solving trainer. Although we had been alerted to the existence of an active and influential parent advisory council, we had little reason to think it would oppose the project. To the contrary, the initial informal meeting with a woman identified as the key parent leader was cordial and productive. She indicated that her group would want some additional information, but she did not signal any serious roadblocks ahead. Mrs. Holmes also strongly, even passionately, confirmed our impression that there were a lot of families who needed help not currently being reached by the school mental health team. She related several cases of child abuse, family breakup and drug abuse for which she herself had been seeking help. Our mention of wanting to work with parents of children struck a particularly responsive chord in this respect.

After this encouraging beginning, we were unprepared for the issues raised at our first meeting with the advisory council. The event took place on an extremely hot and sticky September morning. In a portable classroom that lacked air conditioning, we met—a dozen or so parents, two teachers, the principal, Gesten, Weissberg, and another senior PMHP staff member.

The fact that the meeting was being chaired by another woman, not the person previously identified as the key parent leader, was the first indication there might be a problem. Our chairperson turned out to be a minister who began the session with a spirited reading from the Bible. While extremely assertive during our prior contacts, the school principal was notably less active in the presence of this group. After introducing us as members of the Primary Mental Health Project who were there to talk about two possible new school programs, he remained largely silent during the remainder of the meeting.

Several minutes into our presentation, parents interrupted with a barrage of pointed questions. At first it appeared that their overriding concern was that black children not be used as guinea pigs in some sort of testing program run primarily by white investigators. Attempts to clarify the basis of the group's anxiety proved futile. We could not determine whether concern stemmed from misinformation about our projects or from deeply rooted suspicion. In this context, a great deal of time was next spent listening to parents express their frustration with the school district's central administration for failing to deliver the services the community needed. Although sympathetic, we went to lengths to explain that we were not part of the school district but outsiders interested in assisting their children. To have been closely identified with the power structure would have been to our disadvantage given the alienation this community was experiencing.

Our response to the unspoken racial issue—could white professionals help black children?—was to make it explicit. We did not know all the special strengths and problems of their community, but we were eager to learn if they wanted our help. We also shared our prior program development experience in the inner city. Although the loss of their school would have been a serious setback, we made certain they understood that the decision to become a project school was their own.

In the discussion that ensued, parents legitimately sought reassurance on several critical points. They first wanted to know how much of the project staff would be drawn from their neighborhood. We stated our commitment to hire as many people from the community as possible and solicited their help in recruiting PMHP aides. A second issue related to the duration of funding. This school had witnessed programs come and go as grants were received and then lost just as staff began to see positive change. On this matter we could only commiserate with parents. Our own jobs were tied to the same year-to-year grant that would be providing funds for their school. While working toward securing more stable funding sources, we could not then provide any guarantee for the future. Third, parents wanted to know specifically if this was a research project. Although data would certainly be collected, we reiterated our primary goal—to establish service projects that would eventually become part of the ongoing school program. Once parents understood that this was not a one-shot study, and that evaluation results would be used primarily to modify and strengthen our projects, they gave us the green light to proceed.

Just as we were about to leave, Mrs. Holmes, the parent leader with whom we had initially met, raised a new problem. Pleased that we planned to involve parents, she wanted to know more about the proposed school meetings and home visits. It quickly became apparent that Mrs. Holmes did not share our agenda and was advocating instead another very different program for us to conduct. Rather than concentrating on children at risk via PMHP, and the entire third grade via SPS training, she suggested that we identify a handful of families with the most severe problems and concentrate all our limited resources on them. Evidently this was what Mrs. Holmes had in mind earlier when she had heard we were planning to include parents in our program.

While the proposal had merit and the cases she cited were certainly needy, to have agreed to this change in strategy would have meant the abandonment of our commitment to prevention and required the development of a whole new intervention. We explained that our funding would not allow us to make such a radical change in program direction. Certainly that was so. By way of compromise, however, we agreed to consider ways to strengthen parent involvement in concert with the parent advisory council. Somewhat alarmed by the force with which she had staked out her position, we were relieved when Mrs. Holmes agreed to work with us on this.

With hindsight it can be said that had we not met with parents that day, there would likely not have been a parent training component to the problem-solving program. Their support and active consultation turned out to be critical. For one thing, we had seriously underestimated the difficulty of getting parents to attend school programs. A follow-up meeting with SPS project teachers and Mrs. Holmes revealed that despite an activist parent advisory group, the general level of parent involvement in the school was meager. During open house and parent-teacher conference periods, an average of only four of twenty-five families per classroom was typically represented—despite several announcements and letters sent home with children. Given that we were seeking a much more intensive level of participation from parents—attendance at six weekly evening training sessions—alternative ways to reach and hook parents were needed. The mail and telephone campaign already under way in our two suburban schools could hardly be expected to succeed in the city. Many letters simply never reach parents, and more than half the families lacked telephones.

By the end of this second meeting a solution to the problem of parent recruitment was beginning to emerge. It was decided that Gesten and Weissberg would make a series of home visits to describe the program, sign up parents, and provide a system for getting parents to meetings. Mrs. Holmes was eager to be of help and volunteered time to our group. She was at the same time, however, completing work as a CETA aide and in search of part-time employment. Rather than risk losing our best bridge to the community, we decided to cut budget corners elsewhere and hire Mrs. Holmes on a time-limited basis to assist with home visits.

Though our problems with the parent program were far from solved, adding this parent leader to our team proved to be a significant breakthrough. After making several home visits together and observing her deal with parents' suspicions, we were more comfortable and effective when making visits on our own. Working together we were also able to provide transportation, babysitting, and other services that removed some of the barriers facing parents who would otherwise not be able to participate. In addition to providing a wealth of information about the community, Mrs. Holmes' involvement lent a measure of credibility to our efforts that in her absence would have taken far longer to develop. For her part, Mrs. Holmes was for the first time receiving official recognition for her special skills and role as a school/community liaison. Her interest and obvious success in this work ultimately led to a decision to seek employment in human services.

The inclusion of inner-city parents in the SPS program, while failing to provide a statistically significant advantage over classroom training alone, did have important program benefits nonetheless. Outstanding among these were changes in the curriculum that came about as a result of greater familiarity with local cultural and family patterns.

An excellent example of one such curriculum change derived from one of the few training sessions attended by the father of a child in the program. Not only was a significant proportion of our youngsters from single-parent families, but, moreover, even in cases where both parents were present in the home, we were generally unable to convince the father to attend our meetings. On this occasion the discussion was focused on alternatives to fighting in school as a way of solving problems. Noting from his head-shaking this man's discomfort, we asked what he was thinking. After some hesitation he stated his views very clearly. "Listen, I don't want to tell you how to run your program, but I will tell you one thing. If my boy ever comes home from school after a fight and tells me that he didn't hit the other kid back, I'm gonna take him down to the basement and whip his butt myself."

His remark represented the first time a parent, in our

group of eight, had been openly critical of the program. It led to an excellent discussion of the skills required to survive in a ghetto environment. We ended in agreement that aggression is sometimes necessary and represents a solution we did not want to extinguish. Instead, emphasis during training was placed on expanding the child's repertoire of responses and teaching how and when aggressive solutions, when necessary, could be implemented. Hitting someone back at the end of the day, off the schoolgrounds, had fewer negative consequences than punching that person in the classroom. This distinction was extremely helpful for our city teacher trainees, but it never came up during our pilot year in the suburbs and thus could easily have been missed.

Our expansion to the inner city and our efforts to include parents yielded mixed empirical results (Weissberg and others, 1981) but some straightforward lessons in consultation. We had entered the project too precipitously, confident that our prior work in the black community would greatly simplify the entry process. It did not. Preoccupied with our own needs to get the project going as expeditiously as possible, we had not spent adequate time getting to know our new host agency, its people, and its problems. Furthermore, when the community began to assert itself and exert legitimate pressure to be heard, we misinterpreted their response and assumed they were intent on vetoing the program. In fact, parents' pointed questions and thinly veiled warnings were not designed to scare us away but rather to establish their appropriate role in planning services for their children. Once this had been accomplished, the climate of the meeting and tenor of subsequent relations were considerably more relaxed and cooperative.

Program Continuity. Efforts to ensure program continuity began with the decision to use classroom teachers as trainers, rather than mental health professionals or other support staff. Our goal was to provide teachers with a package that, once mastered and field tested, could be taught to subsequent classes over the years. As of September 1981, after five years, approximately eighty regular classroom and learning disabilities teachers had participated in the program. Assuming twenty-five children per class yields a total of nearly two thousand children taught social problem-solving skills. If only one in four teachers opted to continue the program on their own, this would amount to an additional five hundred children per year receiving training.

Although precise figures have not yet been collected, it is our impression that at least 25 percent of our teachers continue to teach the program formally after the initial year of training. Another 25 percent or more use the curriculum in a more informal or abridged fashion. Although this leaves many children in some of our district schools with no exposure to these principles, it is nonetheless a healthy return on our initial training investment.

By the beginning of the third program year it had become obvious that a more systematic approach was required to help ensure the program's future. Our credibility was by then fairly well established, and it was no longer necessary to commit energy to the individual recruitment of program schools and teachers. To the contrary, we were faced for the first time with the dilemma of having to select from among those interested a smaller group to whom we could deliver quality service. Even with the addition of two capable graduate students to replace those finishing their degree, our resources were pressed to the limit. Unwilling to compromise on the amount of training provided teachers, nor to cut back our commitment to evaluation, another solution was called for.

A decision was made by the authors to phase out our direct involvement with the project and to turn program management over to graduate students and teachers. To accomplish this at a time when more and more teachers were requesting training would also require that certain key project procedures be clarified and simplified whenever possible. After completing a detailed analysis of program tasks and roles, and developing a framework to provide adequate supervision, support, and communication among staff, we were ready to proceed. Over the two-year period that followed, significant changes were made—in the manner of recruiting teachers, the role of graduate student program coordinators, the use of teacher trainers, and the scope of the evaluation.

The selection of teachers during the third and subsequent program years began with the identification of a limited number of schools that provided a supportive, interested principal, a minimum of three teachers at each target grade level, and an agreement to cooperate with our planned evaluation. Second, third, and fourth-grade teachers from each school were next sent a letter summarizing the program's history and concluding with a detailed calendar of critical program dates, goals, and tasks for the current year. A list of specific requirements for participating teachers was provided along with the services and benefits provided by our team.

A variety of teacher options was available, representing points on a continuum of program responsibility. From their responses we were able to identify those who were definitely interested in being trained, a group of "maybes" requiring follow-up, potential controls, teachers who wanted to be contacted again next year, as well as those (a surprisingly small number) who wanted no part of the project. Integrating this information into a sensible intervention research design—given inherent bias due to teacher self-selection, among other factors—proved to be a Sisyphean task. The final plan typically emerged after much debate, compromise, and several diplomatic missions to over and undersubscribed schools. In spite of its complications, the use of these teacher "contracts" helped to clarify mutual expectations and actually simplified recruitment during our expansion phase.

Modification of the role of both graduate students and teachers required negotiation and experimentation and got off to a somewhat shaky start. Two factors that made this transition difficult were the authors' overprotectiveness and the associated reluctance of others to assume what they perceived to be the expert's role. While understanding that it was in the project's best interest that we recede into the background, letting go was not easy. During the first year of the transition the plan was to turn over responsibility for training to graduate students and selected teachers. Unfortunately we ended up conducting or otherwise meddling in too many of these sessions. In so doing, we inadvertently undercut graduate student and teacher trainers at times by communicating to teacher trainees that we, not they, were running the show.

The centerpiece of our attempt to give the program back to the community revolved around the recruitment and utilization of so-called master teachers. These were people who had at least completed SPS training and successfully implemented the program in their classroom. The two most critical requirements, however, were a strong commitment to the program and solid relationships with teacher peers and the school principal. Besides continuing to teach the curriculum to their new classes, these new group members demonstrated many of the lessons during training meetings and shared their program experiences with others. Such contributions from a fellow teacher came to be highly valued by trainees.

Initial feedback was in fact so positive that we decided to upgrade the role of the master teacher. In the past all classroom observations and feedback sessions with teachers had been done by graduate students or senior project staff. Negotiations with school principals led to the release of master teachers for several days each year to perform these duties. Reluctant at first to assume this role vis-à-vis their peers, and unsure of their supervisory skills, at least two of the three participants came to relish this part of their job.

Teachers serving in this capacity received special recognition in the form of a stipend of approximately a hundred dollars per month from our newly acquired grant. In light of their commitment to eight or ten hours a week, and the great number of responsibilities, this was hardly a princely sum. In addition to the responsibilities noted above, for example, teachers presented the program to interested school staff and performed a number of organizational and troubleshooting tasks. In spite of this inequity, teachers expressed appreciation for the money and a satisfaction with their roles that seemed out of proportion to the true value of these reinforcers.

Upon closer examination, however, it is apparent that school settings provide extremely limited opportunities for teachers to receive acknowledgment for their teaching skills. Pay increases are for the most part tied to experience rather than merit. Promotions to an administrative position are limited, not always based on teaching ability, and unattractive to those whose first love is classroom work. Whether because of positive feedback, status, money, intrinsic rewards, or personal characteristics, teachers in this role were extremely hardworking and helped considerably to root the program in the schools where it belonged.

The final set of revisions, designed to help the program continue and expand, related to evaluation. In prior years we had simply done too much testing. Both experimental and control children received an extensive battery of measures requiring at least four hours administration and scoring time per subject for preprogram and postprogram assessments. Continuing in this way would obviously restrict the number of classrooms we could handle and, moreover, would not add much to our knowledge. To make it easier for us as well as independent districts to conduct the program and yet maintain quality control, we cut back on the measures administered and the number of children assessed. In this way, a reasonable balance was struck between the pragmatic demands of program expansion and accountability requirements.

Though the program was not yet self-sustaining, the introduction of these changes helped to provide for its continuity. With the aid of graduate students, teachers were now routinely conducting training for their colleagues. Teacher recruitment and child evaluation procedures were freed from the constraints of a tight research design, making the program more accessible to schools with fewer resources than our own. Other innovations included programs to extend SPS training to kindergartners (Winer and others, 1982) and to provide a follow-up or booster-shot sequence for previously trained youngsters. While districts continued to look to us for overall program leadership and organization, dependence on our staff for key program functions was significantly reduced.

Dissemination

By the end of the third year, local program expansion was increasingly accompanied by requests from outsiders for information and consultation. Additional inquiries resulted from a presentation given at a national conference on prevention (Gesten and others, 1979). Having logged considerable experience in the nationwide dissemination of the Primary Mental Health Project (Cowen, Davidson, and Gesten, 1980), we were reluctant to commit ourselves to another large-scale enterprise. We also thought more field testing was required to clarify inconsistencies in the relationship between social problem-solving skills and adjustment. With some ambivalence we nonetheless began to respond to mail and phone calls about the project.

The events that followed have implications for the consultant interested in change beyond the local community. How does one go about transforming the results of a successful program for use by others? Is the provision of information through the written word sufficient? What other activities are required to ensure that knowledge of innovation is put into use? What, if anything, can be done to ensure that an intervention program, once placed in the public domain, will be used in the manner intended by its authors?

We were persuaded that attempts to spread the word via journal articles would not reach our target audience: school district administrators and policy makers. In search of more effective strategies, we accepted invitations to speak at conferences and conducted workshops for a variety of mental health and education groups. To facilitate implementation in other districts we added a half-day SPS workshop to the annual PMHP national conference in Rochester, New York, attended by school district and mental health representatives. Workshop participants were provided an in-depth exposure to the problem-solving program via videotapes, a newly revised 34-lesson curriculum manual (Weissberg and others, 1980), and role playing.

While such workshops were exciting to conduct, and extremely well received, few of those who attended went on to develop programs of their own. Most participants were better equipped to apply the SPS approach on their own clinical or teaching work than to mount a systematic program. We were also limited by our grant in the type and extent of backup support that could be provided. Developing a program in one's home district, however, required more than mere knowledge of program concepts and individual lessons. The prospective implementer faced a variety of barriers: potentially uncooperative teachers, lack of a district commitment to prevention, limited classroom time—many of the same issues we ourselves had encountered. Surmounting these problems largely unassisted proved too difficult for most.

Our effort to disseminate information about the project was hampered, more than anything else, by the absence of a clear image of what we wanted to accomplish. This shortcoming was brought into sharpest focus by the aftermath of a meeting held with a member of the university's public relations department. Someone from their office had heard about our project and decided it would make good copy for a popular national magazine. Nervous about how badly we might be misquoted, we were at the same time intrigued by the size of the potential audience. It has been estimated that the average professional journal article is read by fewer than ten people. Whatever the real number, it is certain to be far fewer than the readership of these magazines—eighteen million people.

Several weeks later we were interviewed by a freelance writer whose subsequent article appeared in print several months later. We had expected to receive in response a few dozen letters from interested school professionals. Instead, over the next six weeks our mailbox overflowed with more than a thousand requests for information, manuals, professional advice, workshop sites, personal appearances, and the like. Most upsetting were the lengthy, poignant letters from parents having serious problems with their children and wondering if social problem-solving might provide some relief. We were particularly alarmed by one request for materials from a mother who wanted to use the approach with her two-year-old daughter!

This sudden windfall of publicity posed several issues aside from the most obvious one—that is, an absence of time and secretarial support to respond to our mail. How could we prevent parents from misusing the program, frustrating and perhaps upsetting their youngsters in the process? What were our ethical responsibilities to parents who seemed desperately in need of help and expected some response from these new experts? Might a way be found to realize some benefit from this seeming disaster?

In response to these concerns and our secretary's growing anguish, we made several decisions. We would not release the curriculum to parents since the program was developed for teachers and was not easily modified for home use. Parents whose children sounded like they might need treatment or assessment were sent brief individual letters. We explained that while we appreciated their concern, the kind of help they were seeking could not be provided via the mail. We suggested that if they continued to have questions, they should contact their local school or community mental health center, most of which operate on a sliding fee basis. Finally, we sent the remaining parents a form letter providing some program information and stating that if they had further interest they ask a representative of their local school district to contact us. We hoped in this way to promote positive exchange between community members and school officials. Teachers and administrators who wrote in response to the initial article or had been contacted by parents were offered a copy of the curriculum at our cost. Between two and three hundred districts took advantage of this option. Once again, however, we had no confidence that the simple provision of a training manual would lead to program implementation.

At about this point Gesten received an invitation that was hard to turn down. The department of community mental health from a county outside New York City was interested in using the SPS model to introduce the concept of prevention to local school districts. It was agreed that we would begin with a full-day workshop for the twenty or so county school superintendents or their assistants; we would proceed from there if there was sufficient interest. The department's goal was to see active prevention functioning in the schools. Social problem solving was to be the vehicle. Our complementary goal was to determine whether our program could take root and flourish in a distant setting without the day-to-day monitoring that characterized its development in Rochester.

Our two most serious obstacles were the large distance between Rochester and the New York City area and the multiple contracts that would have to be negotiated. The distance meant we would be limited to a handful of visits at most and would need to make good use of each contact. Among the most salient contracts to be negotiated was the one between us and the department, the department's with the school districts, and ours with the individual teachers. Also to be worked out eventually would be a review of understandings with principals, assistant superintendents in charge of instruction, school psychologists, and the like. To develop these contracts and process their outcomes, we requested that one half-day be built into the budget, both before and after the program. We asked in addition that at least part of that time be spent with the commissioner as well as the coordinator of prevention services, our primary contact to date. Both requests were granted.

While the workshop stirred a great deal of interest, the first snag was reached shortly thereafter during Gesten's meeting with the commissioner and his staff. It was his feeling that dollars earmarked for the proposed project evaluation would be better spent on the provision of service—that is, reaching more schools and teachers. Despite objections and justifications from the consultant, it soon became clear that he was immovable. His position was that the program had been both tested and replicated in Rochester; to him that was not only sufficient but represented a more solid data base than most projects under his jurisdiction. In retrospect, responsibility for this outcome rests squarely on our shoulders. We had failed to come up with a cost-effective procedure for assessing the results of such a large-scale project. Though more limited in scope than our university-based evaluations, our proposal was still too unwieldy for a service agency with little evaluation experience.

At the time of this writing, the first year of the project has been completed and the contract has been extended through a second school year. Teacher training was conducted for the first time in an extensive three-day workshop rather than spread over the course of the program. Three subsequent one-day visits included observation of lessons being taught in the school and group meetings to discuss problems and review training material. Approximately twenty of the twenty-eight participating teachers actually taught the lessons and reported positive results. Of the remaining eight, half had been pressured by their principal to attend—despite our insistence that everyone be volunteers. Evidently the principal felt that SPS training would help these teachers with a history of classroom management deficiencies. Whereas some teachers there not by choice were ultimately won over, others were not. Steps have been taken to ensure against repetition of this violation of our contract by two school principals. Nevertheless, viable SPS programs are operating and expanding in the five original school districts. With the help of previously trained master teachers, the program will soon be starting in at least three more.

Lessons in Consultation

Involvement in the SPS program over the past five years has taught us many lessons, sometimes painful, and shaped our views of the consultation process. Three critical concerns emerge that may help to focus the efforts of outside consultants whether seeking entry or with ongoing school involvements. The first two center on the importance of learning: how the school perceives its own needs before intervening and the rules that govern the organization's operation. Third, it seems to us that a prospective consultant must be willing and able to go beyond the simple sharing of information and techniques to develop relationships with key staff members. We were ourselves most successful when these concerns were kept in the foreground and conversely can trace our bigger failures and disappointments to their neglect.

The positive response obtained from suburban teachers during the first project year suggested that our analysis of the pressures they were feeling was on target. Informal conversations and meetings with teachers during the previous year had identified a critical need for which we could shape a solution. In contrast, our hurried, pressured contacts with parent leaders in the inner city resulted in a failure to recognize what they felt to be their greatest need: increased social work services. Leaving aside for the moment the issue of whether a mere interest in traditional mental health services would indeed have achieved the group's ends, we had by that time too much invested in our own solution to hear what they were saying. A second mistake was made when we overestimated the power of the principal in that same school by failing to recognize the discrepancy between de jure leadership and the de facto influence of the parent group on school policy. Once again, in the suburbs where years of contact left us well informed about system procedures, land mines, and facilitators, we had little difficulty. The external consultant is well advised to make time to learn about a new setting even when it interferes with the initial timetable. After moving out of state, one of the authors spent the better part of a year attending psychology staff meetings in one school district getting to know their needs, roles, and rules of operating prior to any formal collaboration.

To promote significant change in a system characterized by suspicion and anxiety demands a high level of trust between external consultant and school staff. To establish this climate requires an openness, flexibility, and comfort with ambiguous rules that some consultants may not possess. Over the course of the project much time was spent listening to teachers express their unhappiness with school policies and personnel entirely unrelated to our mutual contract. To have failed to meet their needs for support in these areas would no doubt have disappointed and alienated some of our teacher colleagues. On the other hand, maintaining the many confidences was at times tricky; and at least one teacher seemed to be asking for therapy rather than occasional information. The consultant who purposely maintains distance and prefers a formal role may enjoy greater success providing information than producing organizational change.

Given finite time and resources to invest in consultation, the external consultant may get further by working in fewer settings over a longer period of time than by attempting to cover a wider turf. Long-range consultation fosters the development of trusting relationships with school staff and enhances one's capacity to do work. As a corollary of this rule—Small Is Better—our SPS experience suggests that it is preferable to begin many intervention projects slowly and with fewer participants (ideally, motivated volunteers) than to respond prematurely to community or school interest and expand beyond one's capacity to deliver quality service. By resisting pressure and temptation to establish our program in an entire system or at least schoolwide from the start, we avoided certain disaster and developed a solid base from which planned growth could occur. The pilot program was established with virtually no budget for equipment and with volunteers. Our receipt of a modest grant that covered two teacher stipends and other expansion-related expenses was due largely to publicity and the availability of empirical data to demonstrate our program's impact.

It is true that our work was facilitated somewhat by the presence of certain luxuries not available to every external consultant. Chief among these was the fact that as employees of the university our salaries were guaranteed, thereby eliminating the need to generate income from our activities. Freelance consultants and those from consultation and education departments of many community mental health centers are by necessity more concerned with such matters. It is likely that schools are a bit more willing to support experimental programs of unproved benefit when consultation is provided free of charge. Nevertheless, final project approval was due in greatest measure to our record and positive history with the district. Many other university and independent consultants offering low-cost or no-cost service continue to be turned down by cautious school officials. The ability to provide an honorarium to master teachers and hire a parent worker was another advantage not available to every consultant. Nonetheless, substitution of teacher in-service credits and use of a small group of parent volunteers would achieve the same end. Thus, while loss of our grant would have required a return to the level of improvisation that characterized our first year, the program would have survived.

Developing an Organizational Team Within a School District

9

Richard S. Schmuck

In Eugene, Oregon, a cadre of organization-development consultants is alive, well, and active in many schools. I helped create that group over a decade ago. This in-district, formal structure is made up of teachers, counselors, principals, and central office personnel; it offers peer (or collegial) consultation on organizational issues. Let me present a few examples of the cadre in action.

Joan, a senior high school principal, Mike, a junior high counselor, and Lynn, a fourth-grade teacher, have been members of the cadre for five years. This year, as a temporary consulting team, they are working with a new middle school in Eugene to help the staff with team teaching. Joan, Mike, and Lynn are not staff members of this new school; they are Eugene educators, however, and have been for ten, seven, and six years respectively. As respected members of the cadre, they were asked by the coordinator, Warren, to spend ten days of release time during the year helping faculty members cope with the stress of moving from isolated positions as self-contained classroom teachers and to facilitate their taking on new roles as team leaders and members.

Joan, Mike, and Lynn ran a five-day workshop before school began during which they trained staff members to use communication skills, to run effective meetings, and to do cooperative problem solving. During the school year, the consultants are rotating their attendance at team meetings at the school, frequently serving as neutral facilitators when interrole or interteam conflicts arise, and during their initial year of the middle school's life there is considerable conflict as teachers articulate their philosophies and negotiate the sharing of space, materials, and time. A serious issue to settle, moreover, is how supervision of instruction should function. The cadre members are helping by convening role-clarification discussions and problem-solving meetings so that the faculty can agree on ways of working together. As the end of the school year approaches, the faculty is taking initiative in solving problems and making agreements for next year. Joan, Mike, and Lynn are free now to work with others in the district.

Once every few weeks John, a professor at the university and a colleague of mine, goes to the central office of the Eugene school district to consult with the superintendent's cabinet. A decade before, John helped me to train the first cohort of the cadre of consultants in Eugene; now he occasionally is asked, as am I, by the cadre coordinator to consult with the cadre or to carry out special assignments too difficult or sensitive for cadre members. John is working on such a task now, helping the central office to build a stronger management team.

Before visiting the cabinet meetings, John talks with whoever is convening the next meeting, both to coach the convener on running the meeting and to find out what has happened since his last visit. A few times he has interviewed all cabinet members one at a time on how the management team is working and what he might do to be more helpful. At the cabinet meetings, John observes how members work together on their agenda. From time to time, he comments on the clarity of communication, how the group collects information to solve its problems, and how it arrives at decisions. He offers summary statements of his interviews to support the observations or to encourage cabinet members to talk about their group's progress.

At an elementary school in the poorest section of Eugene, where several years ago I collected data on classroom climate, two cadre members, Tom, a second-grade teacher, and Lynn, a fourth-grade teacher, feel frustrated with meager parent involvement in their school. Working together on this problem, they persuaded their principal to set aside a small amount of in-service money so that other faculty members could join in planning a parent involvement strategy and next addressed a faculty meeting to explain what they hoped to accomplish and to recruit volunteers for a planning committee. A few weeks later Lynn and Tom organized a half-day meeting at which committee members developed a proposal for a parent task force to be comprised of one administrator, two teachers, a counselor, and three parents—all to be chosen by their respective constituencies.

The function of the parent task force was to plan and coordinate activities in the school that already did, or could, involve parents. The faculty accepted the proposal for such a task force, and the principal agreed to try out the new group if Lynn and Tom would provide consultation. But Lynn and Tom told the principal that it would not be effective for them to act as consultants in their own school. Instead they recommended asking the coordinator to send two other cadre members to the school.

During the next month, two cadre members, Paul, a school psychologist from the central office, and Mary Ann, a third-grade teacher, convened a two-day retreat to train the parent task force in collaborative problem solving and joint decision making. Later, two half-day sessions were held at which the task force suggested innovative activities for parents, eventually deciding on several to try. Paul and Mary Ann were helpful too in getting the committee to plan ways of reporting about their activities and action recommendations to the faculty. Eventually, the faculty voted to support all the task force's suggestions.

The cadre uses a conceptualization of, and a strategy for, school improvement called organization development, or simply OD. It involves the school's members themselves in the diagnosis, transformation, and evaluation of their own school. Rather than being presented with the diagnoses and prescriptions of outside experts, the staff members involved in OD, with the aid of cadre consultants, examine current school problems and their causes and actively participate in the statement of goals, the development of skills, the redesign of structures and procedures, and the evaluation of results. The consulting role, while taken first by cadre members external to the school, can be performed in time by members of the school staff itself.

As experienced educators, cadre members understand that the professionals, parents, and students who make up schools often form into ineffective and poorly coordinated groups and that even those schools in which teachers are working well can improve their educational effectiveness with students and parents. Moreover, cadre members believe that teachers typically do not make deliberate efforts to examine their communication with one another, their customary ways of handling meetings, the ways in which they solve problems and make decisions together, or the impact of their pedagogical efforts on the students.

The OD strategy argues that many of the obstacles that confront schools striving to improve arise from the nature of their interpersonal relations, group procedures, and organizational structures. It is in the dynamics of group interaction, not so much the skills of the individuals, where both the source of problems and the determiner of the quality of solutions can be found. Although group procedures often do obstruct the use of human resources in a school, the cadre assumes that the staff's group procedures can, if consciously coordinated by the staff members themselves, promote the competence and motivation needed for effective teaching and learning.

Because the OD strategy aims to improve the capacity of

a school to solve its own problems, cadre members carry out their consultations with school groups. Such groups can range from teaching teams or academic departments to parent task forces and entire school staffs. The cadre does not usually consult with random collections of individuals, as would many in-service trainers in district workshops, unless the individuals constitute a new group representative of a larger system, such as all the elementary schools of a district or even the whole district itself. While district workshops in communication and problem solving can increase the readiness of key individuals to make use of OD methods, such workshops alone typically have little direct effect on the organization of the school. In contrast to other forms of teacher training, the OD strategy calls for consulting with intact groups in schools so that the staff itself is educated as a unit with colleagues helping one another to make changes they want in the school's interpersonal relations, norms, structures, and procedures.

I have seen the cadre use many different ways of carrying out its OD consultations. They have convened discussion groups in schools to talk about interpersonal relations, norms, roles, communication, and the like. Cadre members have given questionnaires and interviews to find out how the members of a staff feel about specific issues or possible alternatives, and they have reported back the data for subsequent problem solving and action. They have conducted exercises or simulations with school staffs to explore role clarity or other issues such as power, decision making, and communication. They have given faculty groups experience in practicing new ways of operating in staff or departmental meetings. They have attended staff meetings to observe and to give feedback about the group processes. They have brought together total staffs for special purposes like the sharing of innovations and have convened entire staffs and parent groups to work on conflicts. Whatever consultative strategy or procedure is used, the cadre members strive to enable the clients' school to solve its own problems. But before I explain the work of the Eugene cadre in detail, it will be helpful to describe briefly our years of research and development before the cadre.

Before the Cadre

In 1967, Phillip Runkel and I established at the University of Oregon what became the most sustained program of action research on school OD we know of. Over a fifteen-year period, more than a hundred people worked in the program with us and more than a hundred publications were produced. (A list can be obtained from the Center for Educational Policy and Management, University of Oregon.) The most important publication was *The Second Handbook of Organization Development in Schools* (Schmuck and others, 1977). The cadre project, our fourth field study, took place in 1971-72, giving us information from more than ten years of follow-up involvement and study for this chapter. Our first three projects helped shape the goals, design, training procedures, and evaluation methods of this cadre project.

In the first project, Runkel and I tested whether a comprehensive, year-long design for training an entire school staff in OD skills could strengthen the problem-solving capacity of the school. As far as we have been able to discern, it was the first attempt of its kind. We worked with the staff of Highland Park Junior High School in the suburb of Brentwood near a major West Coast urban center. I had met only with the principal prior to the training, so we did not have detailed diagnostic data about the school. We spent the equivalent of twelve days there: five days concentrated before school in August 1967 and the equivalent of seven days spread throughout the 1967-68 school year. Runkel and I were joined by three other experienced consultants in the summer workshop, but we did not have their assistance in the follow-up design. Instead, we were assisted by two advanced graduate students who served primarily as documenters of the project. We trained the whole staff of fifty-eight, including administrators, counselors, teachers, janitors, nurses, and cooks.

Our aim was to help the Highland Park staff to establish skills in describing school goals clearly, in diagnosing its work in relation to those goals, in recognizing discrepancies between the goals and the school's current performance, and to generate action plans to move closer to its goals. The training design started with the practice and gradual development of skills in interpersonal communication. Our intent was to ease communication within the school by having staff members practice the skills of paraphrasing, describing behavior objectively, describing one's own feelings, checking one's impressions of another's feelings, and giving or receiving feedback. These communication skills were practiced in the context of serious simulations such as Five-Square Puzzle, Trip on the Moon, and Planners and Operators. After the communication skills had been practiced in the security of simulation, we encouraged staff members to use them to express frustration or confusion they were experiencing in school, to state clearly important school goals, to identify gaps between the goals and the current situation, and to use a sequence of problem-solving steps as follows: (1) Select the gap between situation and goal; (2) use force-field analysis to analyze the gap; (3) brainstorm alternative actions to reduce the gap; (4) design feasible action plans using the new ideas; (5) forecast consequences of putting such plans into action; (6) take action; and (7) evaluate outcomes of the actions.

A multifaceted evaluation design for the effort was developed by Runkel and me, the two graduate students, and a few of our colleagues at the university. Our design included anthropological observation and interviewing during the 1967-68 school year and before-after questionnaire comparisons with an array of comparison schools. During the former data collections, the documenters noted that the amount of communication and collaboration required to complete the problem-solving sequence reduced some of the staff members' confusion and also brought them satisfaction that they had participated in devising workable solutions. Certain immediate problems were worked on: clarifying and modifying the roles of the school counselors, clarifying the managerial roles of the assistant principals and the department heads, and improving the efficiency of meetings held by teaching teams and subject-matter groups. The documenters also noted that during the school year the staff created several schoolwide committees for continual communication and problem solving involving staff, students, and members of the community. The questionnaire data used before and after the year gave evidence that the project had raised staff morale, improved the organizational climate of the school, and resulted in the new use of innovative instructional techniques in classrooms. We were given an award for a journal article on the project (Schmuck, Runkel, and Langmeyer, 1969), and Runkel and I fully described the details of the project and its evaluation in a monograph (Schmuck and Runkel, 1970).

In the midst of our follow-up consultation at Highland Park, a junior high school counselor from Keele, a school district near another major West Coast urban center, visited Runkel and me to seek consultative help for his district. Keele was growing by leaps and bounds; new teachers were being introduced monthly; and a large number of new central office administrators had just been hired. The district was suffering from poor communication, role confusion, ineffective leadership, and the like. As it turned out, our second project, the Keele project, resulted from a happy coming together of Keele's interests and ours. After several discussions with the superintendent, his cabinet, the school board, and a sample of principals and teachers, we could see that the district needed help in sorting out its problems, while Runkel and I were eager to test our ideas and techniques in a school district. Keele was indeed an organization in need of development, and in our minds Highland Park had a special readiness for OD we did not see at Keele. Besides, Highland Park was but a single school. What about a rapidly growing district with twenty schools? Could OD be effective in enhancing such a district's capacity to solve its own problems?

The Keele project lasted three years, involved hundreds of people, and was made up of fifteen consultative designs, totaling more than eighty-five days, carried out in parallel and integrated into the larger effort for district renewal. Its magnitude was quite a contrast to the twelve days at Highland Park. Building understanding about OD alone took eight months in Keele. From the meeting with the junior high counselor in September 1967 until the first training event the next spring, Runkel and I met three times with the superintendent, six times with his cabinet, twice with the school board, twice with the principals, and once with the staff of the central office. After a planning session with leaders of the teacher association, we ran three large meetings open to all teachers in the district. We answered requests to visit the district's larger senior high, the largest junior high, and three elementary schools. From the outset, the myriad of entry activities that constituted start-up in Keele was immeasurably more complex than my single entry meeting with the principal of Highland Park.

The complexities and weightiness of time-consuming events grew as the training and consultation took shape in Keele. In April 1968 we invited all key personnel performing line functions in Keele to the first training event. Participants included the superintendent and his cabinet, the elementary and secondary school principals, and teacher leaders in the local association including two association leaders from all twenty schools in the district. We sought to commence our OD consutation with the power structure of Keele—a vertical slice of the line. During this event, we sought to involve all participants in listing the organizational issues that would constitute an initial agenda for subsequent problem solving. We also wanted to raise awareness throughout the Keele district that their system could be amenable to renewal and development if only its members could work skillfully together. In September 1968 we ran a workshop for personnel in staff roles in the central office and all the principals in order to clarify communication between the two groups. In particular, the roles of helping, supervising, and collaborating had to be clarified between the central staff and the schools. And from September 1968 until April 1969 we consulted with five school staffs much in the style of our work at Highland Park, not to speak of continuing consultation with the superintendent's cabinet, central office staff, and the principals.

Through all those first-year consultations we sought to increase understanding of how people in various parts of the district affected one another; develop clear communication networks up and down and laterally; increase understanding of the diverse goals present in different parts of the system; develop new ways of solving problems through creative use of new roles in groups; develop new ways of assessing progress toward goals;

involve more people at all levels in decision making; and develop procedures for searching for innovative practices both inside and outside the school district.

I do not have space here to go into the details of the consultations in Keele; the story is long and complex. The reader should study the work of Runkel and his colleagues (1980) for a complete analysis. In this chapter I want primarily to describe how I arrived at the idea of an OD cadre, for it was during this first year of Keele consultation (sometime between June 1968 and February 1969) when the cadre idea was born. The idea entered my mind in a very vague way as we completed the Highland Park design in May 1968. I asked myself: What will keep problem solving going at Highland Park? My answer at the time was: An internal leadership group. Just a few months later, I was involved in our ambitious design in Keele. I could see that we would perhaps improve problem solving in the superintendent's cabinet and that some of our goals would be reached, but it looked like we would only have time to consult in five schools at most and would have insufficient time and staff to do an adequate job even in those schools. As we entered 1969, our efforts had to be herculean. Our progress toward establishing an improved capacity for problem solving seemed too slow. And even as we were achieving progress, how could we reach all twenty schools of the district?

Then the cadre idea came into focus. I learned that Highland Park was searching again for consultative help. The staff had tried to design its own workshops, but a neutral outsider was needed at times when emotions ran high and conflicts deep. The Keele district had a huge agenda for OD, an agenda that could take five years. Keele needed a consultative resource available for at least the next four years. Highland Park's needs were much more modest; still the Highland staff did need a shot in the arm perhaps once a year. And even the highly successful schools in Keele would need a shot in the arm occasionally too. What would be helpful, therefore, was a formal group to carry out OD consultation as needed in the district—a group of consultants on call both for groups in the district in need of in-depth, long-term OD and for groups requiring only periodic help.

In the spring of 1969, we informed Keele personnel that a workshop would be held in June for those wishing to become communication consultants for the district. A circular stated that the trainees would become knowledgeable in communication skills, simulations, diagnosis, giving feedback, problem solving, and drawing up designs for organizational training. We solicited applications from all levels of the district; the twenty-three persons eventually selected represented a wide cross section of the district—teachers, counselors, elementary and secondary principals, specialists in curriculum and student personnel, and assistant superintendents who were members of the superintendent's cabinet.

The first training event was a two-week workshop in June 1969. The goals of the first week were to introduce the trainees to the skills, exercises, and procedures found in the first edition of our *Handbook* (Schmuck and others, 1972), to provide them an opportunity to explore the effect of their behavior on a group, to establish the group as a cohesive, supportive cadre, and to give them practice in leading OD activities. For the second week, they divided into six subgroups, each convened by Runkel, me, or one of our graduate assistants. The entire group determined targets in the district, and each group chose one for its initial work. Among the targets were several schools that were changing their programs, the principal and department heads at a senior high school, the principals and counselors serving elementary youngsters, and a community advisory group made up of parents. Most of the second week was spent establishing goals for the training to be conducted with the targets, gathering diagnostic data about them, analyzing the data to determine organizational forces operating, and designing training events.

From September 1969 to March 1970, we collaborated with the Keele communication consultants as they carried out their consultations. We worked side by side with them, assisting the neophyte consultants and offering them constructive feedback to improve their skills. Approximately ten different training events took place during this period, most of them quite successful in raising district interest in improving communication, group processes, and organizational problem solving, as well as in legitimizing and institutionalizing the Keele communication consultants.

The results of the longitudinal follow-up study of the Keele consultants (Runkel and others, 1980) point out that "the Keele cadre did better than we did. Once a team from the cadre had made entry into a school, its average stay there was longer than ours and its effects often better. . . . When, in this book, the effects of OD training have stood strong and proud, there also has stood the Keele cadre." But in other respects Runkel and I were frustrated by the time and money it took to get favorable effects in Keele. We wanted to establish a district cadre more quickly and more economically than we had in Keele. Before we could try to accomplish that, however, we carried out a third action research project that was to pave the way for our cadre project in Eugene.

In 1970 Runkel and I launched an effort to compare the relative usefulness of two strategies of consultation for enabling six elementary schools to convert from traditional, self-contained structures to a team teaching arrangement (team teaching project 3). The fieldwork ran from the summer of 1970 to the spring of 1971, and all the schools in the project, including the control schools, were in Eugene and the neighboring town of Springfield. Aside from the many insights and new techniques gained from this endeavor (reported fully in Schmuck and others, 1975), we achieved legitimacy and credibility in Eugene, became acquainted with many teachers and principals, and developed rapport with the superintendent and his staff. The most important contacts, however, in terms of the cadre's development were Dick A. and Don E., who, during the 1970-71 school year, were half-time teachers (secondary and elementary respectively) and were employed by the central office the rest of the time to explore the advantages and disadvantages of team teaching and differentiated staffing. As leaders in the Eugene Teachers Association, Dick A. and Don E. were asked by the superintendent to recommend new forms of school staffing that would raise both the responsibility and the morale of teachers in relation to the management of the schools. Among the recommendations made by Dick A. and Don E. was that Runkel and I be asked to help the Eugene district develop an in-district resource for OD—a resource that would draw on the energies and competencies of classroom teachers as one means of extending more administrative responsibility to teachers without taking them out of the classroom. The cadre idea had developed fully and was now ready to become a reality.

Development of the Eugene Cadre

During spring 1971, Dick A., Don E., Runkel, and I collaborated to recruit potential members for the cadre project from throughout the district. We mailed a printed notice in the district's annual catalogue of summer workshops to all certified personnel. We also attended several meetings of the central office staff, the principals, and the teachers association to inform Eugene personnel about the project. Much of the information about cadre was also spread informally at parties, faculty rooms, supermarkets and the like. In all, seventy-two educators responded and each was invited to a two-hour meeting to learn about OD and how it works. After the introductory meeting, interested persons were asked to fill out an application; fifty-one educators handed one in. The four of us, along with the assistant superintendent for personnel, acted as a panel of judges. We selected twenty-six for initial membership: twelve elementary teachers, two elementary administrators, one secondary counselor, four secondary teachers, three school psychologists, and four central office administrators. Those people, selected because of their educational experience in group dynamics, the nature of their announced interest in the cadre, and their diversity in terms of roles, sex, and race, represented fourteen of Eugene's forty-four schools and several different sections in the central office.

The formal training of those twenty-six included two two-hour introductions to OD in May 1971, ten days of workshop in June, five days of workshop in August, and close co-consulting during the 1971-72 academic year. During the initial two short sessions, OD was introduced as a "planned and sustained effort at system self-study and improvement, focusing explicitly on change in organizational norms, structures, and procedures, using behavioral science concepts and the techniques of action research." Each of the important terms in this definition (system self-study, norms, structures, procedures, action research) was elaborated with examples from schools. We used these concepts in a mimeographed copy of our *Handbook*. (There is now a *Second Handbook*.)

The June workshop took place during the ten days just after school was out. We prepared lectures, discussions, and exercises that would help cadre members become knowledgeable about the handbook. Our intention was not to produce sophisticated consultants quickly but to give neophytes a thorough introduction to our communication skills, group problem solving, methods of organizational diagnosis, issues about entry and start-up, designing, evaluation, and the like. We organized the ten-day workshop as follows.

Day 1. After making introductions, cadre members formed triads to discuss "what I hope the cadre can do for me." We gave a lecture on paraphrasing and asked cadre members to use paraphrasing extensively during the workshop. Forming new triads to discuss "what I hope the cadre can do for the district," cadre members listened to another of our presentations outlining the clients, issues, and strategies with which OD is concerned. After we spoke briefly on the skill of behavior description, participants formed cross-role groups to list goals for the cadre. Representatives of the small groups occupied stage center to present their group's list. We then lectured on describing feelings and formed new small groups to build Tinkertoy models of "what this district is like." After discussing what the models revealed about the district, cadre members discussed the group processes they noted while constructing the models. We ended the day with a discussion on checking impressions of another's inner state and asked participants to complete an "expectation survey."

Day 2. We gave a lecture on the technique of survey data feedback, presented data from the expectation survey, and asked new small groups to design and administer a brief questionnaire to the whole group. The new questionnaires were evaluated by us and the participants. Next we asked cadre members to list their personal goals and resources and to share that information. As a homework assignment, we asked cadre members to read the handbook chapters on clarifying communication and establishing goals.

Day 3. After we lectured on constructive openness and the interpersonal gap, we asked cadre members to form new triads to review their personal goals. Following a discussion of using conflict to identify problems, participants formed homogeneous role groups to practice an imaging exercise. They completed stage 1 (generating images of other role groups) and stage 2 (sharing images across groups) before we gave them the assignment of reading the handbook chapter on improving meetings.

Day 4. After going through stage 3 (listing examples of own role behaviors that could contribute to others' images) and stage 4 (sharing examples across groups), cadre members completed the exercise by forming cross-role groups to identify underlying district problems that were brought out during the exercise. The whole group discussed the strengths and limitations of the exercise, identifying contexts in which it could be used. Next we introduced a planners and operators exercise, after which we gave the assignment of reading the handbook chapter on making decisions.

Day 5. After we lectured on task and social-emotional processes in groups, cadre members discussed ways in which these processes are related to making decisions. They formed small groups to list skills they would need as cadre members, later forming pairs of groups to share the lists. Next we lectured on techniques of process observation and feedback, after which the pairs of groups each formed a fishbowl arrangement. The inner groups discussed restraints to the cadre using its skills in the district, while the outer groups acted as process observers. Then the roles and physical positions of the inner and outer groups were reversed to give everyone a chance to play both a content and a process function. We asked all participants to read the handbook chapter on theory and technology.

Day 6. After we gave a lecture on entry and start-up, participants formed into small groups to discuss questions they would raise to get information to facilitate an effective start-up. Following our next lecture on diagnosis, participants received a case to study and formed new groups to make lists of available and required data, to plan for how to collect the data, and to estimate the best ways of tabulating and presenting the data for feedback. Next we lectured on designing and, without another hypothetical case, helped the participants plan a fictitious sequence of consultative events. We asked cadre members to read the handbook chapters on macrodesigning and microdesigning.

Day 7. After we told about the work being carried out by the Keele communication consultants, participants formed four teams and were assigned one OD activity each (Five Square Puzzle, The Trip to the Moon Exercise, Planners and Operators, and One-Way, Two-Way Communication) to role-play with the other three fourths of the cadre. Each exercise was followed by an evaluative discussion focusing on the strengths and limitations of the training procedures used by the role players.

Day 8. After we lectured on follow-up OD designs, participants received fictitious data about a consultation and formed new teams to plan the first day of follow-up consultation. We lectured on problem-solving procedures, formed new small groups to identify potential problems of the cadre, met as a total group to share and analyze the problems, and suggested ways of overcoming the greatest barriers to solving the problems.

Day 9. Small groups from the preceding day finished the problem-solving sequence by making action plans and forecasting potential consequences if the actions were tried. Then those small groups reported their results to the total group, and we led discussion on the strengths and limitations of each plan.

Day 10. Reports, discussion, and critique continued from the preceding day until all groups were finished. We presented a suggested reading list for the summer as well as describing several schools or groups that had requested cadre consultation the coming year. The last few hours were spent with the superintendent who indicated his strong support for the cadre. He also announced that Dick A. would spend half time as the first coordinator of the cadre. Dick A. spent the last half hour leading discussion on the nature of the next five days of cadre training to take place in August.

During those five days, we sought to help cadre members get ready to consult with us during the 1971-72 school year. We wanted to move from the handbook and the rehearsal of specific exercises and procedures toward the cadre's learning more widely applied skills associated with making entry, building contracts, diagnosing client needs, designing at both macrolevel and microlevel, and evaluating their consultative efforts.

We encouraged cadre members to discuss the norms being established within their group. We encouraged them to ask: Are we being open with one another? What does it mean to learn from others? How can resources within the group best be shared? What commitments have we made? What commitments are we willing to make? In addition, we encouraged cadre members to become more self-analytic about the emerging structural arrangements for their cadre. We encouraged them to discuss: What will the coordinator's role be? What sort of governance structure will direct the cadre's actions? How can the cadre work to be accepted by others in the district while maintaining its autonomy and neutrality? We carried out those five days as follows.

Day 11. We formed the participants into six teams for consulting in 1971-72. Each team was made up of four or five members, and each member held a district role different from his or her teammates. We asked the teams to discuss how their group composition would limit or enhance their ability to work effectively and then to brainstorm ways of overcoming the group's potential limitations. In two teams, group memberships were changed. Then we devoted ten minutes to each of the following topics: problem solving, communication, consultation stages, organizational issues, OD procedures, OD exercises, and survey data feedback. We asked participants to spend the last two hours of the day making agreements in their teams about their preferred ways of working together. (For a description of the group agreement exercise, see p. 133, Schmuck and others, 1977.)

Day 12. We asked the entire group to agree on the role of the coordinator, the role and composition of a cadre steering committee, how decisions would be made, and how to deal with ethics. Later in the day, the teams met separately to continue making their own group agreements.

Day 13. The teams continued to work separately while Phil R., Dick A., Don E., and I worked on a demonstration package to offer cadre services throughout the district. Later we presented the package, which included an audiotape slide show (see Arends and others, 1973) and a design with handouts (see Arends, Phelps, and Schmuck, 1973). Cadre members evaluated the package, brainstormed improvements, and planned ways of using it in the district.

Day 14. We asked the teams to select one of their members to serve on the initial cadre steering committee. After selections were made, we led the whole cadre in a discussion about the steering committee's functions. In particular it was decided that the steering committee would design future self-renewal events for the cadre and plan ways to record team activities. We asked the whole group to give us feedback about the handbook (not yet published) and to suggest a list of topics for the self-renewal of the cadre.

Day 15. We asked the teams to complete their planning and the steering committee to decide on self-renewal topics. Later the entire group discussed, revised, and agreed on proposals for self-renewal events, and each team described its group agreements and consultative designs for the coming year to the whole group.

After the Workshop

From August to May 1972, cadre members collaborated with us in carrying out some initial consultations with an assortment of client groups. In addition to three teams who provided follow-up consultation to schools with which we had already worked (team teaching project 3 described earlier in this chapter), one team helped a secondary staff develop the skills and structure for participatory decision making, another team consulted with the superintendent's cabinet, helping it improve both the vertical and the horizontal communications in the district, and the sixth team designed and started an in-service course on communication and problem solving for anyone in the district who might like to attend. While this last group was not doing OD, its work was deemed important both for informing a wider audience in the district about cadre skills and for motivating key teachers, counselors, and principals to request OD consultation in their schools. Each of the consulting teams was aided either by Runkel or me or by one of our advanced graduate students, one of whom at this time was principal of Highland Park Junior High. After May 1972, our active involvement and leadership with the cadre ended; our roles shifted from expert authorities to colleagues and finally to outside resource people. Since 1973 we have continued to provide assistance when appropriate, but only at the request of the cadre.

Since its inception there have been seventy-two cadre members, including twenty-five active members currently. Of the forty-seven former members, seventeen have left the district; thirty are still employed in the district in eleven schools. The twenty-five current members plus the thirty former members have been drawn from twenty of the forty-eight schools in Eugene. These twenty schools include four senior highs, two junior highs, and fourteen elementary schools.

An analysis of the current membership reveals that cadre members average over thirteen years of educational work experience and their average length of time spent in the cadre is just under three years. A typical member has a master's degree or its equivalent. Cadre members have exhibited leadership abilities (eleven members currently have administrative credentials, for example); they are prominent in the district; they represent a balance of district roles; and they have good rapport in the administrative and teaching ranks.

All cadre members function as part-time consultants while carrying out their full-time teaching, coordinating, or administrative responsibilities. They typically work in consultative teams of two to five, depending on the size of the client group. New cadre consulting teams are formed whenever clients in the district request consultation. The criteria for composing teams include a willingness to work with others on the team, a belief that a balanced team has been formed, neutrality in relation to the client group, and an interest in the consultative tasks to be performed.

Perhaps the most important role in the cadre is that of the coordinator, the administrative leader of the group. Since the beginning there have been five cadre coordinators: Dick A. (1971-1973), who served half-time as coordinator and is now an associate professor and my colleague; Bill S., a full-time coordinator from 1973 to 1977 and currently a classroom teacher; Mary Frances C., a full-time coordinator from 1977 to 1980 and now head of an association of school administrators; Barbara K., a half-time coordinator for 1980-81 and now a superintendent of schools in western Canada; and Wayne F., a half-time coordinator from 1981 to the present. Each of these coordinators has managed the activities of consultation teams, assisted and guided the entry and start-up parts of most consultations, worked on consultation teams, provided demonstrations to potential client groups, explained the goals, methods, and work of the cadre to interested persons in the district, arranged for outside consultants when they were required, linked the cadre with district administrators by keeping the latter informed of cadre activities and budgetary requirements, and linked the cadre to groups outside the district—such as universities, other cadres, state department of education, and research and development centers or educational laboratories.

Another important feature of the cadre is its steering committee, which is composed of one representative from each of the current consultation teams plus the coordinator. There have been twelve steering committees in the Eugene cadre. Members of the steering committee link other cadre members to the coordinator, prepare the budget and allocate resources, plan self-renewal events for the cadre, select clients when there are too many requests, and plan for the selection and training of new members.

This last function has been critical in keeping the cadre viable. The continuing development of new technologies for OD has required cadre members to improve their skills continually and remain receptive to new ideas. Moreover, turnover of the membership has meant that the cadre has had to plan ways of ensuring that a reservoir of trained people would be available to replace those who resigned or moved out of the district. The strategy for accomplishing the latter has been to call on those who have completed the in-service course offered by the cadre. This course is designed to last a full year and is divided into three parts: communication and problem-solving skills, group process exercises and procedures, and OD diagnosis and design. A colleague who passes all three is invited to become an intern in the cadre. This past year there were four interns. Over the last decade, it is estimated that two hundred and fifty professionals took the first course, perhaps a hundred took the second, and about fifty took all three. Although there have been a variety of ways of achieving the renewal of the experienced membership, most frequently used have been monthly evening seminars, summer workshops, and an annual retreat of two or three days in August. At these meetings the cadre discusses organizational diagnosis, conflict management, alternative procedures for data feedback, and process observation and feedback.

During its almost twelve years of work the cadre has consulted in every school of the district at least once and with a number of different groups in the central office. We estimate that about three fourths of the professional personnel of Eugene during the past decade have interacted at one time or another with cadre consultants. Over this period the cadre has carried out survey-data feedback designs in twelve schools, organizational training designs similar to the Highland Park effort at five schools, and process observation and feedback with perhaps twenty-five teams, departments, and committees in schools as well as in the central office. It has worked with district nurses, junior high department chairpersons, curriculum coordinators, and citizen groups in the community. It has done on-the-spot coaching with five principals to improve staff meetings, trained student leaders in two senior highs and one junior high, and devised a confrontation design with the parents and faculty of an elementary school.

With regard to the last project, the cadre was assisted by Runkel and me. In a project entitled Bringing a School Staff and Parents into Effective Interaction, Dick A., coordinator of the cadre, received a request for help from a principal of an elementary school who had been shocked to receive a strongly worded letter, signed by seventy-five parents, enumerating the weaknesses of the school and demanding change. The principal wanted to develop a relationship of constructive interaction between teachers and parents but needed help. Dick A., after assessing the strong emotions in the situation, thought the cadre needed help too. Runkel and I agreed to develop and run a constructive-confrontation design along with several months of follow-up work in parent-teacher problem-solving groups. The design worked very well; we and five cadre members collaborated as consultants; and the school eventually developed two schools in one to accommodate the philosophical and pedagogical conflicts present in the situation.

Several years ago the cadre made public its own group agreements for how it aspires to operate:

Group Agreements for Total Cadre Group

1. We regard all cadre information as confidential and will not share it with *anyone* outside the cadre.
2. We will exercise constructive openness with each other.
    a. Be direct.
    b. Report satisfaction and dissatisfaction with how things are going and give and receive positive and negative feedback.
    c. Do perception checks regarding others' feelings.
3. If asked by a potential client to do cadre-type work, we will check with the cadre coordinator before accepting.
4. We will abide by and attempt to implement decisions made at meetings. If a member is not present, she or he will abide by and attempt to implement a decision until it is changed at a subsequent meeting.
5. We will have a prepublished, annotated agenda, a rotating convener, a recorder, and time approximations for agenda items. There will also be set a beginning and ending time of the meeting.
6. The recorder will make special note of decisions and who will implement them. The recorder will give notes to the cadre coordinator for typing and sending to all members.

7. We will make a special effort to attend and be prompt at total cadre meetings (renewals, workshops, business meetings, and retreats). When we cannot attend, we will inform the coordinator, respond to request for input, and make an effort to find out what we missed.
8. We will make a special effort to support good decision making by sharing pertinent information we possess about agenda topics.
9. We assume responsibility for using meeting skills and interpersonal communication skills.
10. Decision making and ratifying decisions affecting the total group will be by consensus of those present.
11. We will be sensitive to the challenges of leadership and agree to support the designated convener.

Evaluation of the Eugene Cadre

Three formal evaluations have been carried out on the work of the Eugene cadre. In the first, Bell (1977) compared the organizational processes of elementary schools that had received different amounts of OD consultation from the cadre. The second study, carried out by Callan (1979), assessed client reactions to a variety of cadre interventions. And in the third study, the most comprehensive evaluation, Callan and Kentta (1979) measured districtwide knowledge and attitudes about the cadre.

Bell developed and pilot-tested a 33-item questionnaire to measure the quality of organizational processes in elementary schools. A factor analysis of results from pilot testing uncovered five highly correlated clusters of items: effectiveness in problem solving; emotional cohesiveness; constructive use of staff resources; collaborative interaction; and schoolwide communication. The questionnaire was administered to teachers and principals of the thirty-two elementary schools in Eugene. The results indicated that the schools that had received the most consultative assistance showed the highest scores on effectiveness in problem solving, emotional cohesiveness, and schoolwide communication. Moreover, the cadre's consultations helped schools with initially low scores on constructive use of staff resources and collaborative interaction to get better. Further, the cadre's consultations helped schools already high on the five factors to maintain high scores, while high-scoring schools with no consultative help had lower scores subsequently. Finally, cadre help was especially useful to schools going through structural changes involving increased complexity as in team teaching and interdisciplinary curricula. Schools that made such modifications without consultative assistance from the cadre typically ran into more serious morale problems—for example, a lowering of the score on emotional cohesiveness. Bell's results must be tempered, however, by a low rate of return and the limitations of change scores.

Callan's study took place the year after Bell's. At the close of nine consultations, clients were asked to evaluate the cadre's work according to six categories using ten-point scales—point 1 indicating a low evaluation and point 10 indicating a high evaluation. The results were as follows. How close did these sessions come to achieving their purpose? (M = 8.19; SD = 1.62) How well did you like the format of the sessions? (M = 8.18; SD = 1.61) How well did you think the cadre members presented the materials? (M = 8.82; SD = 1.52) How interesting *to you* were the session's topics? (M = 8.26; SD = 2.01) Will the information presented be useful to you in your job? (M = 8.23; SD = 1.80) In general, how valuable were these sessions? (M = 8.22; SD = 1.75). Clients also were asked what they liked most about working with cadre and what they liked least. Two responses predominated: Clients liked most "the style of work used by cadre members"; they liked least that there was insufficient time for the consultation.

During the 1978-79 school year Callan and Kentta were asked by the district to assess the cadre's image among the professional educators of Eugene. With the help of Bell, Runkel, and me, an eleven-item knowledge questionnaire and a ten-item attitude questionnaire were developed and tested. The former aimed to assess how accurate district members were about cadre aims and methods; the latter aimed to assess how district members felt about the cadre. Ninety-four percent of the professionals in Eugene completed both questionnaires.

In answering the eleven knowledge items, 2 percent gave

no response to each item while 16 percent answered don't know to each item. Correct and incorrect answers given to each knowledge item were:

1. Cadre is administrators, and management specialists, working with the state department in coordinating districtwide organization. (False; 63 percent correct and 19 percent incorrect.)
2. Cadre gathers information and makes suggestions to the Eugene Education Association regarding negotiations and bargaining with the school board. (False; 70 percent correct and 12 percent incorrect.)
3. Cadre's primary function is to resolve personal problems that arise for members of the district's staff. (False; 52 percent correct and 30 percent incorrect).
4. Cadre provides help with organizational problems and offers training in organizational development. (True; 75 percent correct and 7 percent incorrect.)
5. Cadre supplies a specific sequence of readings and lectures that enable teachers to be more effective instructors. (False; 46 percent correct and 36 percent incorrect.)
6. Cadre will train groups in the skills of problem solving, communication, decision making, and holding productive meetings. (True; 79 percent correct and 3 percent incorrect.)
7. Cadre is from the district and the University of Oregon; it offers sensitivity training and encounter groups. (False; 53 percent correct and 29 percent incorrect.)
8. If individual teachers are having problems developing curriculum for their classrooms, the cadre is a good source of direct help. (False; 58 percent correct and 24 percent incorrect.)
9. Any employee of the district can become a member of the cadre. (True; 56 percent correct and 26 percent incorrect.)
10. Cadre members are district personnel who, in addition to their regular assignments, volunteer consulting services for which they are not paid. (True; 61 percent correct and 21 percent incorrect.)
11. The cadre will work with students, teachers, administra-

tors, classified employees, and parents either individually or in groups. (True; 52 percent correct and 30 percent incorrect.)

In general, the results indicate that the majority of district personnel are knowledgeable of the cadre's purposes and methods. Items 3, 5, 7, and 11, however, received a high percentage of incorrect responses. A number of reasons might be given for the high percentage of incorrect responses on items 3. First, the cadre does deal with organizational problems and many people might think of these as personal problems as well. Furthermore, the cadre's work to resolve organizational problems might reduce individual problems in group work. And even though personal problem solving is not the cadre's primary function, staff members who have been helped may believe that it is. Item 5 received the greatest percentage of wrong responses, but that perhaps is not a significant problem for the cadre. It might be the case that teachers find use for cadre taught concepts, skills, and materials in their classrooms. The high percentage of incorrect responses to item 7 might reflect an assumption that the cadre is still affiliated with the university because Runkel and I occasionally collaborate with cadre members. This probably is not a barrier to cadre work; however, that respondents equate sensitivity training and encounter groups with OD obliges the cadre to distribute more information about the nature of OD to district personnel. Likewise, the high percentage of wrong responses on item 11 means that the cadre must continue to emphasize its availability to anyone in the district.

On all attitude items the percentage of favorable ratings ranged from 7 percentage points to 59 percentage points higher than the percentage of unfavorable ratings. The most favorable ratings were given on items asking about the competence and skill of cadre members. The least favorable were given on items dealing with the value and utility of OD for the school or district. In general, Callan and Kentta conclude that staff members in Eugene feel good about the cadre's efforts. They point out that accurate knowledge is positively associated with favorable attitude both toward cadre and OD. A correlation of +0.45 was obtained between knowledge about cadre and attitudes toward cadre. Also correlated with knowledge and attitude is the number of OD hours spent with the cadre. Thus the picture emerges that with direct experience with cadre services, the Eugene personnel learn what OD is and how it works and develop good feelings both about OD and the competence and skill of cadre members.

Integrating Internal and External Consultation

The cadre idea is being explored in other school districts. Along with Keele and Eugene, for example, cadres of OD consultants have been launched in Boulder, Colorado; Buffalo, New York; Cupertino, California; Palo Alto, California; Polk County, Florida; and Trondheim, Norway. I believe that OD cadres are attractive because they embody the strengths of both internal and external consultation.

On the one hand, cadre members are internal consultants insofar as they are employees of the same district as their clients; they work for the same school board and superintendent, are on the same pay schedule and receive the same benefits, and live in the same sociological context. As fellow employees, their expressed concern for school improvement is easier to trust than similar concerns expressed by socially removed outsiders. As peer-colleagues, they honestly appreciate the day-to-day micropolitics of the district. As volunteers who are not paid extra for their services, their advice to go slowly during diagnosis or to encourage long-term designs with follow-up is more credible than would be similar advice from paid outsiders. Cadre members in a district can establish legitimacy through norms that support teacher autonomy from management, educator equality regardless of rank, and the value of collegial responsibility and collaboration for school improvement.

On the other hand, cadre members are external consultants since they never consult in their own family subsystem—that is, their own department, team, committee, or school. As nonmembers of the client group, they can maintain their composure, disinterest, and neutrality—social-psychological conditions that are typically impossible to achieve for involved group members. As an outside consulting team with a heterogeneous role mix, the cadre consultants can relate to various role takers in their client groups. And when the cadre finds that it cannot be disinterested or neutral, as when conflicts run high or the board wants consultation, it can link potential clients in the district with appropriate external consultants.

I believe that the concept of voluntary, collegial, part-time OD consultation holds a great deal of promise for school districts. At a time when the social distance and suspicion between consultants and educators are growing dangerously stronger in many districts, peer-colleagues as consultants offer a healthy alternative to the traditional, hierarchical, professional-client helping relationships in schools. Will cadres catch on and diffuse to more districts? It will take a decade to answer that question.

Building a Community Group to Improve Local Schools 10

Patrick O'Neill
P. Ross Loomes

Schools must be flexible and offer a broad spectrum of services if they are to meet the challenge of educating diverse groups of children. An important criterion to use in judging the competence of a school system is to see how many students are unserved because they are defined as deviant, how many are unable to use their potential in school, how many have special needs that go unmet. Consultation is often aimed at increasing the ability of schools to tolerate different behavioral styles and to provide services for children who have special talents or handicaps.

In many instances the school, or school system, already contains the resources to meet a broad range of needs. Perhaps the system should be more creative in the way rules are applied; perhaps teachers require additional information to make them more competent in dealing with behavior problems; role definitions might be extended to make more use of staff skills; perhaps the social environment can be enhanced so that peer helping peer becomes the norm. In these and like situations, the consultant can be effective working within the schools.

In many cases, however, the local school system simply lacks the resources to work effectively with groups such as the mentally retarded or the learning disabled. There may be little the consultant can do inside the system. The problem may lie in the relationship between the school system and its own environment. The consultant may see the problem primarily as one in which support must be generated from the political system at large to provide adequate programs for children with special needs.

We offer a case study in which the consultation effort involved building an organization of parents and concerned professionals committed to improving the capacity of schools to diagnose and help children with specific learning disabilities. The major tasks of the organization were to focus public attention on the lack of programs for these children and prod public officials at various levels of government to commit resources to these programs. Our description is limited to the formative phase only—what Sarason (1972) has called the creation of a setting. Since the organization still exists, we have only hints of what it may accomplish.

Much of the literature on organizing has been concerned with the poor (Alinsky, 1946, 1971; Kahn, 1970). But this consultation effort was aimed primarily at members of the middle class. After presentation of case details, we will be in a position to compare our tactics and the problems we encountered with those outlined by Alinsky and Kahn in their experience with poor people's organizations.

The Context

Compared with the rest of Canada, the four Atlantic provinces are like part of the underdeveloped Third World. Natural resources are exported to the central part of the country, and the most able and ambitious young people follow the same road. Those who remain to harvest the sea, the forests, the farms, and the mines receive meager social services and struggle with a low standard of living. Underdevelopment alone does not explain the lack of services. Power shifts periodically between two political parties, called Liberals and Progressive Conservatives, although their policies are neither liberal nor progressive. In frantic attempts to attract industry, these governments are willing to pass antiunion legislation and to ignore pollution and conservation standards. Building highways has a higher priority than creating educational programs and health services of quality.

In our province, one of several significant deficiencies in the educational system is the failure to provide for learning-disabled children. Specific deficits such as those affecting reading or writing give these children, despite their adequate general intelligence, considerable difficulty in school. The many programs that have been developed to help these children in the United States and other parts of Canada have not found their way into our school systems. In most districts the learning disabled were either left to fend for themselves in regular classes of thirty to forty children or dumped into the only special programs available: those created for the mentally retarded.

In a political context where lack of social services is the norm, the failure to meet the needs of these children would be unlikely to attract attention. Neisser (1976, p. 69) points out, "Properties we don't notice are like ideas we have not had. They leave no gap in the world; it takes information to specify gaps." We received information specifying this particular gap in different ways, both largely by chance. One of O'Neill's night school students enlisted his aid to find help for her learning-disabled son. The boy, who had been in school for two years, had a deficit that affected his motor coordination and impaired his ability to write. The boy's mother, a hospital official, had succeeded in getting extensive testing for the child. But official attention to the problem seemed to end with diagnosis. The school filed the neurological findings and continued as before—that is, giving no special attention or treatment to this boy. Working through the local university's school of education, the boy's mother was able to get tutorial help for the boy once a week. The mother reported that the only days her son wanted to go to school were those when he would meet with his tutor. In the absence of other supportive measures in the school, however, there was still not enough progress to advance the child to the next grade. He was held back and his emotional adjustment to school deteriorated.

When Loomes moved into the district, he and his family rented a cottage on the grounds of a new private school for learning-disabled children. The school, an offshoot of a successful program in New England, had been established the previous year; it had taken over a converted motel and was making up its operating deficit by renting out some of the former motel units. The school had twenty-six children in residence and seven staff members. Its program was dramatically successful–in fact, it was showing an average three-year jump in educational level for each half-year semester. Although special techniques were used, the program seemed to succeed not because of any mysterious nostrum but because of sustained focus on the problem and long hours of hard work. Staff members worked with students both day and evening hours, often extending into the weekends.

The cost of the residential program was $8,500, well out of reach of most parents. Even this substantial sum was $2,000 below cost for each student–hence the renting of cottages on school property. Through daily contact with the program and the children it served, and less regular contact with visiting parents, Loomes learned that few of the families could absorb these costs without hardship. Most were middle-class people who ordinarily would never have considered private school among their aspirations. One widow sold most of her assets to raise the tuition so her seventeen-year-old son could have one year in the program. In that year his education level was boosted from grade 5 to grade 11, and his self-esteem was greatly improved. But the fees had drained away most of what this elderly woman counted on for her old age. Loomes reasoned that the public school system must be acutely deficient in serving the learning disabled to prompt parents of average financial means to take such drastic steps to help their children.

After glimpsing the problem through these two different windows, we reconnoitered the situation informally. It took little inquiry to learn about the meager services for the learning disabled in public schools. As noted earlier, the problem was so severe that the schools lacked both programs and even an adequate conception of this need. We felt they were in a position to help effect change. O'Neill taught a graduate course in community consultation; Loomes had a background in learning disabilities and was now completing graduate education in community-clinical psychology.

The first question we had to answer for ourselves was this: What is the appropriate level of intervention? Earlier we outlined the disadvantaged nature of the economy in the Atlantic provinces; yet we did not conceive of learning disabilities as a national issue. Provinces have control over education. The number of children with specific learning disabilities, and the probable cost of providing adequate programs, seemed well within the financial capacity of the province. On the other hand, the problem could not be solved by any teacher or school without the system's support.

We concluded that an effective intervention strategy would have both provincial and local components. The provincial government could make funds available to school districts to cover the costs of programs for these children, earmark the funds so they could not be diverted, and set staffing guidelines that would provide standards of service. Provincial legislation could be introduced to require proper diagnostic screening throughout the province.

Local districts could initiate action by budgeting for programs for the learning disabled and fighting for those programs as high-priority items in negotiation with the provincial government. Local officials would have to justify such expenditures to local taxpayers. If and when money was available, district officials would have to recognize the scope of the problem to spend the funds effectively. Our consultation effort began at the district level, but we knew that a real solution would have to involve new thinking at the provincial level.

Local officials were potential allies but were also potential targets of pressure—an ambiguous situation that presented some problems. If district officials were eventually to help make demands of the provincial government, they would have to acknowledge an unmet need. Rarely do school administrators make such admissions. They find it more comfortable to think they are providing adequate programs to meet all legitimate needs.

In our district, the school board could point to the fact that it had a supervisory staff member who had the title of learning disabilities specialist. Because few other school districts had an official with such a title, local administrators felt they were unusually progressive in recognizing the needs of the learning disabled. The facts were somewhat different. The man who had become the specialist was originally hired to fill the only psychologist position with the school district, but he lacked the qualifications for such a position. In the early months of his employment, while he struggled to cope with the role description of a psychologist, the provincial psychological association was indignantly complaining to the minister of education. When the complaint came under scrutiny from the minister's office, local school administrators eliminated the school psychologist position entirely. They retained the employee but gave him a new title: learning disabilities specialist. The lack of programs for the learning disabled meant the new specialist could continue to perform his old functions.

People become captives of their own fictions. Local officials seemed to forget the odd route by which they had acquired a specialist; they believed with apparent sincerity that his very title indicated they were doing something for the learning disabled. The man who occupied the post also seemed to think that his title, no matter how he came by it, validated his authority. Before we spoke to him we had heard many horror stories about his approach to learning disabilities. After one parent took her child to a major center for neuropsychological assessment, she met with the specialist to explain that her child had been given a battery of tests. He quickly made a sketch of "the brain" on a piece of scratch paper, handed it to her, and asked her to try to remember what the neuropsychologist had said and to indicate on the sketch what sort of disability her child had. Whether such stories were true or apocryphal, they indicated the prevailing view of this man by parents who needed his help. Nevertheless it was important that we talk with him, since he might prove a valuable ally. If he recognized the need for more resources to meet the needs of the learning disabled, the very fact that he was labeled a learning disabilities specialist would work in our favor.

The specialist proved to be somewhat ambivalent about the issue. He knew enough about learning disabilities to realize the need was greater than the resources that had been committed. But he had a stake in believing that he was doing his job—and, by virtue of his title, that job seemed to include providing effective programs for the learning disabled.

The specialist admitted that children with learning disabilities had been neglected, particularly beyond the elementary school level. He was particularly annoyed that the school district insisted on integrating such children into classes intended for slow learners, primarily those children called "the educable mentally retarded." Instead he believed learning-disabled children should be mainstreamed, with additional support provided for regular classroom teachers. The specialist's plan called for reading teachers to serve as consultants to classroom teachers. If a classroom teacher was unable to meet the child's needs, the specialist himself would meet with both the classroom and the reading teachers to find some solution. This rather vague program had several problems. Since there was, at most, one reading teacher in a school, and since few of these teachers had any training in learning disabilities, they were unlikely to offer the classroom teacher much support. Because the specialist still had many duties from his former job description, the effectiveness of his own intervention was doubtful. Finally, his program did not remedy the failure of the school board to provide adequate diagnostic assessment to pinpoint problems.

Despite his evident good intentions, the specialist's program seemed to be an example of what Graziano (1969) called innovation without change. Graziano postulated that in the mental health field most communities have a power structure committed primarily to its own preservation and threatened by any demands for significant change. The power structure has various means of neutralizing true innovation: rejecting outright any plans for change; appearing to support the objectives while building in so many safeguards, such as committees, that no real change can be implemented; incorporating the innovation but altering it to fit the preexisting structure so that nothing is really changed. We seemed to have found an educational analog to what Graziano had discovered in mental health.

In our district the board had recognized the needs of the learning disabled to the extent of giving one official a new title. The new learning disabilities specialist, however, was an individual whose credentials were not strong enough to allow him to exert effective influence on the school board. His own well-meant solutions to the problem required no new staff, no additional expenditures, and no changes in present testing practices. Even while trying to do what had become his job, this man was utterly locked into the strategy of innovation without change.

Graziano's own experience caused him to argue that progress would not be initiated by or through the power structure; it would depend instead on successfully changing or ignoring that structure. We did not think we could afford to write off district officials completely. Yet everything we saw suggested that Graziano was probably right in discounting such a power structure as a willing partner from the outset. We decided to follow his advice and ignore the power structure, at least initially. The task would be to organize parents.

Action: Organizing Parents

Parents of children with learning disabilities had to be located. For several reasons, we did not approach the schools for names. We doubted that formal cooperation of this sort would be forthcoming without considerable negotiation, and such negotiations did not seem worth the effort. Moreover, lack of adequate diagnostic assessment in the schools meant that many learning-disabled children must be going unnoticed. Classroom teachers might know who the children were, but there was no formal mechanism for putting their names in any central register, and no reason for doing so.

There were other routes of this sort that, for similar reasons, we chose not to take. We might have gone to the major urban center in our province, for example, and contacted the children's hospital where neuropsychological testing was usually done. But to release names, the hospital would have had to contact all parents and gain their permission. We knew the first meeting with parents—the way the callers presented themselves and described the project—would be crucial for the success of any organizing venture; so to leave this initial contact in the hands of the hospital staff, over whom we would have no control, was too risky. We had to face the fact that no simple procedure would give us the names we needed.

According to Sarason and colleagues (1977, p. 39), "Networks exist; they are not created." His broad definition of their existence includes the possibility that networks may exist on the conceptual level before there is any regular contact among their members. A community of interest suggests the existence of a network, for example, and the consultant's task may be to draw together those people with common interest. In Sarason's phrase, the network then emerges. For us a potential network existed: parents of learning-disabled children. We wanted to provide the links among these people and then to offer some rationale for maintaining the links.

Sarason and colleagues (1977) have noted that a major purpose of networks is to reduce the sense of isolation that people feel in their lives. We expected this feeling to be particularly relevant in the present case. Parents often feel alone when they discover that a child of otherwise average ability has a specific learning problem that cripples school progress, frustrates teachers, and damages the child's self-esteem. In our district, like most in the province, the loneliness would be accentuated by the lack of information for parents and the lack of programs offering some hope of remedy. While this sense of isolation might help us bring parents together, we knew that it would not sustain a network for long. Parents drawn together by a common problem would expect the organization to work to solve that problem.

A special education teacher in a small elementary school was helpful in locating parents. This woman happened to be very well qualified in the learning disabilities field, but her knowledge and skills were not fully used because the local board ignored the issue. She had no programmatic responsibilities other than working in her own school with children who had problems adjusting to the classroom. Nevertheless, before we became interested in the issue, this teacher had taken on the task of trying to organize parents of the learning disabled. She had done this after hours, with no official sanction, and the attempt had failed. (The reason for the failure, and its relevance to our effort, will be mentioned later.) Of note at this point is that the special education teacher was enthusiastic about our project; she provided us with names of parents involved in her own organizing attempt.

As we contacted parents, we asked them if they knew of any others. This procedure is similar to that used by investigators studying social networks (see Mitchell and Trickett, 1980, for a review); but because our criterion was so specific, our task was in one sense more difficult and in another sense easier. According to Mitchell and Trickett, networks are identified through interviews in which respondents are asked questions like these: Name all the people you consider important in your life; name people to whom you feel close and know well; how many adult friends live within a ten-minute walk from your house; and so on. Our question was this: Do you know any other people who have a child with a learning disability? Because our network was unidimensional and easier to define operationally, our task was easier than it would have been with more diffuse networks. It was more difficult, however, because we had no reason to think that respondents would be able to lead us to others. How were we to build a network?

In a successful consultation, theory informs action. How consultants intervene depends not only on their reading of the situation but also on their theoretical models. Our own work in this case was guided by an evolving model of cognitive community psychology (O'Neill, 1981). We believed research findings from the study of cognitive processes, in particular from social cognition, were relevant to community work. We relied on this assumption to lead us beyond the apparent impasse created by the fact that we had very few names of parents and no formal source to extend the list.

We reasoned that in a district with a comparatively small population, each person hears about a number of others. When one hears information about other people much of it is forgotten quickly, but some is striking. There is ample research evidence establishing the importance of salient information (Taylor and Fiske, 1978). If a parent with a learning-disabled child hears, even in casual conversation, about another person with such a child, this is highly salient information. We thought it would persist in the person's memory because of its emotional significance to the listener.

This is a vivid illustration of the marriage of theory and action. Without the theory, we would not have attempted to build a network unless we had a list of names from some other source. If the theory was wrong, our work would be over before it began. In fact, parents we contacted were able to give us names of others that they knew (or suspected they knew) had a learning-disabled child. Often the parent had never met the person whose name they gave us, but at some point they had picked up this information and, because it created a bond with the listener on an emotional issue, it was remembered.

We were able to locate families, but often we ran into resistance from parents unwilling to acknowledge that their child had a learning disability. In the absence of help in the schools, without even a proper diagnostic testing program, some parents coped with the strain by denying the extent of the problem. The child's unusual difficulty with some aspect of schoolwork was blamed on the teacher, the curriculum, the child's motivation, failure to pay attention, and so on. For these parents, joining an organization specifically aimed at parents of learning-disabled children would stigmatize their child. Their action would acknowledge publicly something they would not acknowledge even to themselves. We found some parents simply were not interested; some were hesitant but willing to explore the matter; some were enthusiastic about any project that might improve a situation they faced alone.

In the initial contact with parents, the problem was to

tell them enough about the proposed organization to whet their interest, but not to impose an agenda that was too specific. We wanted to leave room for the network, as it emerged, to set its own goals and determine its own strategy for achieving them. The caller explained that the first step would be to hold a meeting. He said, "I'll phone you again when the first meeting is set up. In the meantime I'd like you to think about what you'd want from such a group—what it might do." We were making a request that was difficult to refuse: simply asking parents to give the matter some thought. The next step, phoning again, would be ours. We were keeping in mind the social-psychological finding that once someone has complied with a small request, it is easier to get compliance with a larger request—in this case to attend the meeting.

This was another point where we drew on theory to guide action. By asking parents to think about what form the organization might take, we implied that they had responsibility for its fate. O'Neill and Eisner (1981) have shown that inducing a sense of responsibility increases the care with which people weigh options and the commitment they feel once the choice has been made. In their experiments, a sense of responsibility was enhanced when the subjects had choice, when they believed that the decision would have serious consequences, and when they were in a better position to influence the outcome of events than were others. In contact with parents, the caller's approach was to make all these aspects of the situation salient. The proposed organization would have important consequences if it improved education for learning-disabled children. Parents had decision-making power over the organization's form and course of action. Finally, their responsibility would not be diminished by making the new organization top-heavy with local professionals who would influence decisions with their expertise. Apart from heightening parents' sense of responsibility, we had another reason for not involving professionals. That issue will be discussed more fully in a moment, but first we should note that few parents were satisfied with only minimal information. Invariably after we asked them to give consideration to the agenda for the group, parents asked what *we* thought the organization might do. They were told the group would probably put pressure on the government to implement learning disabilities programs in the schools, but whether and how to do that would depend on the members themselves.

One of our first decisions was how broad the network should be. This issue had to be faced early because it dictated who we would contact in the first round of phone calls. We chose not to involve parents if the target child was mentally retarded. Our province and the local district boasted strong organizations to advance the concerns of the retarded. Largely through the lobbying of this group, schools officially recognized the needs of retarded children. One might well argue about the way the school was meeting those needs—segregating the children in special classes—but we were not the ones in the best position to fight that battle. Since there were many more parents of retarded children than parents of children with specific learning disabilities, expanding our membership might swamp the needs of the learning disabled.

A more touchy problem was whether or not to invite parents of children with cerebral palsy. These children have needs that converge with those of the learning disabled at some points but diverge at others. It was just this issue that led to the demise of the organization founded earlier by the special education teacher. She had a particular interest in learning problems of children with cerebral palsy; but when she tried to put together a group, the needs of the two groups were sufficiently diverse to involve the group in endless argument. Nevertheless the reasons for not including parents of the mentally retarded did not apply to parents of children with cerebral palsy. The needs of these children were not being met by the schools, and they had no strong local group to fight for them. Since there were even fewer of these children than those with learning disabilities, we could not argue that needs of the learning disabled would be ignored if we invited parents whose children had cerebral palsy. In addition to all these factors, we were by now relying heavily on the help and enthusiasm of the special education teacher. Her strong interest in cerebral palsy had to be respected. Our solution was to call parents of three children with cerebral palsy. The caller emphasized that the purpose of the organization was to help meet the needs of children with learning disabilities, and if these parents thought they could benefit from such a group, they were welcome. Eventually one of the three did accept the invitation, and the issue posed no further problem.

Another question was whether to invite professionals, and if so which ones. In our district professionals are held in such awe (at least by themselves and other professionals) that they are usually invited to join all organizations of this sort. Local psychiatrists, social workers, school officials, and even a lawyer or two had overlapping memberships on more executives than a General Motors board member. At meetings these people talked loudest, longest, and in the jargon that once caused G. B. Shaw to define the professions as a conspiracy against the laity.

We knew from various published cases, particularly that of Graziano (1969), that professionals would be more likely to protect their own interests and those of their agencies than to join parents in a fight for real change in patterns of service delivery. We also had ample personal experience suggesting that some professionals subvert such groups. One of the authors had been involved in an ambitious attempt by former mental patients in the district to start a halfway house. The house was to be run by former patients, primarily to provide a source of support for one another in times of stress. The organizers obligingly invited a variety of professionals to their formative meetings. These meetings lasted more than a year before the organizers finally gave up. The variety of professionals who attended changed from meeting to meeting. They fell into three groups: a few who had a desire to further the project on the terms set out by the former patients and were willing to follow the lead of these lay people; a group whose institutional affiliation and loyalty prompted them to try to transform the halfway house into a mini-institution in the community, fully staffed by medical personnel, to serve as an aftercare facility for long-term patients; and a third group whose agenda seemed to require that the former patients be put in their place and be shown that people without medical credentials should mind their own business. The latter two groups wrangled from meeting to meeting until the group of sympathetic professionals and the former patients sadly faded out of the picture.

This history led us to be very cautious about the number and quality of professionals we invited. We wanted to keep the special education teacher involved, but for several reasons we thought it would be a liability to invite the learning disabilities specialist. He had a stake in defending what little the schools were doing at present. Some parents already had developed antipathy toward him. Finally, he and the special education teacher were on bad terms, largely because it was she who had the educational background that would have been appropriate for one with his job title. Despite all these factors, we invited him. He was aware of what we were doing because of our initial contact. He would be certain to learn about the meetings as they occurred. We did not want to rule him out as an eventual ally, nor did we want to make him an adversary. He accepted the invitation and even offered himself as guest speaker at some future meeting. The last thing we needed for our credibility with parents was to present a platform for this man to draw diagrams of the brain. These problems were solved, however, when he failed to attend our meetings. This was characteristic of his operating mode, including the way he dealt with problems referred to him in the course of his job: initial enthusiasm with no follow-through. In this case, it worked to our advantage, because we got credit for making the invitation without having to contend with his presence.

Before the first meeting we tried to become familiar with the considerable teaching and research literature on learning disabilities. But just how much should we try to absorb? Sarason (1972) has emphasized the advantage of foreseeing problems before one gets into the heat of battle. He has recounted many examples where new organizations have suffered because their creators failed to predict difficulties that were clearly predictable. On the other hand we could not possibly anticipate every question that might arise. Even if we could, doing so might reinforce the stereotype of the professional as omniscient—and hence as one who ought to make the decisions. That was not the image we wanted to project, nor was it the sort of organization we wanted to build. Reppucci and his colleagues (1973) have shown vividly the disastrous consequences that can come of not acting quickly and decisively. In consultation, preparation can be paralyzing.

In the end, the literature on learning disabilities was of surprisingly little use. It turned out that the most helpful reading we did was on the laws of the province governing education. We learned, among other things, that everything relevant to the quality of education was summed up in a single sentence: The provincial government would decide what constituted proper education. This gave us, as one goal, convincing legislators that specific standards for serving groups with special problems were needed.

When the second round of phone calls was made to set up the first meeting of our emerging network, the response was positive. But one parent announced rather grandly that she was the local representative of a provincewide organization called the Association for Exceptional Children—the AEC. Despite its imposing initials, the activities of this group seemed to have been less than explosive. The AEC had apparently taken as its mandate advancing the concerns of the learning disabled and other groups of children loosely defined as exceptional. The woman who proclaimed herself the local representative clearly believed our new group would be on her turf. She seemed willing to attend the meeting primarily to convince parents that they, or perhaps their new group, should be affiliated with the AEC.

We did some investigating of the AEC. It did exist, but it was all but unknown to other parents in our network. At least in our district, the AEC was not providing links among parents of learning-disabled children. Nor was the organization better known in neighboring school districts. Its principal activity seemed to be the appointing of local representatives like the woman we had contacted. We did hear about one group of parents that had formed, affiliated itself with the AEC, and promptly vanished. We reserved judgment on how useful the AEC would be. The final comment of the local representative before she hung up the phone seemed particularly disturbing: "If this is just going to be another meeting where parents whine about their problems, I'm going to walk out!"

The time for our first meeting had arrived—four months after our decision to found an organization. All three meetings to be described were conducted by Loomes. He introduced himself to the twenty parents assembled and explained that this was the founding meeting of an organization that would press for more resources for educating children with learning disabilities. He reminded the group that the phone calls had produced a consensus on this general objective.

We had recognized in our advance planning that a meeting of strangers would be an uncomfortable affair at first. People would need some direction to get things going, even though we were committed to the organization providing its own leadership as soon as possible. Loomes felt obliged to chair the meeting since he had called it. To involve at least some member of the audience, he asked for a volunteer to take minutes of the meeting. There was a nervous silence and a good deal of staring at the floor. Finally one woman reluctantly agreed to act as secretary—"but only for this one meeting."

We had expected that people would need something to do, so a questionnaire had been prepared and it was given to parents to fill out. It asked such questions as: Do you want to be a member of this organization? Would you be able to contribute time to work for the organization? Would you be willing to serve on the executive? It also asked for names, addresses, and phone numbers so we could keep track of those who might have come without being on our contact list. It turned out this was the only function the questionnaire served; answers to the other questions were negative or vague.

When he had collected the questionnaires, Loomes told the group that this ought not to be a meeting where people talked about their own experiences, such as difficulties their child might be having in school. He then asked for agenda items and was met by stony silence.

We were off to a disastrous start. Up to this point in the meeting, just about every move had been wrong. Handing out a questionnaire that demanded definite assertions of commitment simply reminded parents how little they knew about what they were getting into. Asking them so early to agree to devote time to the group, and even to consider being on the executive, was more likely to prompt a refusal than to get them involved.

The most serious mistake was trying to make an introductory meeting of strangers efficient and businesslike. Since our initiative had brought them together, we could hardly expect them to come with agenda priorities. By telling the group not to talk about personal experiences we were cutting them off from the very objective best served by such a meeting: building a sense of community.

Sarason and his colleagues (1977) have found general meetings of this sort to be crucial for a network. But the importance of such meetings does not lie in their decision making. In fact, Sarason's experience suggests that few decisions are made and no votes are necessary. The meeting has more important purposes. It elicits ideas and encourages broad participation. Subsequent meetings keep network members informed about what various people and subgroups have been doing since they last met. The meeting "confronts the implications of new possibilities, it facilitates exposure to new people and ideas, and it gratifies people's need for a sense of noncompetitive common purpose, as well as for a sense of being part of an extended community of people" (Sarason and others, 1977, p. 83). To create this ambience, the chairperson must overcome a natural tendency to get down to business, keep discussion on track, or measure the success of the meeting by the number of decisions made. People must be allowed to brainstorm, to stray from the point, and to relate personal anecdotes so that others come to know who they are, how they feel, and what they think.

What happened next ranks as one of those unpredictable moments that consultants must watch for. Because no one else was contributing to the agenda, Loomes suggested an item. Without knowing whether the AEC representative was present or not, he told the group about the existence of AEC and indicated that the local representative had suggested an affiliation. He also reported on the apparent consequences of affiliation in at least one case: the demise of a local group.

There was a verbal explosion from the back row. The AEC woman was indeed present. She denounced Loomes for what he had said, though she did not dispute the truth of his report. She was adament that the AEC was doing all that was necessary. Finally, she was scathing in her opinion of a local group of parents trying to do any better. When she finally paused for breath, one man remarked, "I don't think we should join AEC right now." This was the turning point in the meeting. His comment was the first time one of the parents had volunteered an opinion, and in so doing he had confronted a supposed expert. Most important, he had done so in the name of the group, thereby publicly assuming that the new organization actually existed.

Within moments, the group had been cleaved in two. At the back of the room a half dozen parents turned to listen to an angry stream of comments from the AEC representative. Paradoxically (but not really surprising), about half of what she had to say concerned problems her child was having in school—the very sort of discussion she had not wanted to hear. The rest of her comments seemed to be arguments against trying to do anything about the problem. (Later, when we looked at the questionnaire she had filled out, we found she had written that we were "looking for trouble.")

The remaining two thirds of the parents paid this subgroup no further attention. Instead they began an animated discussion consisting largely of anecdotes about their difficulties with the school system. But unlike the focus of comments at the back of the room, these stories seemed to fill parents with enthusiasm. They found that others shared the same problems; perhaps, working as a group, they could do something.

In hindsight, we can see why the AEC representative's manner was a catalyst for this dramatic change. Her insults seemed inappropriate when directed against the rather mild remarks of the chairperson and hence caused others to feel sympathy for him. Her claim that the AEC was doing a good job seemed ridiculous to parents who had never heard of the group. Finally, she belittled the very people sitting before her, heaping scorn on their abilities, a tactic certain to alienate them.

By the end of the meeting, with no formal votes or decisions, the group had been formed. Parents were beginning to feel the emotional ties that would be necessary to sustain a mutually supportive network. Loomes promised to arrange for a guest speaker to address the next meeting and urged parents to bring others who might benefit.

One parent volunteered to help with the telephoning. Loomes eventually made use of her assistance, but for the next meeting he telephoned everyone on the list himself. He wanted to probe, as tactfully as possible, the reasons why those absent had not shown up. Two other parents volunteered to write articles about the meeting for the two weekly papers in the immediate area. One might argue that the group should have been more consolidated before its existence was announced in news stories. After all, if its formation threatened the AEC, the potential for alarming people such as school officials was even more likely. If articles were to be written, perhaps the chairperson should do the job himself to ensure accuracy and present the right impression. Despite these valid considerations, it seemed that recognizing and reinforcing the wish of people to be actively involved was more important. The volunteers wrote their articles, which were both accurate and positive. When the stories appeared, several more sets of parents contacted us. They either knew or suspected that their children had learning disabilities and wanted to join. The membership of the network, at least as measured by our contact list, was more than forty.

The guest speaker was a particularly dynamic woman from the provincial capital. Her expertise in the field of learning disabilities was matched by her conviction that something more should be done to meet the needs of learning disabled children. She was chosen not primarily for her expertise, although it was impressive, but for her ability to infuse a group with both indignation and enthusiasm. When she appeared at our group's second meeting, she began by working the crowd to sell buttons and bumper stickers that advocated programs for the learning disabled. Having made her sales, she promptly turned over all profits to the group. At a stroke she had encouraged members to make a public commitment by buying (and presumably later displaying) these buttons and bumper stickers; she had also founded a treasury. The latter was more important for symbolic value than the actual cash. Once a group has funds, even a token amount, it has to do something with them. Step by step, we were becoming psychologically prepared for action.

Our visitor's speech was as rousing as expected. The enthusiastic discussion after her talk focused on the various tribulations parents had experienced with the district's learning disabilities specialist, who was not present at this meeting or at any other that we held. Parents who had dealt with him were probably comparing his level of competence and his attitude with that of the woman who had just spoken to them. They felt cheated. With increasing heat parents told story after story, each reinforcing their anger.

We were caught in a group process phenomenon that had its dangers. O'Neill and Levings (1979) have investigated the biased scanning of arguments that occurs in group discussion. They found that attitudes become more extreme and harden as group members tend to look at only one side of an issue. The dangers lay in precluding a future relationship between our group and the learning disabilities specialist. If he felt himself to be our target (and his absence from the meeting would not prevent him from hearing about it), he would not welcome our contributions later. Yet if we were successful in getting more resources committed for learning disabilities, he would have an important role in administering the programs. Moreover, if members talked themselves into a hard-line position they would have an obstacle to overcome before they could offer help when it might be useful. It was necessary to intervene, hoping to take some of the edge off these comments. The chairperson pointed out that whatever his own failings, the learning disabilities specialist could not hope to succeed with the resources at his disposal. The demand for change had to be focused elsewhere. It was unlikely that this official would be replaced, and even if he were it would make no difference without allocation of new resources. The discussion was more balanced by the end of the meeting; but once again the report of common experiences, this time in relation to a particular official, had brought our members closer together.

By our third session, we were able to set the framework

for an organization that could accomplish tasks between meetings. The members gave their group a name. A woman volunteered to be corresponding secretary; a husband and wife offered to share the tasks of recording secretary. We noted that while our whole membership could be described as falling into the middle-class financial bracket, these three volunteers were the only ones who actually had their own small businesses.

Four committees were formed to deal with pressure on government, funding of the organization, educating the public about learning disabilities, and direct service to children. The latter committee was considered essential because it could give members a sense of accomplishment whatever the duration and outcome of any campaign undertaken to get more funds from government. Ideal committees probably would consist of people interested in one topic more than the others. But we had to take pragmatic considerations into account. Ours is a far-flung and mostly rural district where traveling is difficult in the winter months, and our committees were formed of people who lived near one another.

Various ideas were suggested by members. They talked about writing newspaper articles, distributing literature, showing films, writing to local politicians. One suggestion that received immediate support was a workshop to show parents how to help their learning-disabled children. Members also spoke of the need to learn more about various aspects of the problem and the sorts of programs that were being provided in other parts of North America. They thought this knowledge would be important for the day when they confronted politicians.

Our organization was formed. The actual details of putting it together have now been given. At the time of writing, the group is girding itself for its various tasks. Some will be difficult —such as the need to persuade government to commit more resources and to specify the programs that local districts must offer. We know we will face the argument that resources are scarce, an argument that has some validity. But we have seen that priorities can be reshuffled, as they were when a strong organization demanded educational programs for the mentally retarded.

In the second year after the organization's founding, the provincial government made what it considered a major concession. Tuition at a private institution would be paid by the province for any learning-disabled child whose needs were not being met in public schools. This concession was problematic for several reasons. It signaled again the provincial government's refusal to accept the responsibility to provide adequate programs in the public schools. And the cost involved in sending children to a private institution, coupled with the lack of diagnostic procedures recognized by the provincial government, almost guaranteed that educational officials would apply the new policy in an arbitrary way. This proved to be the case; children whose learning disabilities had been discovered and diagnosed at the expense of their parents were denied help from the provincial government. Nevertheless the concession really was of significant value. It put the government on record as admitting that there were children whose needs were not being met in the public schools. This admission could be used as a lever in negotiations with the government by parents, including those in organizations such as the one we have described.

Looking ahead, we know some of our tasks will be relatively easy—providing a workshop to show parents how they can work more effectively with their children after school, for example. The greatest challenge to the group will be to maintain a good balance between goals that can be accomplished easily and those that take longer. Although it will be tempting to devote much of the group's energy to workshops, public education, and building a mutually supportive network to help children, these activities might shortchange the need to get more resources committed in the school system.

Implications for the Organizer

After years of working in schools, consulting to schools, and thinking about schools, Seymour Sarason concludes: "The schools will never have resources to deal adequately, let alone excellently, with the problems of children" (Sarason and others, 1977, p. 109). We take this to be a realistic statement of the context in which the consultant works to improve conditions. The fact that resources are scarce does not absolve those who control the public purse from the responsibility of distributing resources wisely and justly. All needs cannot be met completely, but some children have needs that are not met at all. Whole groups, such as the learning-disabled children in our district, may be simply passed over. When that happens, educational consultants may find that the community at large, rather than the classroom, is the appropriate field of action. They may find themselves, as we did, organizing parents to provide advocacy for children whose problems are ignored.

The extensive literature on building poor people's organizations probably can be applied straightforwardly to organizing similar social class groups to fight for educational improvement. But the process may be different when parents are drawn primarily from the middle class. In this section we examine some ideas drawn from the work of Si Kahn (1970) and Saul Alinsky (1946, 1971; Saunders and Alinsky, 1970) and consider their applicability to groups like ours.

In his organizing manual *How People Get Power,* Kahn pointed out that local power structures may have very little real power and few resources at their disposal. "Confrontation tactics are basically aimed at the redistribution of wealth and other resources; and it is not always true that within a given community there is enough wealth to redistribute" (1970, p. 16). We took this observation into account in our preliminary study of the situation for learning-disabled children. The local district could have done more, particularly in terms of recognizing their needs and pressing for programs when submissions were made to the government. Nevertheless, we saw that the issue was best considered on a provincewide scale. Confrontation of the local school board would, at best, shift scarce resources from one area (perhaps from the retarded) to learning-disabled children. We tried to keep open the possibility that local school officials eventually might be our partners in advocacy. This strategy seemed fruitful. When news of our meetings appeared in weekly papers, several school principals expressed interest. They had been concerned about the learning disabled in their schools, although there had been no forum for them to express such concern. They were prepared to cooperate in various ways—from preparing programs that could be instituted when funding was obtained to permitting volunteers to work with children in regular classrooms.

Organizers like Saul Alinsky have been extremely successful in discovering the issues that mobilize poor people and transform feelings of hopelessness into outrage. As one looks around a slum neighborhood, conditions that afflict the poor are usually obvious. Alinsky quotes a prototypical street-corner conversation between a resident and the newly-arrived organizer:

> *Organizer:* Do you live in that slummy building?
>
> *Answer:* Yeah. What about it?
>
> *Organizer:* What the hell do you live there for?
>
> *Answer:* What do you mean, what do I live there for? Where else am I going to live? I'm on welfare.
>
> *Organizer:* Oh, you mean you pay rent in that place?
>
> *Answer:* Come on, is this a put-on? Very funny! You know where you can live for free?
>
> *Organizer:* Hmm. That place looks like it's crawling with rats and bugs.
>
> *Answer:* It sure is.
>
> *Organizer:* Did you ever try to get the landlord to do anything about it? [1971, p. 103]

It is less apparent what conditions will ignite the employed, well-housed, well-fed middle class; but in some situations these people may find themselves among the disadvantaged. In our case the lack of resources for the learning disabled provided a potent issue. It may be that middle-class organizations form best around such single issues with membership largely confined to those affected by the problem at hand.

Kahn (1970) indicates that the port of entry often poses particular problems—and the decision one makes about how to handle those problems will affect the whole project. A fairly common situation in the early days of the civil rights movement was for a young, white, middle-class student from a northern college to arrive in a small southern town and move in with a black family: "Such possibilities as working directly with the power structure or organizing among the poor whites in the community were abruptly ruled out" (p. 3). But if the organizer had chosen to live in the white community, he or she would have found it difficult to work among blacks: "Few blacks could afford to trust or even tolerate anyone working with poor whites or with the white power structure" (p. 3).

In our case the analogous problem concerned the learning disabilities specialist in the district, whose help we might need in the future, and the special education teacher on whom we were relying immediately. Their mutual ill will tempted us to keep them away from the same meetings. But the consequences of such slights were potentially serious. We invited both, but the problem dissolved when one of the two simply failed to attend. Thus we cannot give much information on how the problem ought to be handled in a situation where two people (or factions) do become involved; we can only indicate that this issue is as likely to come up in middle-class organizations as in those composed of poor people.

When an organization finds it necessary to confront the power structure, tactics must be not only effective but also acceptable to the membership. Here we might expect a large difference between organizing the poor and the middle class. In Alinsky's words, "Tactics must begin with the experience of the middle class, accepting their aversion to rudeness, vulgarity and conflict. Start them easy, don't scare them off" (1971, p. 195). In the first few meetings of our organization the most extreme tactic advocated by anyone, and that in the heat of indignation, was to "write letters to politicians." We were a long way from militancy. That is changing, however, as a function of the way politicians answer (or do not answer) those letters. According to Alinsky, "The opposition's reactions will provide the 'education' or radicalization of the middle class. It does it every time" (p. 195). When government officials ignore polite petitions, refuse to make or keep appointments, demonstrate an unwillingness to listen to reasoned presentations—all these responses may make vulgar tactics seem less vulgar.

Middle-class politeness (timidity?) may put the organization at a disadvantage in one way, but social standing also has its advantages. At the office, in church, through the social club, members of our group are more likely to know people who wield influence. Some of our members have political connections that are unavailable to the rank and file in poor people's organizations.

An important difference between the poor and the middle class is their belief about their own influence over social events. Among the poor, the organizer must combat an apathy born of long-term neglect from the power structure in all areas of their lives. In Kahn's view, "One of the most destructive and persistent legacies of paternalism which exists in almost every poor community is the destruction of poor people's faith in themselves and their own abilities" (1970, p. 51). Alinsky has argued that this psychological condition is not confined to the poor: "The middle class are numb, bewildered, scared into silence. They don't know what, if anything, they can do" (1971, p. 194). Our experience is to the contrary: Feelings of personal powerlessness are much less common in the middle class. This has implications for organizing.

It has been pointed out that the sense of powerlessness has contradictory effects on the motivation of people to engage in social action (O'Neill, 1981). The beliefs that individual difficulties lie in the unresponsiveness of a distant power structure, that power is wielded unjustly, and that resources are distributed inequitably can arouse the sort of anger that can be mobilized to build an organization. But, paradoxically, these same beliefs are components of a belief in external control, which contributes to apathy and inhibits action. The successful organizer must deal with both sides of this apparent contradiction. He or she must pinpoint the social causes of unsatisfactory conditions. But the organizer must also convince people that they can do something about the situation. Belief in an internal locus of control must be fostered.

Both sides of this problem have their challenges; it all depends on whether one is organizing the middle class or the poor. The poor are preconditioned by circumstances throughout their lives to accept the view that the power structure is unresponsive, but they are also conditioned to believe that you can't fight city hall. Apathy is the organizer's most serious challenge. The middle class is accustomed to having its efforts pay dividends. You work for what you get, and you get what you work for. This sense of internal control is likely to be the organizer's ally. But those in the middle class are also captives of the view that the political system is run by people like themselves, doing the best they can with the resources at their command. In our case, parents who believed that the schools offer a reasonable quality of education found that no provision had been made for children with special needs—like those who were learning disabled. Some parents could be pacified, for a time, by the explanation that learning disabilities are so rare that it would be unreasonable to expect each school district to fund expensive programs for a handful of children. But when these parents came together they found there were sufficient numbers to justify such programs, and they were willing to challenge the status quo.

Final Thoughts

In their experience with an emerging network, Sarason and his colleagues (1977) found that quantifiable factors—size and so on—were secondary to the conceptual and philosophical characteristics of their activity. They saw the core of their work as clarifying values and ideas. Organizing is, fundamentally, about the way people think.

Each person's belief system is conditioned by widely held social ideas. French critic Roland Barthes (1972) referred to these social ideas as mythologies. A myth is not necessarily false, but it is always a distortion of reality; it robs events of their unique, intrinsic meanings and infuses them with significance derived from powerful cultural beliefs. The organizer must grapple with these myths to achieve the goal summed up by Sarason and colleagues (1977): altering people's conceptions about resources, work roles, and relationships.

A powerful mythology in our society is that of the rugged individual in the context of a competitive society. If people sometimes need nourishment and support they are expected to find it in the family, usually the nuclear family. As we become alienated from those beyond the family, we are robbed of a sense of community. A mythology in which competition and individual enterprises are glorified makes cooperative ventures suspect. In the words of the AEC representative, "You're looking for trouble." The dark side of the individual initiative myth is individual isolation.

Isolation is particularly harsh for those, such as the parents of learning-disabled children, who must struggle with a burden they do not really understand. The nuclear family, even the extended family, has little to offer. Well-meaning family members are all in the same emotional crucible without the special skills needed to help. The mythology feeds on the very isolation it breeds. While they remain isolated from each other, those victimized by a social condition cannot think together or act together. The community psychologist who forges links among such people contributes to a new conception of the problem, including the necessity of social change as part of the solution. The organizer's message to the isolated is, to steal a phrase from science fiction, "We are not alone."

Conclusions: Issues and Similarities Across Cases

Judith L. Alpert

The contributors to this book have presented frank and detailed accounts of their consultation to schools. They have described what happened as well as the puzzles and problems they faced and how they conceptualized the issues. Each author considered the school and community culture and the four phases of consultation: (1) entry, including their formal and informal contract, how it was established, and the entry process itself; (2) diagnosis, including the problem, how it arose, how it was discovered, and the perception of the problem by significant school and community people; (3) the intervention, including what they did and why, the result, and their attempts to sustain the intervention; and (4) evaluation, including how they and others evaluated the intervention. Although different contributors concentrated on different aspects of these consultation stages, all of them commented on these issues. Collectively the ten case studies indicate the varied ways in which successful psychological consultants work in schools and conceptualize their work.

The ten cases differ in many dimensions. In this final chapter I want to consider issues related to two of these dimensions: One is the consultant's relationship to the system with respect to internality/externality; the other is the specificity of the consultation contract. These two dimensions are important with respect to both consultation process and outcome but have not received the attention they deserve in either the literature or practice. Although the ten cases differ in many dimensions, there are similarities with respect to what they have to teach, and these common themes will be considered here also.

Issues

Two dimensions will be considered in this section: the consultant's relation to the school with respect to internality/externality and the specificity of the consultation contract. My intent is to stimulate thinking about the consultant's relationship to the school, the meaning of the contract, and the possible implications of variations among these dimensions.

Internality/Externality. The ten cases vary with respect to the degree that the consultant is internal to the system. Although a consultant's relationship to a system is labeled "internal" or "external," it actually lies somewhere along a continuum. In Medway and Nagle's case, for example, they are external to the system in that they are not full-time salaried employees of the school district; however, they are internal in that they have spent several days a week in the schools over several years. Their relationship is internal too in that it was inherent in the previously established agreement between the school district and the university and did not necessitate negotiation of formal entry into the system. Bardon is more internal to his system than Medway and Nagle in that he is a full-time salaried employee of his "university school district."

Some important differences result from the consultant's

position on the internal/external continuum. What helps me to clarify these differences is an analogy to the family. Before I married I was basically outside my husband's family and fairly objective about them and my husband's relationship with them. Minor injustices were exchanged between us as well as between family members, and I could deal with them in a reasonably objective manner. Over the years I have become more of an insider, although I will never be as internal as those who have been part of the family since birth. Although I know the family system better now, I am part of the dynamics. I squabble with my in-laws, take sides when other family members squabble, and am seen as having vested interests, which in fact I do. I am at various times a reason for guilt, rage, jealousy, warmth, and love, and these charged emotions are mutual. Thus one's position on the internal/external continuum has important consequences indeed. It is not that one is better or worse. Rather, the consultant's position on the continuum has implications for consultative activity. In the following consideration of the issues, I concentrate on the endpoints of the continuum for emphasis although, as indicated, in practice the consultant's relationship to the school lies somewhere in between.

What are the issues? One issue concerns the consultant's knowledge of the system. As I became more a part of my husband's family, I became more knowledgeable about it. Similarly, the internal consultant may know the system better and thus have greater understanding of the context of the problem, the history of the organization, and impending changes. On the other side, as I became more internal my objectivity diminished. The external consultant may therefore have the advantage of objectivity and be able to see the system as it is. From a reading of these ten cases it is difficult to determine whether a case indicates objectivity, although the reader is encouraged to consider the case in this way. Moreover, although it is hard to determine whether the internal or the external consultant knows the system better, the cases by internal consultants Bardon and Carner indicate considerable knowledge of their system.

A second issue concerns the consultant's vested interests. Here the internal consultant seems to be at a disadvantage in that there may be an investment in system maintenance rather than system change or, alternatively, an investment in system change that is consistent with self-interest. It may have been hard, for example, for an internal consultant to help a school cope with its death as I was able to do. As an external consultant I was less personally affected by system change and, in this regard, may have been more willing to accept the school's death and to help school staff and others cope with it. Changing a system involves some risk, and internal consultants may be less willing to take risks that involve the systems upon which they depend.

Whether a consultant is involved in system maintenance or system change clearly depends on more than one's relationship to the school. Such factors as the contract with the system and the type of consultation determine the consultant's focus. Newman and Bloomberg's relationship to the school, for example, falls closer to the external pole on the continuum. However, they contracted to accept the system as it was and work within it.

A third issue concerns the consultant's degree of accountability to the system. As I became more a part of my husband's family, I was perceived as more accountable for my actions. Similarly, the internal consultant is more likely to be seen as accountable and responsible to the system. All the issues presented here are related to each other in a complex way, of course. This issue, for example, is related to vested interests. Given greater accountability, the internal consultant may be less willing to risk system change. While the internal consultant clearly bears the burdens of responsibility and accountability, the external consultant should be cautious in this regard. Sometimes it appears that the external consultant has developed a rationale for never being responsible.

Although it is difficult to determine whether internal or external consultation indicates more or less accountability, the cases by internal consultants Carner and Bardon do suggest a sense of responsibility to the system. While the case by external consultants O'Neill and Loomes may not indicate system accountability, it could certainly be regarded as indicating responsibility to learning-disabled children. Thus we face the issue of "who is your client" in the guise of "accountability." Perhaps internal consultants are more likely to regard the client as the system rather than one group of individuals.

The fourth issue concerns the consultant's involvement with the system. As I became more a part of my husband's family, they perceived me as more stable, continuous, and available—perceptions that had profound implications for our relationship. Similarly, consultants differing along the internal/external continuum are viewed differently with respect to stability, continuity, and availability. Given the internal consultant's greater availability to the system and longer association with it, he or she may build rapport faster and may be viewed as more credible and more legitimate. It is possible, however, that it is the external consultant who is seen as more credible. Frequently external consultants are invited to a school for a specific purpose. External consultant Gesten and Weissberg's expertise on preventive programs was evident to school personnel, for example, and for the most part they were regarded as credible and legitimate in this regard.

Thus internal and external consultants are viewed differently with respect to stability, continuity, and availability, and possibly also with respect to credibility and legitimacy, and these different perceptions have implications for consultation. The external consultant, for example, may want to build in stability, continuity, and availability somehow. In my practicum course in school consultation, students work in schools as consultants for one day a week for an academic year. To build in continuity, these student consultants maintain logs that are available to future consultants. To increase stability and continuity, future school consultants visit their prospective schools with present student consultants the spring before they begin consultation. Moreover, for several years we have had past consultants meet with present consultants either formally or informally. We have been less creative about increasing availability, though. Perhaps we should train a school staff member to serve in our absence or make ourselves more available by means of telephone hours.

Schmuck's case illustrates coordination between internal and external consultants. Schmuck and his staff trained people to function as change agents in the district.Although they do not function formally as change agents in their own schools, they have the appropriate skills and may informally support the efforts of change agents from other schools. Thus the trained consultants, employed as full-time employees in the system, have an opportunity to know the system. The consultants who work in their district, although in another school, are perceived differently with respect to continuity, stability, and availability than the traditional external consultant. Further, as they do not work in the school in which they consult, they may not have as much vested interest as an internal consultant from within the school. Perhaps Schmuck's system combines the advantages of internal and external consultation in promoting system change. As a variation on this theme, an external consultant might promote change within a system whereas the school psychologist or internal consultant could later work to consolidate those changes. When the focus is on the mental health of children rather than the mental health of an institution, such coordination between internal and external consultants may not be indicated.

Specificity of Contract. Another issue on which there is variation concerns the specificity of the consultation contract with respect to the consultant's focus and activities. Here too specificity of contract lies along a continuum. A general contract is exemplified by the case Bardon presents while a more specific contract is exemplified by Gesten and Weissberg's case. Bardon was invited to be the college psychologist. He was asked to help improve the quality of life in the school and to engage in future planning and serve as a developer, intermediary, interpreter, and entrepreneur of educational change. The contract gave him freedom with respect to his activities, and, as the case indicates, these activities were varied and comprehensive. Clearly his task—to improve school life by serving as intermediary and interpreter—could be carried out in a variety of ways. In contrast, Gesten and Weissberg contracted to develop a preventive program; in their case the content of the program, the mental health approach, and the procedure for carrying out the program were fairly specific at the time of system entry and contract negotiation.

Although some contracts remain nonspecific, others evolve and become more specific. The cases by Cherniss, Trickett, D'Antonio, and Tracy and by Medway and Nagle exemplify evolutionary contracts. Medway and Nagle, for example, indicate that initially they did not have a consultation plan or purpose in mind. They learned about the problems facing the students and faculty through informal as well as formal means. From these assessments they developed a number of specific consultative activities. Contracts vary also with respect to other variables such as formality and the degree of collaboration involved in contract negotiation. The focus here, however, is on the specificity of the contract with respect to the consultative focus and activities.

Different issues are raised according to the degree of specificity of the consultation contract. In identifying these issues, for the most part I will consider the endpoints of the specificity continuum. One issue concerns the identification of need. Consultants with specific contracts may find they have contracted to do something that does not need doing or is not a productive use of their time. While such a dilemma is not represented in the cases here, it does occur and is exemplified by the school psychologist who accepts a traditional diagnostic role rather than negotiating a consultative contract. If the need is correctly identified in a specific contract, of course, there is a possibility of meeting the school's need. While there is no guarantee that needs are correctly identified in a general contract, there is more opportunity to determine consultative focus and appropriate consultative activity.

A second issue concerns the expectation of the consultee. With a specific contract the consultee has a clear expectation. While this clarity may make it easier to evaluate consultative efforts later, it promotes a false sense of power in an area where many elements are outside the consultant's control. Gesten and Weissberg's case, for example, involved a specific contract. Their contract may have promoted a false aura of wisdom and power and caused these competent consultants to spend less time learning about the inner-city community in which the expansion program was housed. There are concerns regarding the general contract too. Here there is ambiguity about what the consultant has to offer and why the consultant is at the school at all. The consultees may have few expectations and may even resent consultants and resist their efforts. Some people prefer clarity to ambiguity. This preference may result in premature settling of consultative focus.

A third issue concerns renegotiation. In time a consultant's understanding of a problem may change. Alternatively, the needs of a school may change. With a specific contract, a consultant may be engaged in the consultation activity at hand and may not be aware of new and pressing school needs. Moreover, with a specific contract it may be harder for the consultee to recognize the consultant's expertise in other areas. In contrast, the consultee with a general contract may be open to renegotiation. My initial contract fell closer to the general end of the contract continuum, for example, and was conceptualized as an evolving one: It was agreed that the contract would be renegotiated at various times and that different contracts would exist between different consultant-consultee pairs. In the case I described, the consultative focus seemed less relevant as the needs of the school shifted. It was time to help the school cope with its death. Since the consultants were working on a specific project at the time, it may be that our involvement with the project mitigated against earlier intervention regarding the school's demise. I am not making a case here against specific contracts or focused projects. I am trying to make a case for receptivity to assessment and reassessment and for renegotiation of contracts.

All the cases presented here illustrate concern with the consultation contract; in fact, the focus in Carner's case is on the development of a contract. What the cases indicate is that contracts are important and that they set limits as to what can and cannot be done. Further, the consultant should be aware of the implications resulting from the contract's specificity. The experienced consultants represented here directed exemplary attention to contracting.

Similarities

Models. Another respect in which the cases differ concerns models of consultation. Different models are represented in the book, although I am not convinced there is agreement on which model was actually used in each case. In the consultation literature, the models of consultation (mental health, behavioral, organization development, and advocacy) are defined, described, and compared. The literature will not be summarized here, but I do want to point out that while a consultant may identify with a certain consultative model, it appears that aspects of several models are used simultaneously. In Gesten and Weissberg's case, for example, the training program is a behavioral one; on this basis, some might call Gesten and Weissberg's work an example of behavioral consultation. The focus of their program is on mental health, however, and their work could thus be considered mental health consultation involving the use of a behavioral program. Although their consultation is not organization development, since it is not their primary goal to alter the system, the introduction of a training program to improve teachers' ability to cope in the classroom and to enhance children's adjustment did result in organizational changes as well as a careful consideration of organizational issues. And if advocacy consultation is defined as a question of professional ethics, their work could also be seen as exemplifying advocacy consultation.

Clearly some of the assumptions and intervention techniques may differ according to model and different issues may be raised by different models. Nevertheless, there is a commonality among all these models. Each consultant, regardless of orientation, dealt with resistance and issues relevant to values and ethics. In many cases the answers to various consultative problems have been more a function of the consultants' identity than the model they identified with. Thus, although there are differences in focus among the models, consultants use aspects of several models simultaneously and face many of the same issues regardless of model.

School Level. Another point on which the cases differ concerns school level. The first three chapters mainly concern consultation to elementary schools; the fourth chapter concerns consultation to a middle school; the next two chapters concern consultation to a high school. The seventh chapter involves consultation to a school within a university. The eighth and ninth chapters involve consultation to an entire district. The last chapter concerns consultation outside the school that would involve children at all school levels. Thus levels within the school as well as a relationship outside it are represented in this book. What is striking is the similarity in client problems regardless of level; problems described at one level often appeared at another level. Loneliness, the struggle to deal with children's learning and behavioral difficulties, the heavy teaching loads, burnout—these are common problems whatever the teaching level. Even the less typical problems, a school's death for example, could occur at any level as it did in my elementary school.

The requests for consultative help are similar regardless of level also. Bardon was called into the university to improve the quality of life in the School of Education. This request was similar to what consultants at other levels heard. However, while the problems and requests may be similar at all levels, they may be labeled differently. Absence from school might be called "school phobia" in the lower levels and "truancy" in the upper levels. "Teacher's loneliness" may be labeled as such in the elementary school and be termed "need for sense of community" at the university.

Although there are similar client problems at all levels, consultants must understand the specific content relevant to their level. Although each level presents common problems and, usually, common approaches to consultative process, a different body of knowledge is needed by consultants working at different levels. Consultants need to master different aspects of child or adolescent development and curriculum appropriate to the level at which they work. Bardon was obliged to understand the publication process, for example, while one working in the elementary grades would need an understanding of moral development.

Stages and Approach. In many of the cases similarities were observed despite the many dimensions of difference. The following observations concern not only the four stages of consultation but also the consultant's approach and experience.

Concerning entry:

- Schools and school systems are highly interrelated and complex settings.
- There is a flow of effect in schools: from principals to teachers to pupils.
- The informal and formal power structures in schools are not always the same.
- For the most part, schools are insensitive to individual and group needs.
- Teachers and pupils are lonely and feel powerless.
- Consultants should consider power, flow of information, role, communication patterns, and hierarchical levels.
- Consultants must understand the school's culture before they can determine their approach and expectations.
- Consultants need access to high-level school staff.
- Contracts are important—they set limits on what can and cannot be done.
- Developing a consultative relationship takes time.
- The consultant must earn the right to intervene.

Concerning diagnosis:

- The consultant should consider what is reasonable to accomplish given limited resources.
- Values influence perceptions.
- The perceptions of consultants and consultees may differ.
- School needs change, and rediagnosis may be indicated.

Concerning intervention:

- Change is difficult and slow and not always uphill.

- Chance can influence the outcome of consultation.
- Intervention cannot take place without resources such as administrative support, space, time, and luck.
- There are many ways of intervening.
- An intervention at one level in a school involves changes at several levels.
- There are institutional constraints against change; suspicion and resistance are common.

Concerning evaluation:

- The culture of the school, its history, the history of service to the school, and the consultant's personality and ability interact in a complex way to determine the outcome.
- Consultation does not always work out as planned.
- It is never easy to evaluate consultation efforts, and our evaluation often depends on when we choose to evaluate.
- We should be realistic about what can be accomplished and be grateful for partial success.

These observations apply whether the program is being implemented in a school or an entire system—as indicated by a comparison of Weinstein's implementation of a collaborative team focusing on student problems in a middle school and Gesten and Weissberg's development of a school-based social problem-solving training program throughout a system. The point is that consultative stages are similar despite differences in schools as well as differences in the structure of the consultative relationship. In each setting we enter, regardless of size or level, we go through similar consultative stages, observe similarities in school response, and face many of the same consultative issues. In every setting entry is important and resistance inherent. Although we may give different names to the cast of characters in a setting, there are parallels here too. Bardon's university chancellor and vice-chancellor for academic affairs hold positions similar to Carner's superintendent and assistant superintendent. While Bardon and Carner related mostly to a dean or principal respectively, their chancellors and superintendents were in the district and the presence of these powerful figures was felt. I draw on these parallels for several reasons—first because they exist and second because I hope knowledge of them will enable us to enter new settings with more confidence. In many ways, the contributors to this volume are the pioneers of the consultation world. They have explored new territory and shared with us their discoveries. Now it is time for us to move west.

References

Alinsky, S. D. *Reveille for Radicals.* New York: Random House, 1946.

Alinsky, S. D. *Rules for Radicals.* New York: Random House, 1971.

Allen, G. J., and others. *Community Psychology and the Schools: A Behaviorally Oriented Multilevel Preventive Approach.* Hillsdale, N.J.: Erlbaum, 1976.

Alpert, J. L. "Some Guidelines for School Consultants." *Journal of School Psychology,* 1977, *15* (4), 308-319.

Alpert, J. L. "School Consultation and the Analysis of Faculty Meetings." *Professional Psychology,* 1979, *10* (5), 703-707.

Alpert, J. L., and Trachtman, G. M. "School Psychological Consultation in the Eighties." *School Psychology Review,* 1980, *9* (3), 234-238.

Alpert, J. L., Weiner, L. B., and Ludwig, L. "Evaluation of Outcome in School Consultation." *Journal of School Psychology,* 1979, *17,* 333-338.

Altrocchi, J., Spielberger, C. D., and Eisdorfer, C. "Mental Health Consultation with Groups." *Community Mental Health Journal,* 1965, *1,* 127-134.

Arends, R. I., Phelps, J. H., and Schmuck, R. A. *Organization*

Development: Building Human Systems in Schools. Eugene, Oreg.: Center for Educational Policy and Management, 1973.

Arends, R. I., and others. *Organization Development: Building Human Systems in Schools.* Audioslide presentation. Eugene, Oreg.: Center for Educational Policy and Management, 1973.

Axelrod, S. *Behavior Modification for the Classroom Teacher.* New York: McGraw-Hill, 1977.

Bardon, J. I. "The Consultee in Consultation: Preparation and Training." Paper presented at the Annual Convention of the American Psychological Association, San Francisco, August 1977.

Bardon, J. I. "Educational Development as School Psychology." *Professional Psychology,* 1979, *10,* 224-233.

Bardon, J. I., and Bennett, V. C. *School Psychology.* Englewood Cliffs, N.J.: Prentice-Hall, 1974.

Barthes, R. *Mythologies.* New York: Farrar, Straus & Giroux, 1972.

Bell, W. E. "Impact of OD Interventions Conducted by an Internal Cadre of Specialists on the Organizational Processes in Elementary Schools." Unpublished doctoral dissertation, University of Oregon, 1977.

Berman, P. "Thinking About Programmed and Adaptive Implementation: Matching Strategies to Situations." In D. Mann and H. Ingram (Eds.), *Why Policies Succeed and Fail.* Beverly Hills: Sage, 1980.

Berman, P., and McLaughlin, M. W. *Federal Programs Supporting Educational Change.* Vol. 1: *A Model of Educational Change.* Santa Monica: Rand Corporation, 1974.

Bidwell, C. E. "The School as a Formal Organization." In J. G. March (Ed.), *Handbook of Organizations.* Chicago: Rand McNally, 1965.

Bloom, B. L., Asher, S. J., and White, S. W. "Marital Disruption as a Stressor: A Review and Analysis." *Psychological Bulletin,* 1978, *85,* 867-894.

Brickman, W. W. "Adolescents and Alcoholic Abuse." *Intellect,* 1974, *103,* 165.

Callan, M. F. "Are Cadre Interventions Well-Received?" In M. F. Callan and W. P. Kentta (Eds.), "A Backward Glance over

Traveled Roads: An Evaluation of the Eugene Cadre." Unpublished district evaluation report. Eugene, Oreg.: Eugene Public Schools, 1979.

Callan, M. F., and Kentta, W. P. "A Backward Glance over Traveled Roads: An Evaluation of the Eugene Cadre." Unpublished district evaluation report. Eugene, Oreg.: Eugene Public Schools, 1979.

Caplan, G. *The Theory and Practice of Mental Health Consultation.* New York: Basic Books, 1970.

Cherniss, C. "New Settings in the University." Unpublished doctoral dissertation, Yale University, 1972.

Coleman, J. S. *The Adolescent Society.* New York: Free Press, 1961.

Cowen, E. L., Davidson, E., and Gesten, E. L. "Program Dissemination and the Modification of Delivery Practices in School Mental Health." *Professional Psychology,* 1980, *11,* 36-46.

Cowen, E. L., and Gesten, E. L. "Evaluating Community Programs: Tough and Tender Perspectives." In M. Gibbs, J. R. Lachenmeyer, and J. Segal (Eds.), *Community Psychology: Theoretical and Empirical Approaches.* New York: Gardner Press, 1980.

Cowen, E. L., and others. *New Ways in School Mental Health: Early Detection and Prevention of School Maladaptation.* New York: Human Sciences Press, 1975.

Curtis, M. J., and Zins, J. E. *The Theory and Practice of School Consultation.* Springfield, Ill.: Thomas, 1981.

Elardo, P. T., and Caldwell, B. M. "The Effects of an Experimental Social Development Program on Children in the Middle Childhood Period." *Psychology in the Schools,* 1979, *16,* 93-100.

Finkel, M. C., and Finkel, D. J. "Male Adolescent Contraceptive Utilization." *Adolescence,* 1978, *13,* 443-451.

Fullan, M., Miles, M. B., and Taylor, G. "Organization Development in Schools: The State of the Art." *Review of Educational Research,* 1980, *50,* 121-183.

Gesten, E. L., and others. "Promoting Peer Related Social Competence in Young Children." In M. W. Kent and J. E. Rolf

(Eds.), *Primary Prevention of Psychopathology.* Vol. 3: *Promoting Social Competence and Coping in Children.* Hanover, N.H.: University Press of New England, 1979.

Gesten, E. L., and others. "Training Children in Social Problem-Solving Competencies: A First and Second Look." *American Journal of Community Psychology,* 1982.

Goldenberg, I. I. *Build Me a Mountain.* Cambridge: M.I.T. Press, 1971.

Grady, M. A., Gibson, M. J., and Trickett, E. J. *Mental Health Consultation: Theory, Practice, and Research 1973-1978. An Annotated Reference Guide.* National Institute of Mental Health, DHHS Publication No. (ADM) 81-948. Washington, D.C.: U.S. Government Printing Office, 1981.

Graziano, A. M. "Clinical Innovation and the Mental Health Power Structure: A Social Case History." *American Psychologist,* 1969, *24,* 10-18.

Green, M. "Adolescent Health Care." *Children Today,* 1979, *8,* 8-11.

Gross, N., Giacquinta, J. B., and Bernstein, M. *Implementing Organizational Innovations: A Sociological Analysis of Planned Educational Change.* New York: Basic Books, 1971.

Group for Human Development in Higher Education. *Faculty Development in a Time of Retrenchment.* New Rochelle, N.Y.: Change Magazine, 1974.

Halpin, A. W., and Croft, D. B. *The Organizational Climate of Schools.* Chicago: Midwest Administration Center of the University of Chicago, 1963.

Hefferlin, J. L. *Dynamics of Academic Reform.* San Francisco: Jossey-Bass, 1969.

Iscoe, I. "Community Psychology and the Competent Community." *American Psychologist,* 1974, *29,* 607-613.

Kahn, S. *How People Get Power: Organizing Oppressed Communities for Action.* New York: McGraw-Hill, 1970.

Kelly, J. G. "Qualities for the Community Psychologist." *American Psychologist,* 1971, *26,* 897-903.

Klein, D. "Some Notes on the Dynamics of Resistance to Change: The Defender Role." In W. G. Bennis and others (Eds.), *The Planning of Change.* (3rd ed.) New York: Holt, Rinehart and Winston, 1976.

Kramer, J. J., and Nagle, R. J. "Suggestions for the Delivery of Psychological Services in Secondary Schools." *Psychology in the Schools,* 1980, *17,* 53-59.

Kubler-Ross, E. *On Death and Dying.* New York: Macmillan, 1969.

Levine, M. *Some Postulates of Community Psychology Practice.* In F. Kaplan and S. B. Sarason (Eds.), *The Psych-Educational Clinic: Papers and Research Studies.* Community Mental Health Monograph, Vol. 4. Boston: Department of Mental Health, Commonwealth of Massachusetts, 1969.

Lewin, K. "Group Decision and Social Change." In E. E. Maccoby, T. M. Newcomb, and E. L. Hartley (Eds.), *Readings in Social Psychology.* New York: Holt, Rinehart and Winston, 1958.

Lippitt, R., and White, R. "The 'Social Climate' of Children's Groups." In R. G. Barker, J. Kounin, and H. Wright (Eds.), *Child Behavior and Development.* New York: McGraw-Hill, 1943.

McClure, L. D., Chinsky, J. M., and Larcen, S. W. "Enhancing Social Problem-Solving Performance in an Elementary School Setting." *Journal of Educational Psychology,* 1978, *70,* 504-513.

McLaughlin, M. W. "Implementation as Mutual Adaptation: Change in Classroom Organization." *Teachers College Record,* 1976, *77,* 339-351.

Mann, P. A. "Student-Consultants: Evaluations by Consultees." *American Journal of Community Psychology,* 1973, *1,* 182-193.

Martin, R., and Curtis, M. "Effects of Age and Experience of Consultant and Consultee on Consultation Outcome." Paper presented at the annual meeting of the American Psychological Association, New York, September 1979.

Medway, F. J., and Elkin, V. B. "Psychologist-Teacher Collaboration in Developing and Team Teaching High School Psychology Courses." *Psychology in the Schools,* 1975, *12,* 104-112.

Meyer, J. M., and Rowan, B. "The Structure of Educational Organizations." In M. W. Meyer and Associates (Eds.), *Environments and Organizations.* San Francisco: Jossey-Bass, 1978.

Meyers, J., Parsons, R. D., and Martin, R. *Mental Health Consultation in the Schools.* San Francisco: Jossey-Bass, 1979.

Miles, M. B. "Planned Change and Organization Health." In R. O. Carlson and others (Eds.), *Change Processes in the Public Schools.* Eugene, Ore.: Center for the Advanced Study of Educational Administration, 1965.

Miles, M. B. "Some Properties of Schools as Social Systems." In G. Watson (Ed.), *Change Processes in Public Schools.* Washington, D.C.: National Training Laboratory, 1967.

Mitchell, R. E., and Trickett, E. J. "Task Force Report: Social Networks as Mediators of Social Support." *Community Mental Health Journal,* 1980, *16,* 27-44.

Neisser, U. *Cognition and Reality.* San Francisco: W. H. Freeman, 1976.

Newman, R. G. *Psychological Consultation in the Schools.* New York: Basic Books, 1967.

O'Neill, P. "Cognitive Community Psychology." *American Psychologist,* 1981, *36,* 457-469.

O'Neill, P., and Eisner, M. "Responsibility and Decision Making." *Canadian Journal of Behavioral Science,* 1981, *13,* 288-296.

O'Neill, P., and Levings, D. E. "Inducing Biased Scanning in a Group Setting to Change Attitudes Toward Bilingualism and Capital Punishment." *Journal of Personality and Social Psychology,* 1979, *37,* 1432-1438.

Parker, C. A., and Lawson, J. "From Theory to Practice to Theory: Consulting with College Faculty." *Personnel and Guidance Journal,* 1978, *56,* 424-427.

Pelon, D. H., and Bergquist, W. H. *Consultation in Higher Education.* Washington, D.C.: Council for the Advancement of Small Colleges, 1979.

Rappaport, J., Seidman, E., and Davidson, W. S. "Demonstration Research and Manifest Versus True Adoption: The Natural History of a Research Project to Divert Adolescents from the Legal System." In R. J. Muñoz, L. R. Snowden, and J. G. Kelly (Eds.), *Social and Psychological Research in Community Settings.* San Francisco: Jossey-Bass, 1979.

Reppucci, N. D., and others. "We Bombed in Mountville: Lessons Learned in Consultation to a Correctional Facility for Adolescent Offenders." In I. I. Goldenberg (Ed.), *The Helping Professions in the World of Action.* Lexington, Mass.: Heath, 1973.

Runkel, P. J., and others. *Organizational Renewal in a School District.* Eugene, Oreg.: Center for Educational Policy and Management, 1980.

Russ, S. W. "Group Consultation: Key Variables That Effect Change." *Professional Psychology,* 1978, *9,* 145-152.

Sandoval, J., Lambert, N., and Davis, J. M. "Consultation from the Consultee's Perspective." *Journal of School Psychology,* 1977, *15* (4), 334-342.

Sandoval, J., and Love, J. A. "School Psychology in Higher Education: The College Psychologist." *Professional Psychology,* 1977, *8,* 328-339.

Sarason, S. B. *The Culture of the School and the Problem of Change.* Boston: Allyn & Bacon, 1971.

Sarason, S. B. *The Creation of Settings and the Future Societies.* San Francisco: Jossey-Bass, 1972.

Sarason, S. B., and others. *Psychology in Community Settings: Clinical, Vocational, Educational, Social Aspects.* New York: Wiley, 1966.

Sarason, S. B., and others. *Human Services and Resource Networks: Rationale, Possibilities, and Public Policy.* San Francisco: Jossey-Bass, 1977.

Saunders, M. K., and Alinsky, S. D. *The Professional Radical.* New York: Harper & Row, 1970.

Schein, E. H. *Process Consultation: Its Role in Organizational Development.* Reading, Mass.: Addison-Wesley, 1969.

Schmuck, R. A., and Runkel, P. J. *Organizational Training for a School Faculty.* Eugene, Oreg.: Center for Educational Policy and Management, 1970.

Schmuck, R. A., Runkel, P. J., and Langmeyer, D. "Improving Organizational Problem Solving in a School Faculty." *Journal of Applied Behavioral Science,* 1969, *5* (4), 455-482.

Schmuck, R. A., and others. *Handbook of Organization Development in Schools.* Palo Alto, Calif.: Mayfield, 1972.

Schmuck, R. A., and others. *Consultation for Innovative Schools.*

Eugene, Oreg.: Center for Educational Policy and Management, 1975.

Schmuck, R. A., and others. *The Second Handbook of Organization Development in Schools.* Palo Alto, Calif.: Mayfield, 1977.

Siegel, L. M., Attkisson, C. C., and Carson, L. G. "Need Identification and Program Planning in the Community Context." In C. C. Attkisson, M. J. Horowitz, and J. E. Sorenson (Eds.), *Evaluation of Human Service Programs.* New York: Academic Press, 1978.

Spivack, G., and Shure, M. B. *Social Adjustment of Young Children.* San Francisco: Jossey-Bass, 1974.

Taylor, S. E., and Fiske, S. T. "Salience, Attention, and Attribution: Top of the Head Phenomena." In L. Berkowitz (Ed.), *Advances in Experimental Social Psychology.* (Vol. 11) New York: Academic Press, 1978.

Tharp, R., and Wetzel, R. *Behavior Modification in the Natural Environment.* New York: Academic Press, 1969.

Trickett, E. J., Kelly, J. G., and Todd, D. M. "The Social Environment of the High School: Guidelines for Individual Changes and Organizational Development." In S. E. Golann and C. Eisendorfer (Eds.), *Handbook of Community Mental Health.* New York: Appleton-Century-Crofts, 1972.

Trickett, E. J., Kelly, J. G., and Vincent, T. A. "The Spirit of Ecological Inquiry in Community Research." In D. Klein and E. Susskind (Eds.), *Knowledge Building in Community Psychology.* New York: Praeger, in press.

Trickett, E. J., and Todd, D. M. "The Assessment of the High School Culture: An Ecological Perspective." *Theory in Practice,* 1972, *11,* 28-37.

Vernberg, E. M., and Medway, F. J. "Teacher and Parent Causal Perceptions of School Problems." *American Educational Research Journal,* 1981, *18,* 29-37.

Walberg, H. J. *Evaluating Educational Performance: A Sourcebook of Methods, Instruments, and Examples.* Berkeley: McCutchan, 1974.

Watson, G. "Resistance to Change." In W. G. Bennis, K. D. Beene, and R. Chin (Eds.), *The Planning of Change.* New York: Holt, Rinehart and Winston, 1969.

Weick, K. E. "Educational Organizations as Loosely Coupled Systems." *Administrative Science Quarterly,* 1976, *21,* 1-19.

Weinstein, R. S. "Group Consultation in School Settings: Constraints Against Collaboration." Paper presented at the annual meeting of the American Psychological Association, New York, September 1979.

Weissberg, R., and others. *The Rochester Social Problem-Solving Program: A Training Manual for Teachers.* Rochester, N.Y.: University of Rochester, 1980.

Weissberg, R. P., and others. "The Evaluation of a Social Problem-Solving Training Program for Suburban and Inner-City Third-Grade Children." *Journal of Consulting and Clinical Psychology,* 1981, *49,* 251-261.

Weissberg, R. P., and others. "Social Problem-Solving Skills Training: A Competence-Building Intervention with 2nd-4th Grade Children." *American Journal of Community Psychology,* 1981.

Winer, J. I., and others. "The Evaluation of a Kindergarten Social Problem-Solving Program." *Journal of Prevention,* 1982.

Yalom, I. D. *The Theory and Practice of Group Psychotherapy.* New York: Basic Books, 1970.

Index

F

G

H

R

S

T

V

W

Y

Z